CONTRACT

By

Stephen Woolman, Q.C.

and

Jonathan Lake

Advocate

EDINBURGH
W. GREEN/Sweet & Maxwell
2001

First published 1987
Reprinted 1989
Reprinted 1990
Reprinted 1991

Second edition published 1994
Reprinted 1995
Reprinted 1998

Third edition published 2001

Published in 2001 by W. Green & Son Ltd
21 Alva Street
Edinburgh EH2 4PS

Printed in Great Britain by MPG Books Ltd, Bodmin, Cornwall

No natural forests were destroyed to make this product;
Only farmed timber was used and replanted

A CIP catalogue record for this book is available from the British Library

ISBN 0 414 01293 3

PREFACE TO THIRD EDITION

In preparing this edition, we have tried to reflect developments in the law of contract whilst preserving the character of the book as a short, understandable introduction to the subject. We have aimed to achieve this by three means. The first is to consider only material developments in the law rather than to add new cases supporting established propositions. The second is to reduce emphasis on parts of the law that are of less practical significance. The third is to keep the preface short.

Advocate's Library
September 2001

STEPHEN WOOLMAN
JONATHAN LAKE

PREFACE TO SECOND EDITION

The river of contract law flows on. I have been tempted to add much of the new material which was swelled the casebooks since 1987. However, I have resisted that temptation. I have only added those cases which appear to me of significance. The philosophy of this work remains the same. It aims to be a short, understandable introduction to the subject. It is not a treatise. In this edition, I have attempted to recast some of the discussion to make it clearer or more accurate.

Advocate's Library
February 1994

STEPHEN WOOLMAN

PREFACE TO FIRST EDITION

Contract is a large and complex branch of law. In my view it is also a fascinating one. This short book is aimed at those approaching the subject for the first time. I hope it may serve to key readers into the major principles and issues involved. Because this is an introductory work, I have tried to avoid overburdening the text with too much detail. Fuller citation of authority is to be found in the books and articles mentioned in the select bibliography.

This book was conceived at the University of Melbourne. I am grateful to the members of the Law School there for their hospitality and encouragement. Various parts of the book have been read and commented on by John Blackie, Frank Maher and Colin Tyre. My thanks are due to them. I owe my deepest debt to Hector MacQueen with whom I have debated contract problems over several years and who read and commented on the final draft. The labours of typing and retyping were skilfully undertaken by Mrs Lorna Paterson.

The Old College   S.E.W.
August 1987

CONTENTS

TABLE OF CASES

xiii

TABLE OF STATUTES

TABLE OF STATUTORY INSTRUMENTS

CHAPTER 1

INTRODUCTION

Contracts feature in many areas of our lives. Each day we may be 1.1
involved in a variety of different contracts: buying goods, travelling by
bus, going to the cinema or arranging for a computer to be repaired.
Some of our most important long-term relationships—those concerning
how we earn a living and where we reside—are based upon contracts.
Nor can we fail to be aware that the business world is rooted in contract.
Auctions, hire, share-dealing, insurance and commercial leasing are just
a few examples. The list could be extended almost indefinitely. What
links together these many different arrangements? Let us consider a few
explanations in turn.

One answer that suggests itself is that every contract effects an
exchange. The exchange may take different forms: services for money,
goods for money or goods for goods. The exchange may take place at the
time the contract is made or it may be postponed to sometime in the
future. Most contracts possess this element of exchange. Exchange,
however, cannot be the whole answer because in some contracts no such
element is present. An aunt may draw up a contract under which she is to
pay £500 each year to assist her niece through university. The contract is
valid even though the aunt receives nothing from her niece in return.
Similarly there is no legal objection to an agreement whereby a
sportsman consents not to write newspaper articles about his team. The
agreement can be enforced despite the fact that the sportsman is not paid
nor receives any other benefit for signing the agreement. So while
exchange is a common factor in most contracts, it is not a necessary
ingredient.

Another suggested link between the different types of contract is the 1.2
concept of promise. It is possible to reduce every contract to the form "X
promises the following" and "Y promises the following". Consider a
contract of employment. The employee's main promise is to carry out the
work he is instructed to do. The employer's main promise is to pay the
employee's wages. Defining contracts in terms of promise is useful
because it emphasises the obligatory nature of the transaction. The moral
precept that we must abide by our promises enables us readily to accept
that people who break their legal promises must face the consequences.
So if the employee breaks her promise and does not perform her duties,
the employer has the option of terminating the contract of employment.

Equally if the employer breaks his promise, the employee is entitled to refuse to carry out her duties and to sue to recover the wages.

There are, however, two reasons why it is inappropriate to define contract in terms of promise. The first is that, as we have seen, the great majority of contracts actually do involve an element of exchange. One thing is given in return for another. The concept of promise does not truly explain this reciprocity which is at the core of most contracts. Viewing a contract as a promise distorts the picture by failing to reflect that the promises are the counterparts of one another. A look at a simple contract of sale of goods may help to illustrate this point. The customer who purchases a newspaper can be viewed as promising to pay the price. Similarly the newsagent can be seen as promising to transfer the newspaper. Such an analysis, however, seems artificial—it does not square with the reciprocal nature of the purchaser's and seller's acts.

The second reason for not defining contracts in terms of promise is because in Scots law there is a separate category of obligation which is actually called promise. This category is distinct from that of contract. A promise is an obligation where only one party undertakes to be legally bound and the obligation arises by an act on his part alone. Suppose a newspaper runs a promotional campaign in which it states that £50,000 will be paid to the first person to paddle around the Scottish coastline in a kayak. A person who performed this feat might enforce this obligation as a promise. The newspaper would be bound to pay over the sum to anyone who satisfied this condition. In Chapter 4 we shall see that the dividing line between contract and promise is a narrow one. Nonetheless it is preferable to avoid defining the one, contract, in terms of the other, promise.

1.3   The discussion so far shows how difficult it is to find a definition of contract which will overcome all objections. Some jurists have given up the search as a lost cause. Most, however, have come to the conclusion that a definition can best be framed in terms of the notion of agreement. All contracts involve the parties acting in concert to achieve a particular end. It may involve the construction of an oil tanker, the provision of an overdraft, or the purchase of a bar of chocolate. In each case the parties agree on the nature of their particular bargain. A contract can be said to be a legally enforceable agreement. Two points need to be made about this definition. First the term "enforceable" is used here in a special sense. Most agreements are not enforced in the sense that the parties are made to fulfil their contractual obligations. Instead each party is accorded remedies in the event of the other's failure to perform as agreed. If a builder fails to turn up on the due date to erect an extension to a house, the owner will not litigate to make the builder come and actually build the extension. Instead he will claim damages. Secondly, agreement may be more apparent than real. Does an individual really "agree" to the terms of a car-hire contract? The customer usually signs the form put in front of her without attending in any detail to its terms. If she does read the small print, she may not understand their meaning. Even the most battle-hardened solicitor may sign such an agreement on the footing that he is in no position to negotiate more favourable terms. Defining contract as an enforceable agreement therefore may not satisfy the jurist, but it does provide a working definition.

A query may be put. Even if agreement does link all the different 1.4 types of contract, surely the truth is that the principles relating to each contract form a separate branch of law? There are, for example, special rules relating to marine insurance which are not mirrored in other types of insurance contract, far less in contracts of lease or partnership. Why do lawyers not speak of a law of contracts rather than a law of contract? Paradoxically, the answer to this question stems precisely from the great variety of contracts which exist. The range of contractual arrangements which people can enter into is so vast that it is not possible to lay down specific rules to cover every situation that may arise. Accordingly, when a contractual dispute arises, there is often no special rule to resolve the issue. Recourse must then be made to the general law of contract, because it is a system of general principles rather than particular rules. A new or unusual situation can be resolved by reference to a principle even where the special rules are silent. So in looking at a particular legal problem, it is always necessary to have in mind both the general principles and the special rules relating to the contract in question.

The interaction of the special rules and the general principles is illustrated by the contract of employment. Over the past four decades there has been a colossal growth in employment law. Parliament has enacted a great deal of employment legislation concerning, for example, sexual and racial discrimination, maternity and paternity leave and the right to strike. In addition employment tribunals and the courts have produced a large volume of case law interpreting that legislation. But that has not eclipsed the role of the law of contract entirely. Questions concerning whether a contract of employment has been formed and, if so, on what terms, continue to depend in large measure on the general law of contract. Likewise questions relating to who can sue on the contract and what the measure of damages for breach ought to be. In some rare instances different solutions may be provided. An employee who is sacked may seek a remedy by raising an action of unfair dismissal in an employment tribunal. That is a statutory remedy of the law of employment. But it is still open to an employee to bring the older contractual action of wrongful dismissal in the sheriff court or the Court of Session. This might be advantageous to the employee who has not worked for a sufficient length of time to claim unfair dismissal, or who feels that the financial limits on the awards made by employment tribunals are too low.

In this book we shall discuss the general law of contract. In passing, we shall also consider the law of promise. The principles of contract law will be illustrated by reference to the many different varieties of contract.

As is demonstrated by the example of employment, the law of contract provides a framework of principles into which each individual contract fits. We begin by looking at the development of contract and shall then consider some aspects of contract theory.

DEVELOPMENT

1.5   In primitive societies there is no great need for a law of contract. Individuals tend to live in fixed social and economic positions. Contracts will be relatively simple and will usually involve simultaneous exchange—barter or sale. There is not a great deal of scope for disputes to arise. Both parties can see and touch the commodities with which they are dealing, whether they be gold or grain or animals. Ownership usually depends on an individual's status—as chief, slave or child—rather than on the contracts which he or she makes. The role of custom is more important in individuals' lives than their ability to make contracts. So whether a person owns a particular parcel of land will depend on several factors. On whether land can be owned by an individual in that community. On that person's right to the land by virtue of inheritance or marriage. His ownership will not, however, be determined by reference to his having bought the land from the previous owner. A law of contract comes to be required when there is a development from simultaneous to future exchange. Sometimes this is referred to as the change from "executed" to "executory" contracts.

The Romans were the first to work out in detail the legal consequences of contractual obligations. As Rome developed in commercial as well as in political importance, there was a need to devise laws to regulate the great increase in business transactions which occurred. Originally it was a rather rigid system. Contracts could in general only be enforced if they were real or formal. Real contracts were those which required something more than mere agreement. At first some ceremony would have to be gone through. Later what was required was transfer of the item in question. The transfer could be actual or symbolic. So far as formal contracts were concerned, a set of formalities had to be observed for the transaction to be effective. Instead of two parties merely agreeing that A should sell B a slave, or that X would lease a room in the urbs from Y, formal contracts required that some set pattern of words had to be gone through, or some special writing used. In the later period the jurists succeeded in making the law much more flexible, but it remained a law of contracts rather than contract. This meant that if a dispute occurred, it would be resolved by reference to the rules of the particular contract in question, not by reference to some general body of principles.

1.6   The continental jurist Grotius is generally regarded as the author of the modern law of contract. His achievement was to take the principles laid down by the Romans in their several species of contract and to bind them together into a coherent body of law, animated by the general notion that all obligations should be binding. In other words, failure to comply with formalities and real requirements should not prevent a contract from being enforceable against the parties to it.

The architect of modern Scots law, Viscount Stair, borrowed from a number of sources when writing his magisterial work, the *Institutions of the Law of Scotland*. As well as drawing heavily on Roman law, Grotius and other continental writers, Stair relied on the canon law and the common law of Scotland as it existed in his time. There are two important points to note about Stair's treatment of contract. The first is that his account is a much more substantial, developed treatment than is to be found in contemporaneous English works. Blackstone, for example, hardly devoted any pages to contract law and it can be fairly said that the English did not have a law of contract until the nineteenth century. The second point is that Stair was even more radical than Grotius in his desire to remove formal and real impediments from the law. He adopted the maxim of the canon law: "every paction produceth action". Loosely translated, this means that every seriously intended engagement is binding on the parties, irrespective of the form in which it is couched.

The eighteenth and nineteenth centuries were periods of great social 1.7 and economic change. The shift from agriculture to industry and the urbanisation of the population saw a large increase in the number and range of transactions which took place. Manufacturers bought materials, hired workers, subcontracted work and sold the goods produced; all on a scale hitherto unknown. Law was not immune from this change. Courts had to attempt to deal with a variety of new types of transaction. They responded by fashioning new law to meet the new conditions.

Two interlinked ideas came into prominence: freedom of contract and sanctity of contract. Freedom of contract means that everyone, unless insane or underage, can exercise choice. They can choose (a) whether or not to enter a particular contact and (b) to determine the terms on which it is made. Sanctity of contract is the corollary of freedom of contract. It simply means that all contracts freely entered into are binding upon the parties. In an age of expansion, when Britain's pre-eminence in many spheres, military, economic, and scientific, was at its height, there was a natural reluctance to tamper with the established order of things. While things were going so well for the country as a whole, the argument ran, any intervention might seriously hamper continued prosperity and development. In economic matters this led the government to pursue a *laissez-faire* policy. It did not attempt to regulate markets or manufacturers except in the case of extreme abuses. This was reflected in the legal context, where the courts were unwilling to interfere with the contracts coming before them. Workers were bound by their contracts, however long their working hours or poor their remuneration. It was not for the judges to relieve someone of a bad bargain. Freedom of contract was an application of the utilitarian philosophy that everyone was the best judge of their own interests. Bentham stated that

> "no man of ripe years and of sound mind, acting freely, and with his eyes open, ought to be hindered, with a view to his advantage, from making such bargain, in the way of obtaining money as he thinks fit, nor...anybody hindered from supplying him, upon any terms he thinks proper to accede to"[1]

1.8   Freedom of contract should not be overemphasised in the Scottish context. A study of the contract cases decided by the courts presided over by the greatest Scottish judge of the nineteenth century, John Inglis, successively Lord Justice-Clerk and Lord President of the Court of Session, suggests that the concept never reached the same zenith in Scotland as it did in England. The courts did in general seem more willing than their English counterparts to step in to correct obvious unfairness when circumstances warranted it. However, freedom of contract was and remains an important strand in contract thinking. If the parties are of equal bargaining strength and wish to tailor a contract to their individual wishes, the law has always given them wide scope to accomplish their aim. A successful recording star, for example, might negotiate a contract with a promoter of rock concerts. It may allow for a very high fee to be paid and contain a variety of unusual terms and conditions. Perhaps it is stipulated that champagne will be available in the star's dressing room and that a private jet will convey the star's entourage between cities. Suppose that audience attendance at the concerts are very low and it becomes uneconomic for the promoter to continue with the contract. The court will be very reluctant to interfere with the bargain. It presumes that the parties are the best judge of their own interests and should adhere to the arrangements which they made.

If the nineteenth century can be viewed as a century of *laissez-faire*, then the twentieth century can be seen as one of intervention. Even in the nineteenth century the notion of freedom of contract was largely a juristic abstraction rather than a reality of everyday life. A traveller from Edinburgh to London would have to go by train, by coach or by ship. By the end of the century the train would almost certainly be his preferred mode of travel. As only one company operated the railway line between the two capitals, the traveller had accordingly no choice about the party with whom he contracted. Moreover when he went to the booking desk to buy his ticket, the opportunities for negotiating the terms of travel were non-existent. He either bought the ticket on the railway company's terms or he did not travel. Freedom of contract in such a situation was a myth.

1.9   With the growth of monopolies in various fields, whether government or private, freedom of choice in deciding with whom to enter contracts

---

[1] *Jeremy Bentham's Economic Writings*, (Stark ed., London, 1952), i. 129.

has been eroded. Likewise the opportunity to negotiate terms. Many businesses fix their contractual terms in advance by the use of printed forms. Suppose an individual wishes to rent a television, hire a car or borrow money from the bank. In each case, she normally has to sign a printed form which already has the terms of the contract embossed upon it. There is no opportunity to vary the terms; they must be taken as they stand or left. French lawyers refer to such a contract as a *contrat d'adhesion*—one either adheres completely or not at all. The recognition that all contracts were not freely entered into and freely negotiated led to the development of new doctrines and new principles. But these developments have occurred in the context of a widely held belief that an important feature of the law of contract is its tendency to promote stability by having certain legal rules. People must be able to predict how their contracts will be enforced. And what they themselves have agreed will usually determine their legal rights. So the presumption is to enforce the arrangements that the parties themselves have arrived at. Interference by the courts will only occur in strictly defined circumstances.

CONTRACTUAL THEORY

It is helpful to obtain a mental fix on the place of the law of contract 1.10 relative to other areas of law. On page 8 a broad division of the law is given.

Public Law and Private Law

It can be helpful to think of law regulating two different forms of 1.11 relationship. Public law is that area of law which concerns the relationship of the state with private persons, or of different organs of the state with one other. Thus taxation is part of public law because in matters relating to income or corporation tax, the Crown in the shape of the Inland Revenue is always involved. Disputes may arise between private persons and H.M. Inspectors of Taxes as to the amount of tax due. Similarly, in matters relating to Value Added Tax (V.A.T), the two parties will be the taxpayer and the Commissioners of Customs and Excise. In administrative law, a government department or local authority is always one side of the equation. In criminal cases the state, in the guise of the Lord Advocate or procurator fiscal, prosecutes those who are alleged to have committed an offence.

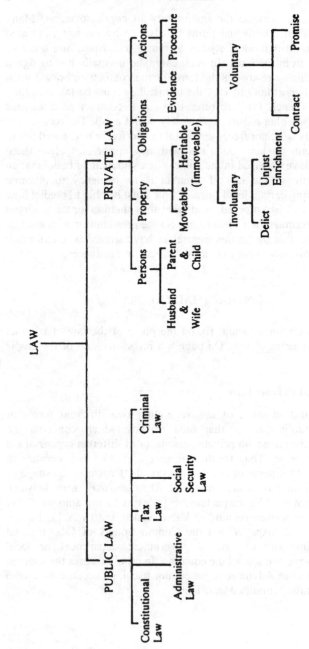

Private law is that body of law dealing with the relationships of private persons. A person can be an individual, a partnership, a voluntary association or a company. So when two neighbours have a dispute about an overhanging branch, or a customer queries the quality of an item he has bought in a shop, or a shareholder wishes to take action against the directors of a company, these are all within the sphere of private law. The Scotland Act 1998 which established the Scottish Parliament defines "Scots private law" as referring to a number of, "areas of the civil law of Scotland", (a) the general principles of private law; (b) the law of persons; (c) the law of obligations; (d) the law of property; and (e) the law of actions.[2]

This distinction between private and public law is more important in English law than in Scots law. The history of Scots law indicates that the courts have been reluctant to differentiate between the two forms of relationship.[3] In any event the boundaries between the two forms of relationship often dissolve. It is still possible, although rare, for an individual to raise a private prosecution. Public authorities are subject to private law. A contract made by a local health authority to build a hospital or to be supplied with laundry is just as much governed by private law as any similar contract made by a private person. This is so even where the contractual dispute may have profound political and social consequences. An example is provided by *British Coal Corporation v. South of Scotland Electricity Board*[4]: 1.12

> In the early 1960s, the South of Scotland Electricity Board (SSEB) resolved to build a new power station in Scotland. The British Coal Corporation (BCC formerly the National Coal Board) was aware that unless the station was coal-fired, it would have a significant and adverse effect on the mining industry in Scotland. After much discussion and negotiation, SSEB determined to build a coal-fired station at Longannet in West Fife. The station was to be supplied from a local seam—the Hirst seam. Extensive works were required to provide the mining capacity to supply the new station. The station itself required special furnaces to burn the type of coal supplied from the Hirst seam. The agreement between SSEB and BCC was recorded in a number of letters which passed between the parties in 1963. One feature of the agreement was that BCC undertook to supply all the station's requirements during its lifetime (which was expected to be about 25 years). The parties concluded various further agreements in the succeeding years, mainly concerned with pricing. In 1988, when the last of these agreements expired, SSEB

[2] Scotland Act 1988, s.126(4).
[3] See in respect of judicial review *West v. Secretary of State for Scotland*, 1992 S.C. 385, 1992 S.L.T. 636.
[4] 1991 S.L.T. 302.

decided to issue an open invitation for the supply of coal to the station. BCC sought an order that SSEB were bound to take all their coal from them. Lord Dervaird upheld BCC's contention that SSEB were bound 'to take exclusively from BCC such supplies of coal as were required for the operation of the power station at Longannet'.

This case may have had a significant bearing upon the local economy of West Fife.

Property and Obligations

1.13   More detailed consideration must be given to the relationship between the law of property and the law of obligations. These two branches of private law often interact, because property is often transferred or affected by a contract such as sale, hire or lease. Property is concerned with ownership, which gives rise to a real right (*jus in re*) on the part of the owner. Obligations, on the other hand, only give rise to a personal right (*jus in personam* or *jus ad rem*). The difference between real and personal rights can best be explained by an example:

When a house in sold in Scotland, the first step is for the purchaser and seller to complete missives. The missives are the letters exchanged between the parties' respective solicitors setting out the property to be sold, the purchase price, the date of entry and so on. Subsequently, the seller grants the purchaser a document known as a disposition in return for the price.

Once the missives are completed, the purchaser has a personal right against a particular person, the seller. This is the contractual stage of the process. Should the seller default in transferring the house, the purchaser can sue him for delivery of a valid title. But if the seller goes bankrupt or sells the house to someone else, the purchaser's right to the house may be defeated. His only remedy may be to attempt to recover damages from the seller. When the purchaser receives the disposition and his title to the property is registered in the appropriate land register, however, he becomes the owner. As owner he has a right of property, a right which is "good against the whole world". He can prevent anyone from defeating his title. A real right involves the idea of a right to a thing, whereas a personal right connotes a right against a person.

1.14   A personal right can only exist if someone has a correlative duty or obligation. Although we term this branch of the law the law of obligations, it would be equally possible to call it the law of personal rights. Viscount Stair explained the relationship between rights and obligations as follows[5]:

> "Obligation is a legal tie by which we may be necessitate or constrained to pay or perform something. This tie lieth upon the debtor; and the power of making use of it in the creditor is the

---

[5] *Institutions*, I.iii.1.

personal right itself, which is a power given by the law, to exact from persons that which they are due."

Accordingly the feature of an obligation is that there is always a correlative right.

Non-voluntary (Obediential) Obligations

Some obligations are imposed by law and are termed obediential 1.15 obligations. There are two types of such obligation: delict and unjust enrichment. The law of delict obliges persons to compensate others for any harm which they have caused to them either deliberately or negligently. This is sometimes called the obligation to make reparation. Suppose a worker is injured in the course of employment, or a pedestrian is knocked down by a car, or a politician is defamed. Any subsequent court action which is brought is an attempt by the person injured to satisfy a personal right. He seeks a court decree requiring the other person to fulfil the obligation of compensation which the law has placed upon him. The second class of obediential obligation, unjust enrichment, relates to situations where one person has benefited at the expense of another. Here the obligation is to restore the parties to the position where neither can be said to be "unjustly enriched". This obligation comes into play, for example, where one person is paid money by mistake, or builds a house on another's property believing it to be his own. Here the respective obligations which arise are for the recipient to repay the money and for the owner of the ground to pay to the extent to which he is enriched. From these examples it can be seen that unjust enrichment is based on equitable considerations.

Voluntary Obligations

There are two types of voluntary obligation: promise and contract. 1.16 Voluntary obligations, by contrast to obediential obligations, arise through choice. Unless a monopoly exists, a person can choose with whom to contract. An individual is not bound to buy cheese in a particular shop, to go on holiday with a particular travel firm, or to take out insurance with a particular company. Any contract entered into is the choice of the parties concerned. It arises out of the parties' own volition. So the difference between the two types of obligation is the difference between imposition and assumption. Obediential obligations are imposed, voluntary obligations are assumed. Stair suggested that voluntary (or conventional) obligations arose through the exercise of will. In the case of unilateral promise it is the will of the person making the promise. In the case on contracts it is the will of both parties to the transaction. For this purpose Stair divided acts of the will into three categories: desire, resolution and engagement.[6] One might conceive a

---

[6] *Institutions*, I.x..2.

desire, and even resolve to carry it out, but neither of these states of mind gave rise to a legal obligation. It was only when there was some definite purpose to do something, manifested by words or conduct, that there could be said to be engagement and consequently that legal rights and duties arose.

This notion of voluntary obligation resting on the idea of will plays an important role in contract law and ties in very closely with the notion of freedom of contract. It will come as no surprise that in England, will-theory had its heyday in the nineteenth century. The basic rationale is fairly straightforward. A person has free-will and can do what he likes so far as he is not restrained by law. By choosing to engage with someone he voluntarily relinquishes part of his independence by granting that person a right against him. As he has chosen to assume this obligation he should be bound by it.

1.17   There are powerful objections to this theory. Adam Smith was one of the first writers to criticise the idea that obligations sprung purely from the exercise of the will. He noted that if someone engaged to do something in the future and subsequently changed his mind then the logical consequence, according to will-theory, should be that he was relieved of his obligation. Yet this was not the case. A person who made a contract could not slip out of it by changing his mind. It was therefore not, Smith suggested, the will of the person engaging which gave rise to the obligation but rather "the expectation and dependence which was excited in him to whom the contract was made".[7] This difference of theoretical approach is of considerable importance. Smith's view was that the law is really concerned with protecting the person to whom the undertaking is made, rather than binding the other person to his statement. It is erroneous to consider the two views as opposite sides of the same coin. If the foundation of the law of contract is the inquiry, "Has a declaration of will been made?" that is very different from the inquiry, "Should we protect the interest of the person who relied upon the other's statement?" In our discussion of the various topics of contract law we shall see that there is a continuous interplay between the consensual approach of Stair and the reliance approach of Smith. In general, the reliance view prevails, but occasionally it is the consensual view which is emphasised.

SCOTS LAW AND ENGLISH LAW

1.18   In many areas of contract law the Scots and English approach is broadly similar. Sometimes, however, the detailed rules differ markedly north and south of the border. Examples are the law relating to formalities, illegality, collateral contracts, capacity, frustration and assignation. Two

---

[7] *Lectures on Jurisprudence* (Meek ed., Raphael & Stein, Oxford, 1978), ii. 56.

recent pieces of legislation have applied solely to Scotland: the Requirements of Writing (Scotland) Act 1995 and the Contract (Scotland) Act 1997. A well-known illustration of the difference between the two countries' laws relates to house purchase agreements. In Scotland the parties are bound at an early stage on completion of the missives. In England the stage at which the parties are bound comes later, when formal documents are exchanged. That is why the practice of "gazumping" is virtually unknown north of the Tweed. Two other major points of difference are privity of contract and consideration. Both these doctrines are part of English but not Scots law. Privity of contract is the principle that only the actual parties acquire rights under the contract. Consideration is the requirement that a contract is only binding if there is some element of bargain or reciprocity in the arrangement. These ideas will be considered more fully in the appropriate chapters of this book.

This does not mean that the solutions to problems which arise differ. It would be odd if a large retailer trading in both England and Scotland found that its ordinary contracts were dealt with in a completely different fashion by the two legal systems. Rather, the solutions are often the same but arrived at by a different route. English authorities must accordingly be used with care. It is as if one is translating from one language into another. The elegance of French poetry can never be matched by a translation into German. So with Scots and English law. A sentence of the great legislative draftsman Sir M. D. Chalmers seems apposite. In relation to the English Statute of Frauds 1677 he noted "it has...never applied to Scotland and Scotsmen never appear to have felt the want of it".[8] The contortions which English law developed to get round the more unhappy applications of that Act and of other doctrines such as privity of contract would likewise not be welcomed in Scotland. One other point about the difference between the two legal systems concerns procedure. Until the late nineteenth century, the common law courts administered different remedies from the Chancery courts. Despite the nineteenth century reforms, English lawyers persist in talking about "common law" and "equitable" rules and remedies. Our courts have always had an inherent equitable jurisdiction (with a small "e") and the different procedural approaches find no counterpart in our law.

Nevertheless the greater size of England and the fact that London is 1.19 the commercial hub of the United Kingdom means inevitably that there are a far higher number of reported decisions on contractual issues there. Many English decisions have either been accepted into Scots law or are of high persuasive value. Accordingly we shall refer to a number of English cases in this book. Differences between the two systems will be pointed out where appropriate.

---

[8] Chalmers, *Sale of Goods Act*, (12th ed., 1945), p. 26.

CHAPTER 2

FORMATION OF CONTRACT—CONCLUDING AN AGREEMENT

When does a contract come into existence? Often the answer will be 2.1
clear. By their conduct, or by means of the written or spoken word, or by
a combination of these methods, the parties will make it plain that a
binding contract exists between them. Setting out contract terms in a
written document and signing it is the clearest method of concluding a
contract. It is, however, far from the only method. At the corner
newsagent, for example, contracts are commonly made without any
words being exchanged. The customer tenders his money, together with
the newspaper, magazine or sweets he wishes to purchase. By taking the
money and placing it in the till, the newsagent concludes the bargain.
Verbal contracts may be struck involving much larger sums of money. A
typical illustration concerns second-hand car showrooms. The
prospective purchaser expresses an interest in a particular model. The
seller indicates a price. The purchaser suggests a different price. After
haggling about this and the other terms of the contract, whether, for
example, road tax or a full tank of petrol is included, the purchaser pays
the price which is finally agreed and drives the car out of the showroom.

Sometimes it may be difficult to determine with precision when, or if,
a contract has been concluded. Suppose Valerie is interested in going on
holiday to Denmark. She telephones a travel company and discovers that
a package holiday is available departing on a particular date. She rings
off to discuss matters with her proposed travel companion. The next day
she sends a booking form to the company. Is the contract complete when
the booking form is signed, when it is sent, when it arrives at the
company's offices or when a deposit on the price of the holiday is paid?
No clear-cut answer can be given. It will depend on the wording of the
booking form, the method by which the parties communicate, their
subsequent actions and the context in which these occur. In this chapter
we shall consider the relevant principles which apply to these issues.

THE BASIC RULE—AGREEMENT

As was discussed in Chapter 1, contract is usually analysed in terms of 2.2
agreement. Formation occurs when the parties reach agreement as to the
essential features of their transaction. This is sometimes referred to as

consensus in idem (meeting of the minds). Agreement does not mean that the parties' minds have coincided on every point. A person cannot know the inner thought-processes of another individual. Accordingly it is not necessary that there is full subjective agreement. Suppose a musician flags down a taxi in the street and is carried to the desired destination. At the end of the journey he refuses to pay the fare unless the taxi driver carries his heavy instrument up three flights of stairs. The taxi driver refuses on the basis that their agreement concerned carriage by vehicle alone. A tribunal asked to resolve the dispute would find in favour of the driver unless the musician could prove that there was a specific agreement to carry the instrument upstairs. The law adopts an objective approach in testing agreement, one which is concerned with the "external indicia of agreement". Instead of looking at what the parties to the contract were actually thinking at the time of contracting, the law looks for those outward indications which evince consensus. The question is, would it appear to a neutral third party that agreement had been reached? In other words, would such a person infer from the contracting parties' words and deeds that a proposal had been assented to?

2.3   Sometimes, parties may have different beliefs at the relevant time. In *Muirhead and Turnbull v. Dickson*[1]:

> The manager of a Glasgow piano shop called on Dickson and his wife at their home. Dickson agreed to take a piano from the shop at the price of £26, payment to be made by way of monthly instalments. No written document was signed. A few days later the piano was delivered. Dickson began paying the instalments but after five months stopped paying. The piano shop raised an action to recover the piano from him. It argued that Dickson had received the piano under a contract of hire-purchase. Under such a contract, ownership of the piano did not pass until all the instalments were paid. Alternatively, the shop contended that the parties had never reached agreement at all, so there was no contract and the shop was entitled to return of the piano. Dickson maintained that he had bought the piano on credit sale. A credit sale contract would have made Dickson owner of the piano and left the piano shop to attempt to recover the balance of the price.

It was held that, viewed objectively, the evidence disclosed that a contract of credit sale had been entered into. A factor of some importance in the case was the relative novelty of hire-purchase. The court thought that the onus was on the piano shop to make it plain that it was this new type of contract which had been entered into. The point to emphasise is that the parties had not agreed as a matter of psychological fact about the terms of the contract they had entered into. Nevertheless they were bound, for even where parties honestly differ, "commercial contracts

---

[1] (1905) 7 F. 686; (1905) 13 S.L.T. 151.

cannot be arranged by what people think in their inmost minds. Commercial contracts are made according to what people say."[2] Accordingly, Dickson was the owner of the piano and the shop could not recover it from him. The shop's remedy was to seek payment of the outstanding instalments.

The corollary is that if parties have proceeded with performance of 2.4 the contract in the belief that it is binding, the courts will not enforce it if they find that agreement has never been reached:

> "It is not enough for the parties to agree in saying there was a concluded contract if there was none, and then to ask for a judicial decision as to what the contract in fact was. That would be the same thing as asking us to make the bargain when our sole function is to interpret it."[3]

In the case in which that statement was made, work was carried out on a garden pond. When the contractors asked for payment for the work the householder refused, claiming that the work was defective. Both in the sheriff court and in the Court of Session the contractors' claim for damages for breach of contract was successful. Nevertheless, on appeal it was decided by the House of Lords that in truth there was no contract between the parties. The contract documents showed that the contractors had offered to hire the equipment. But the householder had purported to accept an offer to hire the equipment and to operate the equipment to clear the pond. As the offer and the acceptance had not met, there was no consensus. Accordingly, the contractors had no contractual claim to recover the cost of the work done on the pond. Instead, their remedy lay in the law of unjust enrichment. This decision is perhaps an extreme application of the objective approach. Where work or performance has followed on an apparent contract which the parties themselves believe to be binding, the courts will normally give effect to that belief.

THE OFFER/ACCEPTANCE ANALYSIS

If contract can be described in terms of agreement, it is essential to have 2.5 a means of determining when the necessary agreement has been reached. Most contracts can be analysed in terms of offer and acceptance: "an offer accepted is a contract".[4] The person making the offer is known as the offeror. The offeree is the person to whom the offer is made, while the acceptor is a person who accepts the offer. In terms of the offer/acceptance analysis, a contract is formed when an offer is met with an unqualified acceptance. If a person who has received an offer replies

---

[2] *per* Lord President Dunedin at p.694.
[3] *Mathieson Gee (Ayrshire) Ltd v. Quigley*, 1952 S.C. (H.L.) 38; 1952 S.L.T. 239.
[4] *Institutions*, I.x.3.

by saying that he or she agrees to the offer but wishes to add conditions of their own, the reply is a qualified acceptance. A qualified acceptance does not conclude a contract. It amounts to a rejection of the offer. It is a counter-offer, which, in turn is open for acceptance. A neat illustration of these points is provided by the case of *Wolf and Wolf v. Forfar Potato Co. Ltd*[5]:

> A Forfar company offered by telex to sell a quantity of Désirée, potatoes to a firm of Amsterdam potato merchants. The offer was open for acceptance by 5pm the following day. An "acceptance" was sent by telex the following morning. In this telex various new conditions were set out. When the Dutch merchants learned from a telephone call to Forfar that these new conditions were not acceptable, they sent a second telex. This second telex was also received before the time-limit had expired. It purported to accept the Forfar terms but reiterated that the Dutch merchants would be glad if their earlier conditions were given consideration by the Scottish company. No further communication was made by the Forfar company and no potatoes were sent. The Amsterdam merchants raised an action of damages for breach of contract. They argued that they had received an offer which they had accepted before the time-limit had expired.

It was held that no contract existed. The first acceptance amounted to a counter-offer which "killed" the original offer. It was, accordingly, no longer capable of acceptance. As the counter-offer had not been accepted by the Scottish company, there was no contract.

2.6   Slightly different circumstances occurred in *Findlater v. Maan*[6]:

> Mr Maan advertised his house for sale. By letter dated March 25, 1988, Mr and Mrs Findlater offered to purchase the property. A qualified acceptance was given by the seller on March 28, 1988. By letter dated March 29, 1988 the purchasers accepted the conditions contained in the seller's qualified acceptance and inserted one further condition. On March 30, and without referring to the letter of March 29, the seller intimated one further condition. On April 6, the purchasers withdrew the condition contained in their letter of March 29, accepted the condition specified in the seller's letter of March 30, and purported to conclude the bargain. By this stage, the seller had changed his mind and did not wish to proceed with the sale. An action of declarator of contract was raised. The Second Division held unanimously that a contract existed.

In distinguishing the case from that of *Wolf and Wolf*, Lord Justice Clerk Ross stated:

---

[5] 1984 S.L.T. 100.
[6] 1990 S.L.T. 465; *cf. Rutterford v. Allied Breweries Ltd*, 1990 S.L.T. 249.

"In my opinion the true approach to be made in the present case is as follows. The letter of 29 March and the letter of 30 March were two offers which existed at the same time, one at the instance of the seller and the other at the instance of the purchaser. They were not written under reference to one another and neither of them superseded the other. They both co-existed. In that situation I am of opinion that it was open to the pursuers to accept the offer contained in the letter of 30 March 1988."[7]

Whether or not an acceptance has been qualified is a question of construction. The response may simply be hesitant or under reservation or a mere request for further information. In such instances the acceptance will not amount to a counter-offer. Where an acceptance contained the phrase "the usual conditions of acceptance apply" and there were no such conditions, the contract was held binding and the phrase ignored as meaningless.[8]   2.7

Where the parties negotiate over a period, there will often be a series of offers and counter-offers before agreement is finally reached. In such cases, the person who was the original offeror may become the eventual acceptor. For instance, A offers to hire B's concert venue for one night at a price of £500. B replies that he is prepared to hire out the venue to A for two nights at a price of £750. A accepts this suggestion. On this scenario, A is the acceptor as well as being the original offeror.   2.8

Because of the importance of offers and acceptance it is necessary to examine the key features of each in more detail.

OFFERS

The Distinction between Offers and Invitations to Treat

An offer may be express—"I offer you £50 for your old lawnmower"— or implied, for example, handing over money for a theatre ticket. The key feature of an offer is that it contemplates acceptance. As soon as it is accepted a contract is formed. No further negotiation is contemplated. Sometimes there is no intention to be bound by the other party's purported acceptance. Instead the person is merely indicating his bargaining position. In effect, he is saying "these are the terms upon which I am willing to negotiate further". Statements of this second type are known as invitations to treat. The difference between the two is important. If a statement constitutes an offer, it is in the hands of the acceptor to form the contract. If the statement is merely an invitation to treat, then the person making the statement will not be bound by the other party's simple assent. If a statement is circulated widely—such as in a hoarding advertisement, newspaper or web site—and amounts to an   2.9

---

[7] p.468.
[8] *Nicolene Ltd v. Simmonds* [1953] 1 Q.B. 543.

offer rather than an invitation to treat, the person making the statement may find themselves in contracts with many more people than they anticipated. An example indicates how important the distinction between offers and invitation to treat can be. In *Carlill v. The Carbolic Smokeball Co. Ltd*[9]:

> The Carbolic Smokeball Co. placed an advertisement in the *Pall Mall Gazette* in November 1891. It stated that the company would pay £100 if anyone caught one of a number of specified diseases after using one of their smokeballs in the prescribed manner for two weeks. The company claimed to have deposited £1,000 in the Alliance Bank to show its "sincerity in the matter". Mrs Carlill bought one of the balls and used it for two months. She caught influenza (one of the specified diseases) and requested payment of the £100 sum. The company refused to pay. Accordingly, an action was raised by Mrs Carlill.

The Smokeball company put up several arguments in its defence to the action. One argument was that the advertisement was merely an invitation to treat. This was rejected. The wording of the advertisement went beyond an indication of the company's bargaining position. As Bowen L.J. put it: "It is an offer to become liable to anyone who, before it is retracted, performs the conditions." The court awarded Mrs Carlill her £100 reward.

2.10   It is not always easy to distinguish invitations to treat from offers. The touchstone, here as elsewhere in contract law, is that of apparent intention. If the person's statements or actions disclose an intention to be bound, it is an offer. If not, it is an invitation to treat. Questions of intention provide the courts with difficult problems. The intention of the alleged offeror must be gathered from the whole circumstances surrounding the parties' communications. In *Dawson International plc v. Coats Paton plc*[10]:

> The defenders, a large Scottish textile company, thought that they were vulnerable to a hostile takeover. In early 1986, representatives of the board of directors met with the pursuers' board to discuss a possible offer from them. It was agreed by the defenders to recommend the pursuers' offer to their shareholders and this was done. Subsequently, the defenders withdrew their recommendation. The pursuers claimed there was a contract in terms of which the defenders would recommend their offer. They sought damages for the abortive costs of their takeover bid. It was held that no such contract existed.

---

[9] [1893] 1 Q.B. 256.
[10] 1993 S.L.T. 80.

Lord Prosser stated:

> "Speaking generally, I would accept that when two parties are
> talking to one another about a matter which has commercial
> significance to both, a statement by one party that he will do some
> particular thing will normally be construed as obligatory, or as an
> offer, rather than a mere statement of intention, if the works and
> deeds of the other party indicate that the statement was so
> understood, and the obligation confirmed or the offer accepted so
> that parties appeared to regard the commercial 'deal' as concluded.
> But in considering whether there is indeed a contract between the
> parties, in any particular case, it will always be essential to look at
> the particular facts, with a view to discovering whether these facts,
> rather than some general rule of thumb, can be said to reveal
> consensus and an intention to conclude a contract."[11]

Two further cases illustrate the narrow distinction between offers and 2.11
invitations to treat. In the first case a dispute arose as to whether there
was a concluded sale of a property in Jamaica called "Bumper Hall
Pen".[12] A telegraphed to B: "Will you sell us BHP? Telegraph lowest
cash price." B telegraphed in reply: "Lowest cash price for BHP £900."
Following this, A telegraphed: "We agree to buy BHP for £900 asked by
you. Please send us your title deed in order that we may get early
possession." No further correspondence took place. It was held that no
contract had been formed.

In the second case a merchant in Leith wrote to a firm in Largo, Fife
as follows: "I am offering today Plate Linseed for Jan./Feb. shipment to
Leith, and have pleasure in quoting you 100 tons at 41s. 3d., usual Plate
terms. I shall be glad to hear if you are buyers, and await your esteemed
reply."[13] The Largo firm purported to accept. The court decided that a
contract had been formed. The distinction to be drawn between the two
cases is that in the first, the party was merely indicating the price at
which he was prepared to contract; whereas in the second the word
"offer" was actually used, a definite quantity and price were mentioned
and the letter looked to the conclusion of the contract by reply.

In several common situations English law has adopted presumptions 2.12
as to whether some statement or action amounts to an offer or an
invitation to treat. Scots law has fewer authorities on this branch of the
law, but it is probable that in most instances we would approach the
matter in the same way. These are only presumptions, not rules of law.
Accordingly they can be displaced if the contrary intention is proved.

---

[11] p.95.
[12] *Harvey v. Facey* [1983] A.C. 552.
[13] *Philp v. Knoblauch*, 1907 S.C. 994; 15 S.L.T. 61.

Shop Displays

2.13 There is no recent Scottish authority in point on shop displays. In one old case it was accepted that such displays were invitations to treat.[14] In England, the two leading authorities which analyse the issue are unusual. Each concerned prosecutions in respect of alleged offences by shopkeepers. Accordingly they were criminal rather than civil cases. The first case concerned the sale of drugs without the supervision of a qualified chemist[15]; the second, offering an offensive weapon for sale.[16] In each case the display was held to be an invitation to treat rather than an offer. A factor stressed by the court was that a shop is a place for bargaining, not for compulsory sales.

The presumption that a display is merely an invitation to treat can be displaced. In one case an individual took a deckchair from a stack on the beach.[17] He was injured because it was defective. The display of deck chairs was held to constitute an offer. The man had then concluded a contract by removing the deckchair and sitting on it: that was the acceptance. It may be that the court was more inclined to reach this result because personal injury was involved.

Auction sales

2.14 The three stages of an auction sale can be analysed as follows:

    (a) exposure of the item for sale   —invitation to treat
    (b) the bid   —offer
    (c) the fall of the auctioneer's hammer —acceptance

Until the hammer falls, the bidder is entitled to withdraw his bid.[18] No contract exists until that moment. Individuals who feel nervous about making inadvertent gestures in salesrooms may be comforted by this knowledge. What of the seller? Like the buyer he too may wish to withdraw after the bidding has commenced. To accomplish this he may put a reserve price on the article to be auctioned. This ensures that the item is not sold below a certain sum.

Advertisements

2.15 Advertisements, whether on television, on hoardings, or in the press are presumed to be invitations to treat. The position is analogous to that of shop window displays. An advertiser is granted the right to determine the person with whom it contracts. If an advertisement was an offer, the

---

[14] *Campbell v. Ker*, 24 Feb. 1810, F.C.
[15] *Pharmaceutical Society of Great Britain v. Boots Cash Chemists (Southern) Ltd* [1953] 1 Q.B. 401; 1 All E.R. 482.
[16] *Fisher v. Bell* [1961] 1 Q.B. 394.
[17] *Chapelton v. Barry U.D.C.* [1940] 1 K.B. 532.
[18] *Fenwick v. Macdonald Fraser & Co.* (1904) 6 F. 850.

advertiser might be contractually bound to persons which it was unable to supply. Suppose a company advertising beds was faced with unusually heavy demand. It would be unfortunate if it were held liable in damages to all persons who sent cheques in response to the advertisement, irrespective of the availability of the beds. In appropriate circumstances, however, the general presumption can be displaced. For this to occur, the advertisement must clearly indicate that the advertiser intends to be bound upon acceptance. This was the case in *Carlill*.[19]

Vending Machines

These present particular difficulties. Who makes the offer: the machine 2.16 or the customer? In one English case involving a ticket machine at the entrance to a car park, it was argued that the machine made a standing offer because it had to deliver the ticket to any person who put the correct money in the slot.[20] It had no discretion to accept or reject a particular person. This is probably the correct analysis, even if it may seem rather surreal to apply the concept of intention to machines. That objection loses force when it is remembered that it is not the intention of the machine itself which is relevant, but rather that of its owner.

Tenders

A tender or quotation to carry out work is an offer. For example, a letter 2.17 from a plumber which states that a new bathroom will be installed at a specified price is converted into a contract by simple acceptance. In some instances, for example in relation to car repairs, the repairer may be unwilling to give a definite quotation. Then the parties must reach some agreement as to the manner in which the price is to be fixed. It is common to stipulate that express authorisation is required for repairs beyond a certain maximum cash limit, or that the car owner will pay for all costs reasonably necessary to obtain an M.O.T. certificate.

Features of Offers

Who May Accept

In some instances an offer is made to the world at large. Such offers are 2.18 capable of acceptance by anyone who sees or hears the offer. The case of *Carlill* is a good example. The offer of reward was addressed to everyone who happened to read the advertisement. Normally, however, an offer is made to a particular person and the rule is that only that person can accept the offer. A purported acceptance by another person is accordingly invalid.

---

[19] [1893] 1 Q.B. 256.
[20] *Thornton v. Shoe Lane Parking Ltd* [1971] 2 Q.B. 163; 1 All E.R. 686.

Revocation

2.19 An offer may be withdrawn at any time before acceptance. This is an important feature of offers and is known as *locus poenitentiae* (the opportunity of withdrawing). Right up to the moment the acceptance is given, the offeror can change his mind. The bidder at an auction has the right to withdraw his bid until the hammer falls. Apart from express revocation, an offer is impliedly withdrawn by the death, insanity or bankruptcy of the offeror.

To take effect, the revocation must actually be communicated to the offeree. This can be done verbally.[21] It is not necessary for the retraction of the offer to be actually brought to the attention of the offeree. Doing all that is reasonable to bring it to his notice, such as delivering it to his normal business address, is enough.[22]

Termination

2.20 Another method by which an offer comes to an end is termination. Where a time-limit for acceptance is attached, the offer automatically falls on the expiry of that time-limit. Of course, the offeror can waive the time-limit if he so wishes. Where no time-limit is stated, an offer only remains open for a reasonable time. An early American case provides a colourful example.[23] In May 1837 an offer of reward for the "apprehension and conviction of incendiaries" was issued. Relevant information was given to the authorities in 1841. It was held that no obligation to pay the reward remained, as the time lapse was unreasonably long. What amounts to a reasonable time will depend upon the circumstances of the case. Where the contract concerns the sale or supply of a commodity for which there is a ready market, acceptance will usually require to be by return of post. In *Wylie and Lochhead v. McElroy and Sons*,[24] a delay of five weeks in accepting an offer to carry out ironwork at new stables was held to be unreasonable. At the time the price of iron was fluctuating from day to day. To allow the client to wait and accept the offer when the price of iron changed in his favour would be unfair. It would allow him to speculate at the expense of the offeror.

It is possible in Scots law for a person to bind himself to keep an offer open for a specified period. Suppose X writes to Y on Monday stating: "I offer to sell you my house for £150,000 and will keep this offer open until Friday at 12 noon". X will be liable to damages to Y if he breaks this promise and sells to Z on Thursday. We shall discuss this situation in Chapter 4.

---

[21] *McMillan v. Caldwell*, 1991 S.L.T. 325, 329L *per* Lord Kirkwood.
[22] *Burnley v. Alford*, 1919 2 S.L.T. 123.
[23] *Loring v. City of Boston* (1844) 7 Metcalf 409.
[24] (1873) 1 R. 41.

Referential bids

A fixed bid is one in which a definite price is mentioned. A "referential 2.21
bid" is one where the bidder offers a certain sum in excess of any other
bid made. An example is: "I offer £500 more than the highest bid you
receive from any other party." Sometimes the two are combined, as in: "I
offer £500,000 or whatever is offered by party B plus £5,000, whichever
is the greater." The House of Lords has held that such bids are only valid
if reasonable notice is given to all parties that such bids may be used.[25]
Otherwise the person making the referential bid would always succeed
against a rival bidder making a conventional bid. This would be plainly
unjust. A further problem which could arise if referential bids were
widely used would be that it might lead to no valid bids being submitted.
Such bids depend upon at least one person using a fixed bid, so in the
absence of such a bid there would be no reference point upon which the
other bids could be based.

ACCEPTANCES

An acceptance is a final unqualified assent to an offer. Like offers, 2.22
acceptances can be express or implied. The action of a check-out
assistant in taking a customer's basket and ringing up the items on the till
indicates implied acceptance of the customer's offer to buy. Silence does
not generally, however, constitute acceptance. A man who sends a letter
offering to sell beehives to a neighbour cannot assume that a binding
contract has been formed simply because he does not receive a reply to
the contrary. The neighbour's silence does not amount to acquiescence.
Nor is it possible to stipulate that silence on the part of the offeree is to
be regarded as effective. An offeror cannot say: "I offer to purchase your
record collection for £400 and if I do not hear from you by Wednesday I
shall take it that you agree." If this rule did not exist persons could have
contracts imposed upon them without their consent. Despite this
principle, in the 1960s certain traders sent unsolicited items through the
post and then demanded payment if the goods were not returned within a
specified time. People who were unsure of their legal rights thought they
were bound to pay for these items. To deal with this problem, Parliament
enacted the Unsolicited Goods and Services Act 1971. It provides that
recipients of unsolicited goods can treat them as their own if they are not
reclaimed by the sender within a certain period. There is no obligation
upon the recipient to return them. Exceptionally, however, silence may
amount to valid acceptance. This might happen where there is a history
of dealing between the contracting parties, or where there have been
prolonged negotiations. In the beehives example, there may have been

---

[25] *Harvela Investments Ltd v. Royal Trust Co. of Canada (C.I.) Ltd,* [1986] A.C.
207; [1985] 3 W.L.R. 276; [1985] 1 All E.R. 261.

several prior transactions and on each occasion the neighbour has
omitted to give any positive acceptance but has simply paid for the
beehives when delivered.

One must be careful to distinguish situations where the offeree is
silent, from situations where an offer is followed by actings by the other
party. An express offer followed by actions by the offeree consistent with
acceptance is enough to infer the existence of a contract.

COMMUNICATION OF OFFERS AND ACCEPTANCES

2.23   In general, neither offers nor acceptances take effect if they are not
communicated to the other party: "An offer is nothing until it is
communicated to the party to whom it is made."[26] This seems obvious.
Imagine that a promoter had written out, but not posted, an offer to book
a particular musician for one of his venues. If the musician
surreptitiously found out about the offer he is not entitled to accept it.
The same is true in respect of acceptances. The offeror cannot divine
when the offeree mentally assents to the offer. He requires
communication of the acceptance before a binding contract exists.

As with many rules, there are exceptions. An offeror may waive the
need for express communication of the acceptance. In *Carlill*, the
contract was formed when the smokeballs were purchased. Mrs Carlill
did not require to write to the company intimating that she accepted the
company's offer of reward should she succumb to one or other of the
specified diseases. The terms of the advertisement demonstrated that no
communication of acceptance was required.

Mode of Communication

2.24   An offer may be intimated by any mode of communication. The offeror
can, however, prescribe the manner in which the acceptance is to be
communicated. He may stipulate that communication is to be made by
letter, by telex, by telephone, by e-mail or by facsimile. Where such a
stipulation is made, communication of the acceptance by other means is
invalid. In one case the exercise of an option to purchase a piece of land
was required to be "by notice in writing to the intending vendor."[27] It
was held that notification by telephone to the vendor's solicitors did not
satisfy this requirement. What was required was written intimation to the
vendor himself.

If the offeror does not prescribe the mode of communication, the
acceptance can be given in any competent manner. Normally it should be
given in the same mode as the offer. Accordingly, an offer made in
writing should be accepted in writing. There is a measure of common-

---

[26] *Thomson v. James* (1855) 18 D. 1 *per* Lord President McNeill at p.10.
[27] *Holwell Securities Ltd v. Hughes* [1974] 1 W.L.R. 155.

sense to be applied here. Whilst a telex acceptance to an offer posted by second class post is likely to be legally effective, the converse probably does not hold. This is because a telex offer suggests that a speedy response is sought. By contrast, the use of second class post indicates a more leisurely mode of proceeding.

When Does an Acceptance Take Effect?

The answer to this question determines when a contract is made. The general rule is that an acceptance only takes effect when it is received by the offeror. That is the case in respect of telephone,[28] telex[29] and fax communications.[30] The burden is upon the offeree to ensure that his words are communicated and understood. Should, accordingly, a telephone line go dead during the course of negotiations, it is up to the offeree to ensure that his acceptance has been heard. If he does not telephone back to check matters, and any dispute arises, no contract will have been concluded.[31]   2.25

There is a different rule for postal communications. In *Dunlop v. Higgins*[32] the House of Lords held that the acceptance was made when the offeree put it in the post.[33] This rule can have startling consequences. For instance:

(1) Where an offer is only open for a specified period, acceptance is effective when the acceptance is posted within the time limit, even if it is not received until some days later. So, where an offer to purchase goods stated: "This for reply by Monday, 6th inst."[34] a letter posted on the evening of the 6th, which only reached the offeror the following day, was held to be timeous acceptance.

(2) In one English case, the rule was taken to its logical conclusion and a contract was held to have been concluded even though the acceptance went missing in the post and was never received.[35] One Scottish judge, Lord Shand, doubted whether the same solution should be applied in Scotland.[36] His view is surely the better one. It is one matter for an offeror to be contractually bound for a day or two before the offer is actually received, quite another when the acceptance is never received at all.

---

[28] See *Entores Ltd v. Miles Far East Corpn.* [1955] 2 Q.B. 327.
[29] *Brinkibon Ltd v. Stahag Stahl* [1983] 2 A.C. 34; [1982] 1 All E.R. 293.
[30] *McIntosh v. Alan*, 1998 S.L.T. (Sh.Ct) 19.
[31] *Entores Ltd v. Miles Far East Corpn.* [1955] 2 Q.B. 327.
[32] (1848) 6 Bell's App. 195.
[33] *per* Lord Chancellor Cottenham at p.207.
[34] *Jacobson, Sons & Co. v. Underwood & Son* (1894) 21 R. 654.
[35] *Household Fire Insurance Co. v. Grant* (1879) 4 Ex. D. 216.
[36] *Mason v. Benhar Coal Co.* (1882) 9 R. 883 at p.890.

(3) We have seen that an offer can always be withdrawn before acceptance but that the revocation must be brought to the attention of the offeree if it is to take effect. If the acceptance is posted while the revocation of the offer is in transit a contract will come into being before the revocation takes effect.[37] A contract may thereby be formed even though there is never a point in time when the parties have reached *consensus in idem*.

2.26   In essence this rule of acceptance "effective on dispatch" is an arbitrary one. It means that in the interval of time between one party knowing that the contract is concluded and the other finding out, the law favours the acceptor. He can rely on the contract at the moment of posting. If, of course, the offeror does not wish this to occur, it is open to him to prescribe another method of communication. He can "contract out" of this rule should it not suit him.

The logical consequence of the "postal" rule should be that once the acceptance is posted, it cannot be revoked. After all, that acceptance is the point at which the contract comes into being. Surprisingly, in the only case upon the issue, *Countess of Dunmore v. Alexander*, it was held that the postal acceptance might be revoked.[38]

2.27   In the case of sales under the Uniform Laws on International Sales Act 1967, the postal rule is set aside in favour of the principle that acceptance is effective on receipt. Where, accordingly, a contract is made under the provisions of the Act and an order for goods is placed with a foreign company the contract will only be deemed to be concluded when an acceptance arrives at the ordering company's offices.

2.28   As the use of computers to conclude contracts becomes more common, issues may arise as to the time at which a contract has been formed. Contracts made by means of e-mail and the internet can be analysed in the same manner as oral and written contracts. The technology is simply the means by which the parties communicate with a view to reaching, and possibly recording, consensus. Where e-mail is used, an analogy can be drawn with postal communications - instead of instantaneous communication a message is sent which may take time to arrive. Where the contract is concluded over the internet, the situation is closer to that of faxes or phone calls in that there is a "conversation" of sorts.

---

[37] *Thomson v. James* (1855) 18 D. 1.
[38] (1830) 9 S. 190.

The Consumer Protection (Distance Selling) Regulations 2000

These regulations[39] implement a European Union directive.[40] Essentially,   2.29
they aim to safeguard individuals who purchase items by mail order, over
the internet or otherwise than "face to face". They do not change the
rules as to creation of a contract by means of offer and acceptance. They
do, however, suspend the effect of an acceptance in some situations by
introducing a right for a consumer to cancel the contract.

When do the Regulations Apply?

The Regulations apply only to "distance contracts". To be a "distance   2.30
contract" a contract must have the following features.[41]

(1) It must concern goods or services.

(2) It must be concluded between a "supplier" (a person who acts in
a commercial or professional capacity) and a "consumer" (a
person who is not acting in a business capacity).

(3) In concluding the contract, the supplier must have made
exclusive use of one or means of "distance communication".
This includes the post, order forms in newspapers, catalogues,
telephones (including faxes), teletext, email and television.[42] If
there has been any face to face meeting between the supplier
and the consumer prior to conclusion of the contract, the
Regulations will not apply.

(4) The contract must have been concluded "under an organised
distance sales or service provision scheme run by the supplier".
This expression is not defined. It appears to require that it is the
intention of the scheme that contracts should be concluded
without the parties ever being in each other's presence. It would
therefore not suffice merely that the parties had not met. For
instance, the Regulations would not apply to a contract
concluded when a motorist phones a garage to arrange that her
car be serviced on a certain date or a contract concluded when a
house buyer phones a surveyor to instruct a survey.

(5) It must not fall within the list of excepted contracts which
include contracts for the sale of land, contracts relating to
financial services and contracts concluded at auctions.

---

[39] S.I. 2000 No. 2334.
[40] Directive 97/7/EC [1997] O.J. L144/19 of the European Parliament and the
Council on the protection of consumers in relation to distance contracts.
[41] reg. 3(1) and Sched. 1.
[42] Sched.1.

The Effect of the Regulations

2.31   The Regulations have three main effects:

   (1)   they require information to be given to the consumer;
   (2)   they give the consumer a right to cancel; and
   (3)   they imply a term as to when the contract should be performed.

2.32   (1) **Information to be given to the consumer.** Certain information regarding the supplier, the subject matter of the contract and key contract terms must be given to the consumer by the supplier prior to the conclusion of the contract.[43] This information need not be provided in writing. There is a further requirement to provide information in writing to the consumer.[44] The information which must be provided in writing also includes details of the supplier, the subject matter and key contract terms. In addition, the written information must also include details of the consumer's right to cancel the contract, after sales service and guarantees. This written information must be provided either (a) before the contract is concluded, or, (b) in the case of a contract for services, during the performance of the contract, or, (c) in the case of a contract of sale in which the goods are to be delivered to the consumer rather than a third party, at or before the time of delivery. A failure to provide information under the first obligation would not affect a contract. A failure to comply with the second obligation—to provide information in writing within the time limits—will, however, affect the right of the consumer to cancel the contract.

2.33   (2) **Consumer right to cancel**. The most significant change introduced by the Regulations is the right given to the consumer to cancel the contract after it has been concluded.[45] The period in which this right may be exercised could be as short as seven days after the contract is made or the goods are delivered. But if the required written information is not provided, it could be extended by up to three months. Although "cooling-off periods" have existed before in relation to certain types of contract, this right applies to all contracts falling within the Regulations. The result of the new rules is that where the Regulations apply, it will not be possible to assume that there is a contract when an offer is met with an unqualified acceptance. Before the supplier can be sure of the contract he or she must wait for the cancellation period to expire. If cancellation takes place, the contract is treated as if it had never been made.

2.34   (3) **Implied term as to when contract should be performed.** The third effect is in relation to performance of the contract. The supplier must perform the contract within a period of 30 days. If he does not, after that period the contract shall be treated as if it had not been made other than for the purposes of such rights and remedies as the consumer has.

---

[43] reg. 7.

[44] reg. 8.

[45] reg. 10.

INCOMPLETE AGREEMENTS

Sometimes it is not easy to tell when the parties have completed their 2.35
negotiations and have moved to the stage of concluding a contract. The
parties may be discussing several different aspects of their proposed
relationship—some which are critical to determine the obligations they
are willing to undertake and others which are less important to them. On
some occasions there may be one particular aspect of the contract which
remains outstanding after *consensus in idem* has been reached on all the
other points. When this occurs disputes may arise as to whether or not
there is a contract.

For some agreements to be enforceable, agreement of certain key
matters is required. The classic instance is the contract of lease. The
essential elements are (a) the identity of the parties, (b) the property to be
leased, (c) the rent and (d) the duration of the lease. If an essential term
of a contract is not agreed, then the contract cannot be enforced. Two
examples may help to illustrate this principle. (1) Suppose Humphrey
agrees to buy Greta's car. Until they settle upon the price neither could
force the other to go through with the bargain. (2) Ginger negotiates with
Fred to rent his holiday cottage on Shapinsay for £300 per week. Until
they have agreed the dates of the proposed let, it would not be possible to
enforce any agreement.

Apart from the question of whether it is possible to enforce a contract 2.36
in the absence of an essential term, that absence may indicate that the
parties were still negotiating and had not reached the point of concluding
a contract. In certain circumstances, however, the absence of an essential
term may not be decisive. The parties may indicate that they had in fact
moved beyond negotiation and concluded an agreement.[46] So where the
parties expressly agreed that "the prices [are] to be mutually settled at a
later and appropriate date" it was held that a contract had been formed.[47]
Alternatively, the circumstances may indicate that the parties had in fact
passed the negotiation stage and concluded a contract. For example,
despite the fact that a key part of the contract has not been agreed, one
party may start to perform its obligations under the contract and the other
party may permit this. This is illustrated in *Avintair Ltd v. Ryder Airline
Services Ltd*[48]:

> The parties were negotiating a contract under which Avintair would
> attempt to introduce Ryder to clients who would provide Ryder with
> work. No agreement was reached regarding the commission that
> Avintair would receive from Ryder in the event that it managed to
> introduce such new business. Later Ryder contacted Avintair and

---

[46] *Neilson v. Stewart,* 1991 S.L.T. 523.
[47] *R. & J. Dempster Ltd v. Motherwell Bridge and Engineering Co.,* 1964 S.C.
308; 1964 S.L.T. 353.
[48] 1994 S.L.T. 613.

said that it did not wish to proceed. Avintair claimed that it had
already provided new business to Ryder. It raised an action against
Ryder seeking payment for the services it had provided. Ryder
defended the action on the basis that there was no concluded
contract as the parties has still been negotiating about the price.

The court held that Avintair was entitled to reasonable remuneration.
The services provided to Ryder were not intended to be free of charge.
There was therefore a contract with an implied term that Avintair would
be paid a reasonable sum. A contract was not excluded merely because
the parties had continued to carry on negotiations. While it might appear
odd to impose a term as to payment when the parties were still
negotiating about that very matter, it is clear that what happened was fair
in that Ryder had benefited as a result of Avintair's work.

2.37   If a contract is to be enforced in these situations a term must be
implied in place of the "missing" term. In *Avantair* it was that Ryder
would pay reasonable remuneration for the services they received. Some
other examples of terms that are implied in such situation are: (a) in a
contract of sale of goods, if no price is specified, then the buyer must pay
a reasonable price[49]; (b) in a contract of lease, if no period is specified, a
period of one year will be presumed[50]; (c) in a contract of loan, it is
presumed that the money is repayable on demand[51]; and (d) in a contract
to carry out works, if no remuneration is specified, a entitlement to
reasonable remuneration will be implied. The general rules for implied
terms are considered in a later chapter.

LIMITS OF THE OFFER/ACCEPTANCE APPROACH

2.38   Although most agreements or apparent agreements can be analysed into a
sequence of offer, counter-offer, acceptance, and so on, it is not always
possible to do so. Hiring a taxi, buying a newspaper and many of the
other common transactions of everyday life are, on one view, only
capable of an offer/acceptance analysis by adopting an artificial
approach. Few people think in terms of offers and acceptances when they
make such agreements. It is only in relation to a small number of
contracts, such as auction sales and written estimates for building work,
that the offer/acceptance analysis is readily apparent. But in general, such
an analysis is helpful. It enables one to break down and isolate each
component part of the transaction to determine what the respective rights
and duties of the parties actually are at any particular stage. Some
specific situations call for comment.

---

[49] Sale of Goods Act 1979, s.8(2).
[50] *Gray v. University of Edinburgh,* 1962 S.C. 157; 1962 S.L.T. 173.
[51] *Neilson v. Stewart,* 1991 S.L.T. 523.

Identical Cross Offers

If A writes to B offering to sell B his car for £500 and simultaneously B   2.39
writes to A offering to purchase the car at the same price, then it would
appear that consensus has been reached. The parties' minds are *ad idem*
with regard to the essential features of the bargain. Normally of course,
the parties will be delighted to go through with the bargain in such
circumstances. However, if one of the contracting parties changes his
mind and refuses to go through with the transaction, an offer/acceptance
analysis suggests that there is no contract. Neither party has received an
acceptance and therefore neither can be bound. This may appear a rather
rigid adherence to the requirement of offer and acceptance at the expense
of the true issue in question, namely whether the parties are in
agreement.

Members of a Club

When individuals join a club or society, few legal rights or duties will   2.40
normally arise. Often the only obligation on members is to pay a
subscription. But what is the position if individuals voluntarily submit to
some legal liability in relation to other club members? It is difficult,
applying an offer and acceptance analysis, to unravel the legal
relationship of club members with one another. In one case, competitors
in a yacht race agreed under club rules to pay full compensation to any
other boat which they damaged during the event.[52] This waived the
statutory rule which limited the liability of boats by reference to the
tonnage of the yacht in question. While there was no doubt that the
competitors had agreed to full liability, it was difficult to identify any
process of offer and acceptance which had occurred between the
individual entrants. The contract (if any) appeared to be between each
competitor and the club. Nevertheless the court held that there was
indeed an offer by one competitor to the next. It has been pointed out
that, even if the analysis holds in relation to later competitors, it cannot
logically explain the position of the first entrant who had not received
any offer.

The Battle of the Forms

It has become increasingly common for businesses to contract on printed   2.41
forms. These forms are prepared in advance by legal advisers and
amount to "package contracts". When each party uses its own standard
form and neither form refers to the other, it may appear that there is no
consensus. If, however, performance follows and a dispute arises it
seems inappropriate to hold that there is no contract. Accordingly the
trusty offer/acceptance analysis has been pressed into service in this

---

[52] *The Satanita* [1895] P. 248, aff'd, *sub nom, Clarke v. Dunraven* [1897] A.C.
59.

arena as well, although it may not appear the most suitable approach. An example is provided by the case of *Continental Tyre and Rubber Co. Ltd v. Trunk Trailer Co. Ltd*[53]:

> Company T ordered a quantity of tyres from Company C. The order was placed on company T's standard printed purchase form. No written acceptance was given, but company C proceeded to supply tyres in a number of consignments. Each consignment was accompanied by a "delivery note" and several days after each delivery, company C sent an invoice to company T. Both the "delivery note" and the invoice sought to incorporate the sellers' terms into the contract. Those terms were materially different from the buyers' terms. A dispute arose regarding the quality of the tyres supplied. The sellers sought to rely on a term which operated in their favour and was included in their own standard form. It was held that the buyer's terms ought to prevail. The contract was complete when the first batch was delivered in response to the purchaser's order. The purchaser had made the offer which the seller had impliedly accepted. Accordingly, the delivery note and the invoice came too late to be the basis of the contract.

Whether, however, this is a useful analysis is a questionable proposition. In an earlier English case, Lord Denning M.R., had noted the difficulty of applying an offer, counter-offer, acceptance analysis and suggested that,

> "the better way is to look at all the documents passing between the parties and glean from them, or from the contract of the parties, whether they have reached agreement on all material points, even though there may be differences between the forms and conditions printed on the back of them."[54]

Certainly we need to look carefully at such situations to see whether an alternative approach might be formulated.

---

[53] 1987 S.C.L.R. 58.
[54] *Butler Machine Tool Co. Ltd v. Ex-cell-o Corp.* [1979] 1 All E.R. 965; [1979] 1 W.L.R. 401.

CHAPTER 3

FORMATION OF CONTRACT—ENFORCEABLE AGREEMENTS

The presence of *consensus in idem* may not by itself be sufficient to form   3.1
a contract. Various other features must be present.

INTENTION TO CREATE LEGAL RELATIONS

Not all agreements are contracts. Suppose Marlene agrees to have dinner   3.2
with a friend, or consents to a proposal made by a fellow member of a
committee. Neither of these agreements amounts to a contract. In such
cases the law deems that the parties did not intend to create legal
relations. This is not an additional requirement for, as we have seen, a
contract is only formed when a serious offer is accepted. If the offer is
not serious, acceptance cannot create a contract. On grounds of policy,
however, there are several categories of agreement which the law
declines to enforce. In such cases there is a presumption that the parties
did not intend to create binding relations. No legal rights and duties flow
from such agreements and they cannot, accordingly, be enforced.

Social Agreements

In the host of everyday arrangements made by individuals, a large   3.3
number are presumed not to create legal relations. An agreement to invite
an acquaintance to a concert does not give rise to legal liability if broken.
Of course one can figure exceptions. To request a neighbour to purchase
expensive tickets for the opera on your behalf may well give cause for
legal action if you fail to pay for them. The question in each case will be
whether a reasonable person would have assumed that legal
consequences would flow from the agreement.

Domestic Agreements

It is not desirable for one party to threaten the other with legal action in   3.4
the event of a row in the home. Domestic harmony is ill-served when
appeal can be made to courts of law over disputes arising between

husband and wife, or parent and child.[1] Accordingly, the courts are reluctant to uphold domestic agreements as contracts. A wife who looks after her husband during an illness is presumed not to do so under an implied contract.[2] This is deemed to be part and parcel of their married relationship.[3] In the past, agreements relating to maintenance payments between separated spouses were held to fall within this exception. But the great incidence of such arrangements today has led to their more often being enforced than not. Indeed, it is always possible for the presumption to be displaced where it is clear that the parties intended to put their relationship on a legal footing.

Commercial Agreements Binding in Honour Only

3.5   Moral obligations do not always bring legal obligations in their train. A debtor compromised a sum which he owed by paying one half.[4] In granting a receipt, the creditors stated that it was "understood that [the debtor] will pay the balance of 10s. per pound whenever he is able to do so." On the same date the debtor wrote to the creditor and stated "I beg to assure you that I will pay up the deficiency as soon as I am able to do so". It was held that the arrangement to make payment of the balance was an "honourable understanding" which did not import any legal obligation. Similarly, a "letter of comfort" from a parent company stating that it was their policy to ensure that one of their subsidiaries was in a position at all times to meet its liabilities did not render them liable for a £10 million bank loan when the subsidiary went into liquidation.[5]

In the above situations the court inferred that the agreement was not binding from the terms of agreement and the circumstances. The parties themselves may stipulate that their agreement is not to be legally binding. Such arrangements are rare, because a party is unlikely to consent to a position whereby he cannot apply to the court for redress should the other party fail in his obligations. In the leading English case on the matter, *Rose and Frank v. Crompton Bros.*, a clause stating that the agreement was to be "binding in honour only, and not subject to the jurisdiction of the courts", was upheld.[6] Actual deliveries which had taken place under the agreement were, however, to be paid for on the basis that they formed individual contracts of sale. Clauses of this nature could enable parties to evade their normal legal liabilities. Happily the use of such clauses is rare. The cases that have come before the courts

---

[1] *Balfour v. Balfour* [1919] 2 K.B. 571.

[2] *Edgar v. Lord Advocate*, 1965 S.C. 67.

[3] Compensation in respect of such services is, however, now available under statute in certain actions of damages for personal injuries, Administration of Justice Act 1982, s.8.

[4] *Ritchie v. Cowan & Kinghorn* (1901) 3 F. 1071.

[5] *Kleinwort Benson v. Malaysia Mining Corpn. Berhad* [1989] 1 W.L.R. 379; [1989] 1 All E.R. 785.

[6] [1925] A.C. 445.

have shown that judges do not approve of these arrangements. In one case, an agreement was made in terms of which a government department agreed to make *ex gratia* payments in respect of harbour dues.[7] Although the Lord Ordinary recognised that agreements could be entered into which were not legally enforceable, he held that the department were bound to pay the dues. The words "*ex gratia*" were not in his view enough to remove the intention to effect legal relations.

Collective Agreements

Agreements between employers and trade unions are known as collective 3.6 agreements. Often they are of great length and cover every aspect of pay, conditions and work practices. For a long time the status of such agreements was unclear, but in the late 1960s it was decided by an English court that collective agreements were not presumed to effect legal relations.[8] Breach of the terms of such an agreement could not therefore be remedied by litigation. This principle is now enshrined in Trade Union and Labour Relations (Consolidation) Act 1992, section 179. Unless the collective agreement is in writing and has an express stipulation that it is to have legal force, no action will lie if one side defaults in its obligation under the contract. The collective agreement is a statement of aspiration and an indication of good faith, rather than a legal document. If the collective agreement is in writing and has an express stipulation that it is to have legal force, then it is conclusively presumed to be a legally enforceable contract.

Voluntary Organisations

It is presumed that persons join clubs, whether sporting, political or 3.7 recreational, for mutual association, not to assume legal rights or liabilities. So long as such bodies conduct their affairs according to the canons of natural justice and within the provisions of the race and sex discrimination legislation, no legal rights arise. The law will not intervene to say who is properly entitled to enter a particular competition or uphold the right of a sportsman to play a particular game. But the law will intervene when it is clear that the parties have intended legal relations, as in the case of the *Satanita*,[9] where all the competitors had signed a carefully worded document. An intention to effect legal relations will also be deemed to be present where a member's financial (or "patrimonial") interest is affected by the action of the club or voluntary association.

---

[7] *Wick Harbour Trs. v. The Admiralty*, 1921 S.L.R. 109, *cf. Edwards v. Skyways Ltd*, [1964] 1 All E.R. 494.
[8] *Ford Motor Co. Ltd v. A.E.F.* [1969] 2 Q.B. 303; 2 All E.R. 481.
[9] *The Satanita* [1895] P. 248, aff'd, *sub nom, Clarke v. Dunraven* [1897] A.C. 59.

A patrimonial interest is a property interest: one that can be valued in money terms. This question of patrimonial interest concerns persons who hold offices in voluntary associations and in particular, ministers of religion. So far as the Church of Scotland is concerned, deprivation of office is a matter within the jurisdiction of the General Assembly of the Church. In non-established churches, however, the position is less clear. Where actual loss of office, or even loss of status, is concerned, the law has in the past intervened and adjudicated upon the rights and duties of the parties.[10] But the law steered clear of controversial theological matters. Thus a minister who claimed a change in his church's doctrine meant he would have to relinquish his post in accordance with his conscience had no redress.[11] More recently there have been two cases in England which deny that a minister has a contract.[12] The view seems to be that the spiritual nature of a clergyman's calling ousts the temporal. The practical consequence is that a clergyman is not entitled to sue for unfair dismissal in an employment tribunal, because that right only exists if there is a contract of employment.

Gaming Contracts

3.8   The winner of a bet cannot enforce it against the loser or bookmaker.[13] Nor can a casino correct an error by a croupier in giving a customer too many chips after a win on the roulette wheel.[14] A written admission of the debt will not render a wager enforceable. Football pools fall within this category.[15] Television plays and the seamier sort of novel suggest, however, that non-legal sanctions for the enforcement of such matters are a good deal more effective than the courts.

There are several justifications for not enforcing these agreements. In *Ferguson v. Littlewoods Football Pools Limited*,[16] Lord Coulsfield summarised the reasons evident from earlier cases as:

(a)   the parties cannot have intended the agreement to have legal consequences;

(b)   it would be beneath the dignity of the courts to rule on the matter in dispute;

(c)   gambling agreements do not have commercial significance; or

(d)   a judicial disapproval of gambling.

---

[10] See, *e.g. McMillan v. Free Church of Scotland* (1861) 23 D. 1314.

[11] *Forbes v. Eden* (1867) 5 M. (H.L.) 36.

[12] *Davies v. Presbyterian Church of Wales* [1986] 1 W.L.R. 323; [1986] 1 All E.R. 705; *President of the Methodist Conference v. Parfitt* [1984] Q.B. 368.

[13] *Wordsworth v. Pettigrew* (1977) Mor. 9524.

[14] *County Properties & Developments Ltd v. Harper,* 1989 S.C.L.R. 597.

[15] *Ferguson v. Littlewoods Football Pools Limited,* 1997 S.L.T. 309.

[16] 1997 S.L.T. 309.

Very few propositions in contract law are absolute. Such is the case here. If the contract is truly collateral or incidental to the gaming contract itself it may be enforced. This is what occurred in *Robertson v. Anderson*[17]:

> The pursuer and the defender were close friends. On 21 November 1997 they went to play bingo together at the Mecca Bingo Hall in Drumchapel. They had done so many time before. That night, the defender won over £100,000 on the national jackpot. The pursuer claimed that there was a long standing agreement between her and the defender that they would split their winnings. This was disputed by the defender.

After proof, Lord Carloway held that there was an agreement. This issue was therefore whether it was enforceable. It was held that it was because the wager was between the defender and Mecca. The agreement between the pursuer and defender was collateral to that wager and involved "no gamble in itself". In his opinion, Lord Carloway indicated that it would not be difficult to raise questions about the validity of the rule that the courts would not enforce gaming contracts.

Social Work "Contracts"

It has recently become more common in the welfare field for social 3.9
workers, parole officers and even headmasters to enter into written "contracts" with their clients and pupils. General practitioners routinely require heroin addicts to agree to certain terms about the use of the surgery before they agree to administer Methadone programmes. These agreements list the obligations that each party is supposed to fulfil but are clearly not legally enforceable. The fact that they are made at all perhaps shows the potency of the idea of contract. Persons entering such arrangements regard themselves as morally bound to uphold the obligations to which they have agreed, even though there are no legal sanctions in the event of breach.

UNCERTAINTY

Even where there is consensus between the parties and an intention to be 3.10
bound, an agreement will not be enforceable if it is lacking in certainty. For example, Clarke plc wishes to licence software to be developed by HAL Ltd. The parties have been discussing exactly what the software should do, when it is to be delivered and what licence fee should be

---

[17] Lord Carloway, 15 May 2001. This case had not been reported as the time of writing.

payable. In order to get the contract signed, they agree that "the customary level of support will be provided during reasonable hours for the usual remuneration". If a dispute arises as to the level of support it is unlikely that a court could enforce this term. It is simply too vague.

The test that the courts use to determine whether an agreement is too uncertain is to ask whether it would be possible to frame a decree of specific implement requiring a party to perform its obligations under the contract.[18] If this cannot be done, the contract—or part of it—is said to be void for uncertainty. The leading case on this issue is *McArthur v. Lawson*[19]:

> McArthur had been taken on by Lawson as an employee. Their contract provided for payment of a salary for a period of two years. It also stated, "At the expiry of the second year I engage to give you a substantial interest by way of partnership in my business, so that your annual income may be considerably increased." When the two years was up, Lawson refused to give McArthur any share in his business. McArthur sought damages in respect of Lawson failure to make him a partner in his business.

The court considered that none of the terms of the partnership were spelled out in this contract. They would therefore have been unable to grant a decree of specific implement. On that basis the clause was void. Because it was void, it was not possible even to give damages rather than enforce the partnership. In the words of Lord President Dunedin, "A contract which cannot be enforced by specific implement…is no contract at all, and cannot form the ground of an action for damages".[20] It is nevertheless common for such imprecise expressions as "reasonable remuneration", "best endeavours" and "best practice" to feature in contracts. Sometimes it is the very fact that they are imprecise that makes these terms attractive to the parties—each assumes that the term will have the meaning that best suits them. The courts recognise that these terms are used by parties and attempt to give such terms meanings where the circumstances make it possible to do so.

3.11   Uncertainty may strike at only part of the contract. If that is so, the issue of whether the contract as a whole may survive will depend on the importance within the contract of the terms rendered void. If it touches the core of the agreement it is likely that the whole agreement will be considered void. If the term in question is more peripheral, it may be ignored and the remainder of the agreement may be given effect.

---

[18] Specific implement is considered in more detail in relation to breach of contract.

[19] (1877) 4 R. 1134.

[20] p.1136.

WHEN IS THE CONTRACT BROUGHT INTO OPERATION?

In some instances the parties to the contract may wish to postpone its 3.12 legal enforceability. It is competent for the parties to provide that the contract shall not take effect until a particular date or event occurs.

> *Example*: A may agree to buy B's car provided that the car passes an M.O.T. test. A is not bound to buy the car unless and until the car passes the test.

Not all conditions have the effect of postponing or suspending the operation of the contract. The legal effect of a particular condition will depend on a number of factors. If the condition refers to a future certain event such as a particular date, or the death of a named individual, then the obligation is constituted immediately: "In truth such an obligation is a present obligation which is to be discharged in the future".[21] So if A agrees to pay a debt when A's grandfather dies, that obligation exists from the moment it is entered into. It is only performance which is postponed. But where the condition refers to a future uncertain event— that X will reach the age of 18, or that Y will swim the Channel—its effect will either be suspensive or resolutive. Suspensive, if the obligation only becomes enforceable when the uncertain event occurs; resolutive if the obligation exists immediately, but is to come to an end if and when the uncertain event happens. An example of a suspensive condition would be where a job is offered subject to a medical examination being passed. Only when a satisfactory medical report is received does a contract of employment arise. But an offer of employment subject to documentary proof that the individual held the academic qualifications which he claimed, would be a resolutive condition. The contract of employment would arise when the individual accepted the offer. If, however, he could not confirm his qualifications the employment would be deemed never to have arisen. These two examples demonstrate that sometimes, there is no more than the thickness of a cigarette paper between the two types of action.

A common expression in English law is that the agreement will be 3.13 "subject to contract". Most agreements for house transfers in England include such a clause. Its effect is to suspend the operation of the contract until written documents are signed by the parties. This has led to the practice of "gazumping". A seller who has agreed to sell to a particular person subject to contract may renege on his agreement and decide to sell to someone else. As there is no legally enforceable obligation the seller is entitled to do this. The different method of buying property in Scotland has prevented such a practice arising.[22] Under Scots law there is no

---

[21] Smith, *A Short Commentary on the Law of Scotland* (Edinburgh, 1962), p.617.
[22] There are proposals for a change in the law to prevent it occurring in England.

conclusive answer regarding the effect of a "subject to contract" clause.[23] It will always be a question of construction. Should it be clear that the parties did not intend to be bound until a formal writing is signed, then the contract does not come into existence until that condition is satisfied.

---

[23] *Erskine v. Glendinning* (1871) 9 M. 656; *Stobo v. Morrison's Gowns Ltd*, 1949 S.C. 184.

CHAPTER 4

PROMISE

Apart from contract, Scots law recognises a second type of voluntary 4.1
obligation known as promise. Stair described a promise as "that which is
simple and pure, and hath not implied as a condition the acceptance of
another".[1] A clear case of promise is an undertaking to make a gift.

> *Example:* Rudolph, a wealthy philanthropist, visits an exhibition of
> watercolours by Zeke. Two days later Zeke receives a signed letter
> from Rudolph. It states that Rudolph is impressed by Zeke's
> paintings and that he promises to send Zeke £2,500 to assist him in
> his work.

Rudolph is legally bound to honour this obligation. He has incurred
the obligation despite the fact that Zeke has done nothing. Indeed Zeke
may be completely unaware of Rudolph's intention until he receives the
letter. But once Rudolph declares his intention, Zeke acquires a personal
right-a right to sue Rudolph for £2,500. Rudolph must fulfil his promise
if required to do so by Zeke.

PROMISE OR CONTRACT

When is a particular obligation analysed as a promise rather than a 4.2
contract. In particular, what are the differences between promise and
offer? They can be listed as follows:

(1) A contract arises out of the will of two parties. A promise is the
product of one person's intention alone. No acceptance is
required to create a binding obligation.
(2) An offer is revocable until it is accepted. A promise is binding
and irrevocable from the moment it is made.
(3) A promise places an obligation on one person alone. By
contrast, contracts place obligations on both parties to the
contract. In theory this is true even of gratuitous contracts. For
instance, if A offers to gift a statue to his local council and it
accepts, the council is under an obligation to take the statue.In

---

[1] *Institutions*, I.x.4.

the case of a promise the council would always have a right to reject the statue.

The apparent simplicity of this account is belied by the problems which occur in practice in attempting to distinguish a promise from a contract. A person giving an undertaking will not normally have in mind the relevant legal rules. The words used will not be particularly precise or technical. In some instances there will be no words at all but simply acts or a mixture of words and acts. It is then necessary to analyse the circumstances to determine the exact nature of the obligation in question. This is not always an easy task. The problem of classification can be illustrated by reference to two cases. In the first, *Morton's Trs v. The Aged Christian Friend Society of Scotland*[2]:

> Morton wrote to a committee which was promoting a charitable society. He offered to pay the society £1,000 by 10 annual instalments of £100 if certain conditions regarding its constitution were observed. Morton's offer was accepted by the committee, the society was formed and the conditions in the offer complied with. During his lifetime Morton paid the instalments every year, but he died leaving two instalments unpaid. A dispute arose as to whether his estate was bound to pay the remaining instalments. It was held that the society were entitled to recover the outstanding sum from Morton's estate. There was a binding contract between Morton and the society.

4.3   By contrast in *Smith v. Oliver*[3]:

> During the course of her life Mrs Oliver had given money from time to time toward the cost of certain structural alterations to a church in Dalry, Edinburgh. After her death the trustees of the church raised an action against her executor, claiming that Mrs Oliver had promised to provide £7,000 in her will for the remainder of the outlay involved. No such provision in the will had been made. The trustees said that they had relied on the assurances that Mrs Oliver had given in arranging for the work to be undertaken.
>
> There was held to be no contract here, only a promise. As the trustees did not have the appropriate evidence to prove the promise, their action failed.

The substance of the transaction in each case was the same. Both Mr Morton and Mrs Oliver wished to make a gift, one to a charity, the other to a church. Can we explain why different legal analyses were applied? The answer lies in the circumstances in which the obligation was undertaken. Mr Morton had actually used the word "offer" several times in his letters to the committee. It was not disputed that they had accepted

---

[2] (1899) 2 F. 82; 7 S.L.T. 220.
[3] 1911 S.C. 103; 1910 2 S.L.T. 304.

the offer. Mrs Oliver's case was different. She had not committed her thoughts to writing. The church trustees could only point to various oral statements which she had made. No offer could be inferred from these statements, nor had there been any definite acceptance: "There is in truth no contract at all averred here, but merely a promise to pay".[4] Without a signed statement from Mrs Oliver, the promise was unenforceable.

The guidance to be derived from these two cases has not proved particularly helpful to subsequent judges. Where possible they have avoided committing themselves to one analysis or the other. In *Bathgate v. Rosie*, a young boy broke a shop window while out playing one evening.[5] His mother told the shopkeeper's wife that she would pay for the cost of a replacement. However, when the window was installed, the mother refused to pay. The sheriff held that the mother was bound to pay the replacement cost because she had given an unqualified undertaking to do so, but he did not specify whether it was a promise or a contract. What is clear is that a promise cannot be converted into a contract. In the old case of *Miller v. Tremamondo* it was alleged that a man had married a lady on the strength of certain financial assurances made by her father.[6] When these assurances were not realised, the husband sued his (now) father-in-law to fulfil his promises. It was decided that the alleged assurances were promises and the mere fact that the husband-to-be had acted on the faith of the promises did not convert them into a contract.

A Presumption in Favour of Contract

There is no doubt that through time there has developed a general presumption in favour of an analysis in terms of contract rather than in terms of promise. Several cases can be cited in support of this proposition. In *Malcolm v. Campbell* a lady signed a document before witnesses which said "I have agreed to sell my house for £150 to Miss X" and delivered the document to Miss X.[7] The court decided that the lady was not bound by the document as it was only one side of a bilateral arrangement. The circumstances of *Paterson v. Highland Railway Co.* arose out of the First World War. Various railway companies undertook to maintain freight rates for timber at a fixed rate while an arrangement they had with the government remained in force.[8] The companies sought to increase the rates before the arrangement had terminated. It was held that the undertaking did not amount to a contract and was therefore unenforceable. In *Muirhead v. Gribben* an assurance was given by one firm of solicitors to another.[9] They stated that the second firm's fees

4.4

---

[4] *per* Lord President Dunedin.
[5] 1976 S.L.T. (Sh.Ct) 16.
[6] (1771) Mor. 12395.
[7] (1891) 19 R. 278.
[8] 1927 S.C. (H.L.) 32.
[9] 1983 S.L.T. (Sh.Ct) 102.

would be paid if they transferred to the first firm papers belonging to a particular client. This was held to be a contract rather than a promise.

Three factors have had a bearing on this preference for a contractual analysis. First, many situations which might possibly be regarded as a promise involve the satisfaction of a condition. The condition is that some act be performed. Let us take an example. Suppose a wealthy businessman makes the following statement: "I promise to pay £150 to the first person to climb Ben Nevis wearing roller skates." The businessman does not receive a return promise for his own obligation. No one is bound to fulfil the condition. But it is clear that if performance is made he must pay the sum stipulated. Now an offer can be viewed as a promise to perform, subject to a condition being satisfied, *viz.* that acceptance be given. It is not therefore difficult to view fulfilment of the condition by performance as implied acceptance. This is the line that the courts have tended to adopt.

4.5 Secondly, there is a strong presumption against donation in the law. The law is reluctant to hold that a person intended to benefit another without receiving anything in return, unless clear evidence of that intention is present. All promises appear on their fact to be gratuitous and, therefore, to be treated with caution. In a contract, even a gratuitous contract like the one in *Morton,* both parties know of and assent to the creation of the obligation. Clear evidence of both parties' intention is therefore present and it is expected that the person benefited will rely on the obligation. The third factor which has led to a presumption in favour of contract rather than promise is the influence of English law. A short excursus into English law is therefore required.

THE ENGLISH REQUIREMENT OF CONSIDERATION

4.6 In England obligations are enforceable only when supported by "consideration". In essence, consideration means that there must be some reciprocity, or element of bargain, in the transaction. English law will not enforce a bare promise where the promisor receives nothing in return. Consideration is therefore an additional technical requirement beyond offer and acceptance which must be satisfied before obligations are upheld. A classic example of consideration in English law occurs in *Stilk v. Myricklo*[10]:

> Nine seamen had been engaged to sail a ship on a return trip from London to the Baltic. Two of the crew deserted at Kronstadt. The captain promised the remainder of the crew extra wages if they would work the ship home shorthanded. However, when the ship arrived back in Britain, the owner refused to pay the extra amount and an action was brought by one of the seamen for the increased

---

[10] (1809) 2 Camp. 317; 6 Esp. 129.

wage. He was unsuccessful. It was held that there was no consideration for the captain's promise—the crew were under an existing contractual duty to bring the ship home. The captain's promise to pay them extra was unsupported by consideration. He received nothing in return for his promise which he was not already due.

In theory, therefore, there is a wide gulf between the position of English law and that of Scots law. North of the border, the concept of simple promise is recognised. South of the border it is not. However, the true picture is less clear cut. In England, even where consideration is absent, a person can make a binding unilateral obligation in a deed under seal. This is not a difficult requirement to satisfy. All that is required is that a simple adhesive wafer be attached to the deed. This is the manner by which a parent in England might covenant to pay sums to a child at university in order to secure tax advantages. In addition, the concept of consideration has over the years become somewhat elastic. The English courts have been prepared—rather artificially—to "find" consideration in many instances. A promise in return for a promise is good consideration. So is an act in return for a promise. In determining whether or not there is consideration, no inquiry is made into the value of the other party's performance. It is enough that something is given in return, no matter how low in value. That is why the term "peppercorn rent" can be literally as well as figuratively true. If a landlord stipulates that the rent for premises shall be 3 peppercorns, this will be binding. An example of this approach is provided by *Williams v. Roffey & Nicholls (Contractors)*[11]:

> Building contractors contracted to refurbish a block of 27 flats. Their contract provided that they would have to pay penalty damages in the event that there was a delay in completion. They subcontracted the joiner-work to a carpenter at a price of £20,000. The carpenter ran into financial difficulties. The contractors agreed to pay him an extra £10,300 to complete the work on time. He went on to complete several flats but only received one further payment of £1,500 from the contractors. He sued for the extra sum. The contractors maintained that there was no consideration. The Court of Appeal held that the advantage to be secured by the contractors in not having to pay under the penalty clause, nor having to find another subcontractor, amounted to consideration.

It follows that in practice, the difference between the two legal systems is often not very great. But the underlying theory of consideration has resulted in English lawyers preferring to analyse all types of unilateral undertaking in terms of contract. By an unfortunate process of osmosis, this approach has become accepted in Scotland, a

4.7

---

[11] [1991] 1 Q.B. 1; [1990] 2 W.L.R. 1153; [1990] 1 All E.R. 512.

result which can lead to strained and artificial reasoning in analysing common situations where such undertakings occur.

THE PRACTICAL APPLICATION OF THE CONCEPT OF PROMISE

Firm Offers

4.8   The first situation where the concept of promise is useful is in connection with promises to keep an offer open. In *Littlejohn v. Hadwen* the estate of Renniston was being sold.[12] In a postscript to a letter containing details of the estate, the seller's solicitor wrote "it is understood that Mr Littlejohn has the offer of the estate of Renniston for ten days from this date". Lord Fraser regarded this as "an obligation, no doubt unilateral, but still binding upon the offeror during the appointed period". Unless something was given in return for such a promise in England, it would not be binding upon the promiser. There is no consideration. Yet if the offerer truly intended to keep his offer open for a certain period it seems appropriate that the law should uphold this undertaking, as in Scotland.

Third Party Rights

4.9   The concept of promise has allowed Scots law to develop the principle that third persons may acquire rights under a contract to which they were not parties. Two contracting parties can bind themselves in favour of a third. This is known as *jus quaesitum tertio* and will be discussed in Chapter 9.

The Reward Cases

4.10   Those cases where a promise to pay a reward in the event of a condition being fulfilled are referred to generally as "the reward cases". Before the late nineteenth century, the precise analysis of such cases in Scotland was unclear. This can be seen by examining the case of *Petrie v. Earl of Airlie*[13]:

> The Earl of Airlie did not vote in support of the great Reform Bill which extended the franchise for the House of Commons. Subsequently, a poster appeared accusing the Earl of Airlie and others of conduct amounting to treason by not supporting the measure in Parliament. The Earl stated that he would pay 100 guineas reward for information leading to the detection of the author and printer of the placard. The reward was to be payable on conviction. Petrie informed the Earl that his brother and another person were the printers. When the Earl passed this information to

---

[12] (1980) 20 S.L.R. 5.
[13] (1834) 13 S. 68.

the authorities, however, they declined to prosecute and he himself did not initiate a private prosecution (which was more common then). Accordingly, there was no conviction and the Earl refused to pay the reward. Petrie was successful in recovering the reward money when he sued the Earl. The opinion of the Lord Ordinary (Corehouse) was affirmed by the Inner House without their giving reasons.

Professor Smith regarded the case as being one of conditional promise.[14] Professor Walker states that it could have been dealt with on this basis, but in fact it was treated as a case of contract.[15] It is not clear from the opinion of Lord Corehouse which view is correct. He did not distinctly analyse the basis upon which the obligation was founded.

In the early twentieth century there were several Scottish cases   4.11 dealing with rewards.[16] All proceeded on the basis of contract rather than promise, probably because of the influence of *Carlill*. The divergence between the two approaches has practical consequences. This is clearly demonstrated by considering an Australian case, *R. v. Clarke*[17]:

A reward for information leading to the arrest of certain alleged criminals was issued by the Government of Western Australia. If the information was provided by an accomplice it was further promised that he would receive a free pardon. Clarke, who was himself under suspicion of the crime provided information. Later he found out about the reward and claimed payment.

The High Court of Australia held that Clarke was not entitled to the reward. In issuing the reward, the State Government was making an offer. Clarke gave the information without reference to that offer. There was therefore no acceptance and no contract. The Australian Chief Justice (Isaacs) instanced the case of an offer of £100 to anyone who would swim 100 yards in the harbour on the first day of the year. In his view, someone who had been thrown overboard and was simply swimming to save his life was not entitled to the sum. This argument reflects a hostility to persons acquiring money on a "something for nothing" basis. As the person would have given the information or swum the distance stipulated anyway, irrespective of the reward, the other person should not be bound to pay him anything. Perhaps it ultimately depends on one's moral perspective. On one view the condition is satisfied so the undertaking should be fulfilled. A person who issues a reward but wishes to withhold it from certain persons can do so by

---

[14] Smith, *A Short Commentary on the Law of Scotland* (Edinburgh, 1962), p.748.
[15] Walker, *Contracts* (3rd ed., 1995), 2.34.
[16] See, *e.g. Hunter v. General Accident Corp.*, 1909 S.C. (H.L.) 30; [1909] A.C. 404; 1909 2 S.L.T. 99.
[17] (1927) 40 C.L.R. 227.

express stipulation. If he fails to make such a qualification, then he should be bound.

4.12   Another problem of analysing the reward in cases in terms of offers concerns the right to withdraw. When precisely does the offerer lose his right to cancel the reward? We have seen that offers can always be withdrawn before acceptance. How does that principle apply here? Suppose a man puts a notice in his local newspaper that he will pay £50 to anyone who will return his lost kitten "Shuggie" to him. A promise analysis means that the man must pay the money to anyone who satisfies the condition by returning the kitten to him. But if it is an offer, is the right of revocation lost when someone spies Shuggie, or picks him up, or starts going towards the man's home? English law has been over-elaborate in its attempt to explain why the offerer should be prevented from withdrawing his offer before acceptance is made. The approach of Scots law does seem both clearer and more appropriate.

Options

4.13   A typical option occurs where there is a provision in a contract which allows one party to acquire certain specific rights in the future by issuing a notice to the other party.

> *Example:* A agrees to lease B's estate for 15 years. Clause 3 of the lease allows A to purchase the estate after eight years have elapsed. In order to exercise the option, A must issue a notice by means of recorded delivery letter served on B. The price for the estate will he its market value as at the date the option is triggered, which will be assessed by independent surveyors.

Some contracts are exclusively about options. A contract relating to the right to film a novel would fall into this category. A studio might agree to pay an author £20,000 in return for an option to film her novel within the next two years. Lord Ross suggested that the better view is to regard options as a type of promise, rather than as an offer.[18] In effect, the granting of an option means "I oblige myself to do such and such provided you exercise the option." In our example, B promises to enter into missives to sell the estate to A provided that the option is exercised in terms of Clause 3. This overcomes the problem that arises with offer/acceptance, where an explanation must be given as to why the option is irrevocable even before any acceptance has been made.

---

[18] See *Stone v. MacDonald*, 1979 S.L.T. 288.

THE POTENTIAL FOR DEVELOPMENT

The discussion above highlights a number of areas where the concept of 4.14
promise might be useful. There are other areas where promise might
potentially be employed.[19] A bank cheque-card, for example, can be
viewed as a promise by the issuing bank to honour cheques drawn on a
particular account up to a certain amount. A similar approach might be
adopted in relation to "letters of intent".[20] These are documents where
one person indicates to another that he intends to enter a contract with
him if certain events occur. They are commonly used in the building
trade, where a main contractor may request a subcontractor to provide a
tender for certain specialist work such as plumbing. In return, the main
contractor will provide a letter of intent, which indicates that he proposes
to take the subcontractor on if he is awarded the main contract. Such a
letter of intent might, in appropriate circumstances, be regarded as a
promise. Requirements contracts, where contractors undertake to take all
their supplies from a particular supplier or retailer, might also yield to a
promise analysis. These are areas where the concept of promise may
provide a template for future legal development in Scots law.

CONCLUSION

(1) Scots law recognises the unilateral voluntary obligation of 4.15
    promise. It is not bedevilled by the notion of consideration.
(2) A promise is irrevocable from the moment it is made and does
    not require acceptance.
(3) There is a presumption in favour of analysing situations in terms
    of offer and acceptance.
(4) Promise is largely an undeveloped concept in Scots law despite
    the fact that it may provide a more accurate analysis of several
    common situations.

---

[19] MacQueen, 1987 S.L.T. (News) 1.
[20] See *Uniroyal v. Miller*, 1985 S.L.T. 101.

CHAPTER 5

CAPACITY AND FORMALITIES

CAPACITY

Everyone aged over 18 years and in full command of their faculties can   5.1
make contracts. Such persons are said to have full capacity. Special
provisions apply to young people and to those who are not in full
possession of their mental faculties.

YOUNG PERSONS

So far as age is concerned, the law is contained in the Age of Legal   5.2
Capacity (Scotland) Act 1991.[1] The 1991 Act distinguishes a person's
capacity to act into three periods. In general, a person under the age of 16
is deemed to have no capacity to enter into transactions.[2] Any important
legal step will generally be taken by that person's legal representative.[3]
Parents are usually the legal representatives.[4] However, the general
principle has an important qualification. Children are entitled to enter
into transactions provided two conditions are satisfied. First, the
transaction is of a kind commonly entered into by persons of that age and
circumstances. Secondly, the terms of the transaction are reasonable.[5] If
the two conditions are not met, however, the transaction is void.[6]

> *Examples*: (1) Ingrid is eight years old. If she buys a bus ticket or a
> comic at face value, the contracts made will be binding. (2) Archie is
> 11 years of age. He makes a contract, in terms of which he agrees to

---

[1] As amended in part by the Children (Scotland) Act 1995.
[2] 1991 Act, s.1(1)(a).
[3] 1991 Act, s.5 (as amended) and Children (Scotland) Act 1995 Act, ss. 1(1)(d),
2(1)(d) and 7(5); and see Law Reform (Parent and Child) (Scotland) Act 1986.
[4] Children (Scotland) Act 1995 Act, ss. 1 and 2.
[5] 1991 Act, s.2(1).
[6] There are two further, limited exceptions. Persons aged under 16 have capacity
to act (1) as the legal representative for a child of their own (Children (Scotland)
Act 1995 Act, Sched. 4(53)(2)(b)); and (2) to instruct solicitors for legal
proceedings (Children (Scotland) Act 1995 Act, Sched. 4(53)(3)).

buy one computer game per month for a 10 month period. The price of each game is £200, which is well above the retail price. There is no provision in the contract which allows Archie to cancel. The contract is void on the basis that it is not common for 11-year-old children to enter contracts of this type and that the terms are unreasonable.

5.3   When a person reaches the age of 16 years, the position changes. Upon attaining that age, the general principle is that a person acquires full legal capacity.[7] If, however, between the ages of 16 and 18, someone enters into a "prejudicial transaction" then he or she is entitled to apply to the court to have the transaction set aside. A prejudicial transaction is defined by the Act as one which:

(a)   an adult, exercising reasonable prudence, would not have entered into in the circumstances of the applicant at the time of entering into the transaction; and

(b)   has caused or is likely to cause substantial prejudice to the applicant.

The application must be made before the person reaches 21 years of age. A party may be reluctant to enter into a transaction with a person between 16 and 18 years old, because of the possibility that the agreement might subsequently be set aside on the ground that it is prejudicial. In such a situation, a joint application can be made to have the transaction ratified by the court.[8] The court is required to scrutinise the bargain before ratifying it. Where a transaction has been ratified, it cannot be challenged on the basis that it was prejudicial.[9] Over the age of 18 years, a person has full capacity.

Summary	Under 16 years	— Limited capacity
	16-18 years	— Qualified full capacity
	Over 18 years	— Full capacity

MENTAL CAPACITY

5.4   Insane people have no capacity to make contracts. The law intervenes to protect such people by making their contracts void. A curator must be appointed to make contracts on behalf of such a person. Accordingly if an elderly person becomes demented such that they are deemed incapable of managing their own affairs, a *curator bonis* may be appointed to supervise that person's affairs. This can be an expensive and

---

[7] 1991 Act, s.1(1)(b).
[8] 1991 Act, s.4(1).
[9] 1991 Act, s.3(3)(j).

time-consuming process. It is often difficult for relatives to deal with an insane person's affairs expeditiously because of the need for a curator to be appointed.[10]

A less important category of persons deemed to have no capacity are intoxicated persons. Persons who are drunk or under the influence of drugs can make contracts so long as they are not totally incapacitated. Erskine summed up the position as follows: "Persons while in a state of absolute drunkenness and consequently deprived of the exercise of reason, cannot oblige themselves, but a lesser degree of drunkenness which only darkens reason, has not the effect of annulling the contract."[11]

FORMALITIES

Introduction

"Formalities" means that the law lays down further requirements beyond 5.5 those of formation in order to the contract to be brought into existence. How does this work in practice? In contracts where no formalities are required, a person wishing to prove that a binding agreement exists can rely on all relevant evidence. Witnesses can be heard and documents examined. But should a contract fall into a class where a particular formality is required, the validity of the contract will be determined by whether or not that formality has been complied with. The most common formality is to require some form of writing.

The general principle is that no special formalities are required to make a valid contract. This has always been the approach in Scots law. Stair said we had adopted the canon law approach by which "every paction produceth action."[12] If, accordingly, the twin elements of agreement and intention to be bound are present, the contract is complete. This means that in Scotland most contracts have legal effect no matter what their form—whether written, oral or arising by implication from the way the parties act. Accordingly a verbal bargain to sell an Aston Martin, or a block of shares valued at £5 million, is binding on the parties. In the next section we shall examine the exceptions to this general principle.

Reasons for Requiring Writing

It would be possible for a legal system to require no formalities for 5.6 contractual obligations. Every contract could be made in any fashion and

---

[10] This will change when the Adults with Incapacity (Scotland) Act 2000 (asp. 4) comes into force on April 1, 2002. After that date "guardians" will be appointed in terms of the Act.

[11] *Institutions* I.iii.16.

[12] *Institutions* I.x.7.

proved by any means. No system, however, entirely dispenses with formalities and there are several interlinked reasons for this:

5.7 (1) **To show that the transaction is authentic.** A formality demonstrates that a particular person truly intended to conclude the transaction. In the early law seals were used. Because seals could be easily lost or forged, signed writing came to be required as a better means of authenticating a person's intention. Today we regard signed documents as a mark that the signatory clearly intended to enter the transaction. Even in electronic commerce, it may be necessary to have some means of authentication to show the identity of the party entering into the transaction.

5.8 (2) **To emphasise the importance of transaction.** Formalities may impress upon the contracting parties the importance of their acts. In some societies in the past, the requirements have been startling: "Herodotus tells us that the Scythians, when they desired to make a contract entirely binding, drew blood of one another into a bowl, dipt their arrows in it, and afterwards drank it off."[13] By putting their contract into writing, signing it and having the signatures witnessed, the parties are made aware of the serious nature of the transaction they are undertaking. The formality should deter them from entering contracts on a whim. It allows parties to pause and reflect before entering serious undertakings. The contracting party "is awaked from his reverie by the entrance of two or more people called in to witness what is going on" and "he will be more upon his guard and deliberate more coolly upon what he is doing."[14] When confronted by a car hire contract on holiday, however, there are few of us who actually comply with this approach.

5.9 (3) **To produce certainty.** When negotiations have been going on for a period, there may be certain issues which each contracting party thinks are settled. If, however, the agreement is oral and a dispute arises, each party may find that his recollection of the terms differs from that of the other. A written contract provides a fixed record of the agreement. This allows disputes to be resolved more easily than by recourse to the parties' (or other peoples') impression of the terms of the agreement.

5.10 (4) **To protect one of the parties.** There are some instances where it is helpful for one of the parties to have a written record of the terms of the transaction. A tenant or an employee may find himself in a situation where it is important to have in writing a statement of the terms of the contract. This can be particularly true where there is the possibility of exploitation by the stronger party. Some statutes require that one party's rights are to be specifically declared in the contract. Where goods are bought with finance provided by a credit company, for example, it is incumbent upon the company to provide a written statement of the

---

[13] Smith, *Lectures on Jurisprudence* (Meek ed., Raphael & Stein, Oxford, 1978), ii. 70.
[14] *Crichton and Dow v. Syme* (1772) Mor. 17047 (said in relation to signature authenticated by witnesses, see below).

contract to the consumer. This statement must include information telling the consumer about his rights.[15] Under the Timeshare Act 1992, businesses which offer timeshares in holiday apartments must give written notice to purchasers that they have a right to cancel the agreement within 14 days.

THE REQUIREMENTS OF WRITING ACT 1995

The development of the present Scots law of formalities can be traced   5.11 back to several statutes passed from 1540 onwards, which are known as the Authentication Statutes.[16] Those Acts laid down a variety of rules regarding the requirements to be satisfied to make a document legally binding. Subsequent cases amplified when and how these rules were to apply. The later statutes passed in relation to this topic possessed a common element, namely the relaxation of the more strict requirements of the earlier legislation.[17] Nonetheless, the law in this area remained unsatisfactory. The Scottish Law Commission considered the matter in detail.[18] The Commission concluded that while it might be prudent in many fields for parties to record their contracts in writing, it was doubtful that the law should make this compulsory. The Commission recommended that the law be reformed. That proposal was accepted and the result was the Requirements of Writing Act 1995 ("the 1995 Act").[19] That Act sets out the general rules as to the need for formalities for contracts generally. There are other statutes and regulations with rules for particular forms of contract and these continue to have effect.[20] However, as the 1995 Act provides a scheme for contracts generally, it is the only one we shall consider in detail.

When Writing is Required

The Requirements of Writing Act 1995 sets down the general rule and   5.12 the exceptions to it. The general rule is that writing is not required to constitute a contract or unilateral obligation.[21] The exceptions for which there is a requirement for a written document in the law of contract are:

---

[15] Consumer Credit Act 1974, ss. 58, 60, 61.
[16] The most important of these are the Acts 1540 (cap. 117), 1579 (cap. 80), 1584 (cap. 4), 1593 (cap. 179), 1681 (cap. 5) (Lord Stair's Act).
[17] See Conveyancing (Scotland) Act 1874, Conveyancing and Feudal Reform (Scotland) Act 1970.
[18] Scottish Law Commission No. 112.
[19] (c. 7).
[20] *e.g.* the Consumer Credit Act 1974 requires all hire purchase agreements to be legible, to embody all the terms of the agreement, including those prescribed by the Act, and to be signed by both hirer and creditor.
[21] s.1(1).

(1) Agreements relating to land and buildings.[22] The Scottish Law Commission recognised that many contracts are made for far greater sums of money than those which relate to land. Nonetheless, the purchase of a house is still the most important contract entered into by most people. They considered it desirable to have a rule which allows time to consider the proposed contract and discourages the formation of informal contacts without legal advice.

(2) A gratuitous unilateral obligation other than an obligation undertaken in the course of a business.[23]

A variation to a contract or obligation falling within either of these categories is treated in the same way.[24]

The Requirements Imposed

Writing

5.13 The first requirement is that there must be a written document.[25] The only definition of "document" states that it includes an annex to a document. In its present from, the term would exclude "writing" contained on or in electronic media. The Electronic Communications Act 2000, however, includes a power to alter legislation so as to facilitate electronic communication.[26] This appears to raise the possibility that in future "writing" might consist of an electronic record.

Signature

5.14 The second requirement is that the granter or granters sign the document.[27] Individuals must sign with one of the following:

(1) the full name by which they are identified in the document or testing clause[28];

(2) his or her surname preceded by (a) at least one forename, (b) at least one abbreviation or familiar form of a forename (*e.g.* "Willy" instead of "William"), or, (c) at least one initial of a forename; or

(3) a name or description or an initial or mark which is his or her normal method of signing documents of the type in question and is intended as a signature.

---

[22] s. 1(2)(a)(i).
[23] s.1(2a)(a)(ii).
[24] s.1(6).
[25] s.1(2).
[26] s.8(1). At the time of writing, this section is not in force.
[27] s.2(1).
[28] See below.

If the document consists of more than one page it is enough that it is signed on the last page.[29] It is possible for an offer to be contained in one or more documents and for the acceptance to be contained in another document or other documents provided that each document is signed by the granter or granters thereof.[30] Once again, the Electronic Communications Act 2000 provides for the possibility of an electronic signature.[31]

Although simple signature is all that is required to render the contract 5.15 enforceable, it is open for the parties to have their signatures witnessed. The effect of having the signature witnessed is that it is presumed that the person who bears to have signed the document did so and, if the document bears a date, that it was signed on the date stated.[32] Only one witness is required. The witness must be over 16, have full mental capacity and know the granter and must not also be a granter of the document. Both the granter and the witness must use one of the first two forms of signature set out above and the witness must sign after the granter. The process of the granter signing or acknowledging his signature and the witness signing must be a continuous one. The name and address of the witness must be set out in the document or in a testing clause but this can be added any time before the document is registered of founded upon.[33]

Contracts are bilateral obligations and the use made of the terms "granter or granters" in Act is therefore odd. Where the contract is contained in one written document the Act envisages that it will be signed by all the parties and that each party to the contract will be considered to be a "granter". In a situation in which the offer is contained in one or more documents and the acceptance is contained in another document or other documents, the "granter" or "granters" is/are the person or persons making the offer or acceptance as the case may be. The person(s) making (or granting) the offer must sign all the documents that make up the offer and the person or persons giving (or granting) the acceptance must sign all the documents that make up the acceptance.

The ability to have the offer and acceptance contained within separate 5.16 documents is essential if the law is to recognise as valid contracts concluded by communication passing back and forwards between the parties. This would include order forms, faxes and exchange of letters. A common example of a contract which requires writing and is constituted by means of exchange of letters is missives for the sale of a house. These letters, usually passing between the solicitors for the buyer and the seller respectively, make it possible to adjust the terms on which the sale will take place. The original offer to purchase will normally be met by a

---

[29] s.7(1).
[30] s.2(2).
[31] s.7.
[32] s.3(1) and (8).
[33] ss. 3(1), 7(5) and 10.

qualified acceptance amending several of the suggested terms. This may in turn be met by a further qualified acceptance and so on until the terms are agreed. When this occurs, the final qualified acceptance will be met by a "clean" acceptance. To require the results of this exchange of correspondence to be incorporated into a further document encompassing all the terms would have been unnecessary and would not reflect the means by which the contract was concluded. Instead, to conclude the contract the final qualified acceptance refers to and incorporates the terms as agreed in the preceding correspondence and is by an acceptance. What is required for the contract to be formally valid is that the last qualified acceptance (the offer) and the "clean" acceptance (the acceptance) be signed by or on behalf of the parties making them.

In determining what level of formalities to require in order to conclude a contract it is necessary to balance competing interests. The advantages of a written contract must be balanced against the imposition of unnecessary obstacles to concluding a contract. This balance is reflected in the level of formalities required. The level of formality required by the Act is not great. A signed letter from a prospective buyer of a house stating that he would like to buy the house for £50,000 and enquiring whether the owner would sell for that sum would, if met by a signed reply accepting the offer, form an enforceable contract. In such a situation, the expressed intention of the Scottish Law Commission—to ensure that parties had a time to consider their bargain and would not conclude contracts without legal advice—would not be realised.

The Effects of the Absence of Writing

5.17 In the cases where the Act says that formalities are required, the general rule is that failure to have a written document signed by the granters means that there is no contract. This is despite the fact that the parties may have agreed on all the terms that were to regulate their relationship. This rule could produce results that would be unduly harsh for a party who believed that he or she had concluded a contract. For instance, assume that Marlon concludes an oral agreement with Cary to purchase a hotel from him. On the basis of that agreement, Marlon begins to advertise the business that he will conduct from the hotel, buys equipment for the hotel and starts to engage staff to work in the hotel. If the operation of the rules as to formal validity of contracts were applied then, even if he knew of the actions being taken by Marlon, Cary would be able to withdraw from the "contract" at any time. This would be manifestly unfair. The 1985 Act therefore defines circumstances in which a party will be prevented from relying on the lack of formality in the conclusion of the contract to escape their obligations.[34] These rules replace and, to some extent, repeat the old doctrine of *rei interventus* which formerly addressed this problem.

---

[34] ss. 1(3) and (4).

For a person to be prevented from relying on a lack of formality all of the following requirements must be satisfied:

(1) The party seeking to uphold the agreement must have acted or refrained from acting in reliance on it. It is necessary that what has happened can be said to have been in reliance in the contract as opposed to something that would have happened in any event or was done in reliance on some other factor.

This rule is broader than that which existed in the doctrine of *rei interventus* in that it includes refraining from acting as well as acting on the basis of the agreement. Under the law prior to the Act it was possible for the party seeking to uphold the contract to rely on the doctrine of homologation. That doctrine looked to the acts of the party seeking to escape from the contract to render it enforceable. That is no longer possible under the new rules.

(2) The party seeking to escape from the agreement must have known that the other party was so acting or refraining from acting and acquiesced in it. This is part of the purpose of the rule in achieving fair play. It is not necessary that the party has encouraged incited or in any way approved of the action or restraint—it is enough that they merely knew of it. Therefore once the party has knowledge of what the other party is doing or intending to do, if they wish to avoid being bound by the agreement, they must immediately notify the other party that they do not consider the contract to be valid.

(3) The position of the person seeking to uphold the contract must have been affected to a material extent by having acted or refrained from acting. This imposes a threshold for the application of these rules and means that they will not apply where the actings in question are minor. For instance, the fact that a party who intended to purchase a house has bought paint to decorate a bedroom would be unlikely to justify application of the rules.

(4) The effect of allowing one party to withdraw must be that the position of the party seeking to uphold the contract would be adversely affected to a material extent. This follows from the last rule. It provides a threshold for the rules to apply. In imposing a requirement that the party seeking to uphold the contract would be adversely affected the rule is limited to those situations in which the notion of fair play requires the contract to be maintained.

CHAPTER 6

GROUNDS OF INVALIDITY

Even where a contract complies with the rules relating to formation and to formalities, one party may still seek to have it declared invalid. In order to challenge the contract successfully, that party must show that there is some fundamental infirmity or defect in its constitution. The bases on which such a challenge may be made have one thing in common—the allegation that one party did not truly consent to the contract. Challenge on that ground is in accordance with the notion that contracts are based on consent of parties to be bound. However, as noted in Chapter 2, the law also recognises that bargains are made by what people say or do and not by what they think. Therefore a balance must be struck between, on the one hand, not enforcing contracts where there is no true consent and, on the other hand, not allowing one party to escape an apparently valid contract for reasons unconnected with the other party. To reconcile these two factors the law has developed grounds on which the validity of a contract may be challenged. These are considered below. 6.1

THE GROUNDS OF CHALLENGE

Force and Fear

The clearest case of invalidity is where some form of coercion or unfair pressure is applied to secure consent to the contract. A person who is threatened with a gun to make him sign a contract cannot be regarded as acting freely. Were the law to hold such bargains binding, this would legitimise terrorism and extortion. In Scotland, this ground of challenge is known as force and fear.[1] It is the subversion of consent by fear, rather than the force, which is important: 6.2

> "Although…we couple together force and fear as one ground of reduction, the act of force is truly…only one means of inducing fear, the true ground of reduction being extortion, through the influence of fear, induced in the various ways".[2]

---

[1] *vis ac metus.*
[2] *Priestnell v. Hutcheson* (1857) 19 D. 495 *per* Lord Deas at p.499.

An early and colourful example of force and fear is provided by the case of *Earl of Orkney v. Vinfra*[3]:

> The Earl sued Vinfra for payment of 1,000 merks that he said were owed to him under a deed which Vinfra had signed. Vinfra claimed that he had initially refused to sign but then "the said Earl was so offended that with terrible countenance and words and laying his hand upon his whinger [short sword], he threatened with execrable oaths to bereave this Vinfra of his life and stick him presently through the head with his whinger, if he subscribed not."

The Earl maintained that he had only used boisterous words. The court preferred Vinfra's account of events and held the contract invalid.

Threat to do an Unlawful Act

6.3 Sometimes lawyers speak in this connexion of the "overborne will." However, we should be clear that the person threatened has a choice—he chooses the lesser of two evils. He consents to sign the document to avoid the threat being carried out. Indeed, the greater the threat, the more likely it is that the person will do the act in question. It is not therefore strictly correct to say that one person's will is actually overborne. That is simply a convenient way of expressing what happens. More accurately, the person threatened is influenced or pressurised in such a way as to choose one course of action instead of the course he would have adopted had he not been subject to such pressure. So it is the illegitimacy of the threats which is the crucial factor. Some forms of pressure will not ground an action for force and fear. It is legitimate, for example, for one party to tell the other that he will resort to litigation. A creditor can tell his debtor that he will raise an action for payment unless the debtor agrees to pay off the debt. This is a proper course of action for, "If the only threat is a threat to do a lawful act then the plea of force and fear must fail."[4] In *Hunter v. Bradford Property Trust Ltd*[5]:

> Two sisters were in financial difficulties. They signed an agreement with a property company. The terms of the agreement were that the sisters would be paid certain sums of money when the company sold properties belonging to them. On the night before the sale was due to take place, one of the company's directors found that the written contract did not accurately record the agreement that he thought had been reached. He told the sisters that unless they signed a second contract, he would cancel the sale. After discussions long into the night, the sisters signed. They sought to reduce this second contract

---

[3] (1606) Mor. 16481.
[4] *Hunter v. Bradford Property Trust*, 1977 S.L.T. (Notes) 33 *per* Lord Migdale at p.34.
[5] 1977 S.L.T. (Notes) 33.

on the ground that it had been signed through force and fear. They claimed that they were anxious about their financial position should the sale not go ahead the following day. It was decided that the sisters had not made out a case of force and fear. The threat to cancel the sale could not be regarded as unlawful and could not therefore be a ground for setting the contract aside.

In England, for a time, it was considered that an action for duress might succeed even where the acts threatened were lawful. In one case a contract induced by a threat to take lawful industrial action was reduced.[6] Most recently however, the Court of Appeal has said that it would be rare for "lawful act duress" to occur in a commercial context. The court considered that such a rule would create uncertainty in commercial dealings and would involve the court determining what was morally or socially acceptable in any case before it.[7]

Severity of Threats

The threats employed to induce the contract must not have resulted in 6.4 "vain or foolish fear".[8] Rather, they must have been such as would have overcome the fortitude of a person of reasonable constancy. Where a weapon is used, or actual violence is threatened, then the issue is clearcut. Usually, however, some more insidious pressure is brought to bear. Then it is a question of evidence as to whether or not the plea of force and fear is made out. The question is, was consent subverted or not? A good illustration is provided by *Hislop v. Dickson Motors (Forres) Ltd*[9]:

The cashier of a garage in Forres was confronted by her employer. He shouted at her and accused her of embezzling sums from the garage accounts. She admitted the allegation and agreed to try to repay the sums. The next morning the employer arrived at her home with another director of the company. She handed over her car registration documents and keys together with a blank deposit-account withdrawal form which she signed. The directors drove her car away and withdrew all the money from her deposit account (£385). At the bank, they found out that the cashier also had a current account. They returned to her house and after further argument obtained a signed blank cheque from her which they used to withdraw the total credit balance (£195) from her current account. Subsequently the cashier was prosecuted in respect of the sums that had disappeared from the garage accounts. A not proven verdict was

---

[6] *Universe Tankships of Monrovia v. International Transport Workers' Federation* [1983] 1 A.C. 366; see also *Dimskal Shipping Co. S.A. v. International Transport Workers' Federation* [1992] 2 A.C. 152.

[7] *CTN Cash & Carry Ltd v. Gallaher Ltd* [1994] 4 All E.R. 714.

[8] *Institutions*, I.x.14.

[9] 1978 S.L.T. (Notes) 73.

returned. She raised an action for reduction of the two transactions
with her employer on the ground of force and fear. It was held that
the transaction involving the car and deposit account was valid, but
that the transaction involving the current account was invalid
through force and fear.

It is not easy to draw a clear distinction between the two transactions.
On both occasions, the pursuer was prepared to trade off her assets
against the threat of a criminal prosecution. Although her optimism on
that point proved unfounded, that was not a relevant factor in the
decision reached. The line drawn by Lord Maxwell was to say that in
giving over the documents relating to the car and the deposit account the
cashier was acting voluntarily: she was handing them over in return for
not being prosecuted. On the second occasion, however, she was not
acting voluntarily. Instead, she was coerced by her two employers into
handing over the blank cheque in respect of an account about which she
thought they knew nothing. By disclosing certain of her assets, she was
indicating the extent to which she was prepared to go to avoid
prosecution. But when she was confronted by the two men returning with
information which she had not volunteered, no true consent on her part
was discernible. Accordingly the second arrangement was struck down.
This is probably the correct analysis of a fact situation where,
superficially at least, it is difficult to measure the consent given and the
degree to which it was undermined.

Economic Threats

6.5   Some English cases have given colour to the notion that there can be
economic duress, as opposed to physical duress or pressure to the person.
Thus, where a creditor accepted a lesser sum from the debtor than that
due, solely because he himself was in difficult financial circumstances
and the debtor took advantage of his position, the bargain was declared
invalid.[10] The threat by the debtor not to pay at all unless the lesser sum
was accepted amounted to unfair pressure. It followed that the balance of
the debt was recoverable. Similarly, in the case referred to above of a
contract induced by a threat to take industrial action, the contract was
reducible on the ground of economic duress.[11] As yet there has been no
detailed discussion of such types of pressure in Scots law. In the case of
Hunter, referred to above,[12] although the pressure brought to bear was
economic the court of first instance held that the defenders had been
entitled to cancel the sale that was scheduled to take place and the issue
of the nature of the threat did not therefore arise. The essence of force

---

[10] *D. & C. Builders Ltd v. Rees* [1966] 2 Q.B. 617.
[11] *Universe Tankships of Monrovia v. International Transport Workers'
Federation* [1983] 1 A.C. 366; see also *Dimskal Shipping Co. S.A. v.
International Transport Workers' Federation* [1992] 2 A.C. 152.
[12] 1977 S.L.T. (Notes) 33.

and fear, however, is that agreement is extorted from one party by the other's use of illegitimate pressure. Today that pressure can be as effective economically as physical violence was of old.

In all the cases referred to above, the pressure to induce the contract has come from one of the parties to the contract. For some time the law appeared to be that this was necessary if a challenge was to succeed on this ground. For example, in *Stewart Brothers v. Kiddie*,[13] Mrs Kiddie sought to challenge an agreement whereby she agreed to accept a sum of money in full settlement of a claim for damages on the basis that her paramour had pressured her to sign. The court said that because the other party to the contract did not know of the improper pressure they were not affected by it and the challenge on that basis failed. More recently, in *Trustee Savings Bank v. Balloch*,[14] the court stated that if the effect of the force and fear is that there is no consent the result is that the contract is void and it does not matter who it was that exerted the force. This latter approach has recently been referred to with approval in the House of Lords.[15]

Facility and Circumvention

A contract is reducible for facility and circumvention when, for example, 6.6
a weak-minded [facile] party has been imposed upon unfairly and misleadingly [circumvented]. Facility and circumvention involves one party taking unfair advantage of another who, for some reason, is in a vulnerable state.

> *Example*: Motorist X is in a state of shock after a car accident: Y takes advantage of X's condition to purchase X's car from him at 25 per cent of its market value.

Three elements must be present before such a challenge will be successful. The person attempting to set aside the contract must prove:

(1) weakness and facility (if the person is insane rather than merely weak-minded then he is incapable of giving consent);
(2) circumvention; and
(3) loss (lesion).

The greater the facility and loss, the less circumvention required. In 6.7
each case it is a question of degree. The court will examine whether the person seeking to be released from the obligation was easily influenced or preyed upon because of his or her vulnerable mental state at the time. A person who is ill and in hospital is not on that account alone "of facile

---

[13] (1899) 7 S.L.T. 92.
[14] 1983 S.L.T. 240.
[15] *Smith v. Bank of Scotland* 1997 S.C. (H.L.) 111 at 117D; 1987 S.L.T. 1061 at 1065H.

disposition"[16] but a recently bereaved widow may be in such a condition.[17]

For a challenge to succeed on this ground, the acts of circumvention must have been carried out by or on behalf of the other party to the contract.[18]

Undue Influence

6.8 A contract obtained in consequence of the abuse of a position of influence by a person in a position of authority or trust may be reducible. The law recognises that where parties are not at arm's length, any transactions between the parties must be closely scrutinised to make sure that one party does not abuse his position. As Lord President Inglis put it in the leading case of *Gray v. Binny*[19]:

> "If...the relation of the parties is such as to beget mutual trust and confidence, each owes to the other a duty which has no place between strangers...the party trusted and confided in is bound, by the most obvious principles of fair dealing and honesty, not to abuse the power thus put in his hands."

There, a 24-year-old man, on the advice of his mother and the family solicitor, sold his inheritance rights for an inadequate amount. It was decided that if he could show that he had only entered the contract because of the advice he had received, it could be set aside.

6.9 At one time, it was thought that the classes of relationship which could ground an action of undue influence were closed. It is now accepted that it is always a question of fact whether such a relationship is present and it can exist as much between client and art-dealer as between doctor and patient, or parent and child.[20] The issue is whether one person actually did repose trust and confidence in another; and whether that confidence was abused. The difficulty with challenge on this ground is that the influence may be exercised in such a way that there is no independent evidence of the abuse. To counter this problem, the courts are willing to infer that there has been undue influence where there is a relationship of the type referred to in *Gray* and the following two conditions are met:

(1) the party with the influence has received a material and gratuitous benefit to the prejudice of the party trusting him/her; and

(2) the party disadvantaged did not have independent advice.

---

[16] *Mackay v. Campbell*, 1967 S.C. (H.L.) 53; S.L.T. 337.

[17] *MacGilvary v. Gilmartin*, 1986 S.L.T. 89.

[18] See *Smith v. Bank of Scotland* 1997 S.C. (H.L.) 111 at 117C; 1987 S.L.T. 1061, 1065F.

[19] (1879) 7 R. 332 at p.343.

[20] *Honeyman's Exrs v. Sharp*, 1978 S.C. 223.

Here too, for a challenge to be successful it is necessary that the undue influence be exerted by or on behalf of the other party to the contract.

Extortion and Inequality of Bargaining Power

So far we have been considering grounds of challenge where it is alleged 6.10 that something improper has occurred in the course of the bargaining process, such that one party's consent has not truly been given. However, it may be that without being able to point to anything specific at the time of negotiating, one party claims that the contract should not be enforced because its terms are grossly unfair. In common parlance, someone has made a "bad bargain" and seeks relief. This can occur where there is a gross disproportion between the relative bargaining strengths of the parties. Take, for example, a contract between a small business and a large multinational company. Because of the company's superior bargaining strength, it may be able to ensure that the contract terms are weighted heavily in its favour.

There is some early authority in Scots law to the effect that such 6.11 bargains may be reducible.

> "All bargains which from their very appearance discover oppression, as an intention in any of the contractors to catch some undue advantage from his neighbour's necessities, lie open to reduction on the head of dole or extortion, without the necessity of proving any special circumstances of fraud or circumvention on the part of that contractor."[21]

Despite this statement, at common law no such general ground of challenge on the basis of extortion of inequality of bargaining power now exists in Scotland. The general principle is that such contracts must stand. The courts have been unwilling to intervene directly to decide whether a bargain is or is not unfair. To do so, it is argued, would be to usurp the function of the parties in making their own contract. It is not for the court to determine whether or not a person has made a good or bad bargain. A flood of claims would occur, it is argued, if the courts had power to set aside a bargain on the ground of "fairness" alone. Reduction can probably only be granted where a contract is so inequitable in its terms as to raise an overwhelming presumption that it has been involuntarily granted.

In certain areas, however, legislation has intervened.[22] For example, 6.12 there are regulations relating to licences and levels of interest to cover those involved in money-lending and consumer credit agreements.[23] An

---

[21] Erskine *Institutes*, IV.i.27.
[22] Some contracts are considered in Chap. 9.
[23] Consumer Credit Act 1974, Pts III and IX.

extortionate credit bargain can be re-opened by the court.[24] There is a "cooling-off" period for those entering distance contracts, consumer credit agreements, time-share agreements and life assurance transactions other than on trade premises.[25] This gives individuals an opportunity to pause and reflect before committing themselves to such major financial relationships. In addition, the courts have power to consider the fairness of non-negotiated terms in consumer contracts.[26]

6.13   A move toward a general principle of inequality of bargaining power was at one stage discernible in English law.[27] Lord Denning M.R. suggested that the court might intervene to protect a person

> "who, without independent advice, enters into a contract upon terms which are very unfair...when his bargaining power is grievously impaired by reason of his own needs or desires, or by his own ignorance and infirmity, coupled with undue influences or pressures brought to bear on him by or for the benefit of the other."

Although such a test found some favour in Australia[28] it has been rejected by the House of Lords. In *National Westminster Bank plc v. Morgan*, Lord Scarman, after considering Lord Denning's dictum, stated in relation to contracts:

> "I question whether there is any need in the modern law to erect a general principle of relief against inequality of bargaining power. Parliament has undertaken the task (and it is essentially a legislative task) of enacting such restrictions on freedom of contract as are in its judgment necessary to relieve against the mischief...I doubt whether the courts should assume the burden of formulating further restrictions."[29]

Error

6.14   If one or both parties to a contract enter into it under some misapprehension, can the contract be declared invalid? Suppose, for example, that a person buys a car by phone and only discovers when it is delivered that it is a left-hand drive vehicle. Or imagine a person booking tickets for a performance of Carmen only discovers after paying the price that it is a film rather than a live performance. In both cases the purchaser

---

[24] Consumer Credit Act 1974, ss. 137–140.
[25] Consumer Protection (Distance Selling) Regulations 2000, reg. 10; Consumer Credit Act 1974 ss. 67–73; Timeshare Act 1992; Insurance Companies Act 1982, s.76.
[26] Unfair Terms in Consumer Contracts Regulations 1999.
[27] *A. Schroeder Music Publishing Co. Ltd v. Macaulay* [1974] 1 W.L.R. 1308 and *Lloyds Bank v. Bundy* [1975] Q.B. 326.
[28] See *Commercial Bank of Australia v. Amadio*, (1983) 57 A.L.J.R. 358.
[29] [1985] 1 All E.R. 821 at p.830.

has made a mistake. Can the contract be set aside on the basis that it would never have been made if the true situation had been known? This is the key question to be discussed under the heading of error, which is one of the most controversial topics in contract law. The nub of the problem is the conflict between two different theoretical approaches to contract law. A subjective approach suggests that where error is present there can be no true consent and therefore no contract. In our examples, this would mean the contracts would be set aside. The purchasers never intended to make the bargains in question. The objective approach, on the other hand, takes the view that parties are bound by what they say, not what they think. So the purchaser in our examples would be bound by the respective contracts they had entered into. This conflict can be seen as far back as Stair. In an early passage in the *Institutions* he seems to take a broad subjective approach: "These who err in the substantials of what is done, contract not."[30] But later on he narrows the compass of this passage considerably: "But the exception upon error is seldom relevant, because it depends upon the knowledge of the person erring, which he can hardly prove."[31] By and large it is the objective approach that has prevailed.

Classifying Error

Error is capable of arising in a number of ways and may relate to many features of the contract in question. For instance, a party buying a painting could be in error as to something as important as the price to be paid for it or something as minor as its size. The error might be in the mind of one party or in the minds of both parties. It may have come about through ignorance, misunderstanding, or something said by the other party. It is therefore necessary to consider the means of classifying error.   6.15

The subject matter of the error. Clearly there is more justification for holding that the consent to the contract is invalid where the error goes in some respect to the root of the contract rather than dealing with peripheral matters. The issue is therefore what constitutes the root of the contract for this purpose.   6.16

Stair's view seems to have been that error in the substantials would render a contract void. It remained to lay down with precision what constituted error in the substantials (or essential error). The formulation of another Institutional writer, Bell, was expressly adopted by Lord Watson and is generally regarded as the correct statement of the law[32]:

"I concur...as to the accuracy of the general doctrine laid down by Professor Bell [*Principles*, s.11] to the effect that error in

---

[30] *Institutions* I.x.13.

[31] *Instituitions* IV.xxxx.24.

[32] *Stewart v. Kennedy* (1890) 17 R. (H.L.) 25 at p.28.

substantials such as will invalidate consent given to a contract or obligation must be in relation to either (1) its subject-matter; (2) the persons undertaking or to whom it is undertaken; (3) the price or consideration; (4) the quality of the thing engaged for; if expressly or tacitly essential; or (5) the nature of the contract or engagement supposed to be entered into. I believe that these five categories will be found to embrace all the forms of essential error which, either *per se* or when induced by the other party to the contract, give the person labouring under such error a right to rescind it."

6.17   We can illustrate the five categories of essential error as follows:

(1) Subject Matter	—A thinks he is buying wheat from B, B thinks he is selling barley to A
(2) Identity	—A thinks he is contracting with B, whereas he is contracting with C
(3) Price	—A thinks the price is £1,000, B thinks it is $1,000
(4) Quality	—A thinks he is buying a stallion, when in fact the beast is a gelding
(5) Nature of the Contract	—A thinks he is signing a lease, whereas in fact the document is a guarantee

If the error is not essential, the contract stands. For example, A's belief that he will make a profit from his contract affords no ground of relief should he prove mistaken. His error is one of motive, so it does not affect the contract.

6.18   **How the error affects the minds of the parties.** (a) *Unilateral error*. As its name indicates, in unilateral error only one party is mistaken as to some feature of the contract.

Example: X believes the painting he is buying is an original by Max Ernst. The seller Y knows it is a copy.

A unilateral error is usually treated as irrelevant. In one case, parties were negotiating an out of court settlement. A number of communications took place between the parties' solicitors. One issue which required to be resolved was the date from which interest was to run on the settlement sum. For most of the negotiations, this date remained constant. Finally, one party's solicitor accepted an offer to settle the action, omitting to notice that the date on which interest was to run had been altered.[33] The mistake could not be relied upon in order to avoid the transaction. The solicitor ought to have read the offer more carefully, as it clearly stated the new date from which interest was to run.

---

[33] *Steel v. Bradley Homes (Scotland) Ltd*, 1974 S.L.T. 133.

Similarly, if a company erroneously believes that a property being sold by it is subject to a lease of 990 years, rather than 99 years, it will not be relieved of that mistake unless it is engendered by the other party.[34] Even a lay person is expected to understand that a document signed by him gives rise to obligations. In *The Royal Bank of Scotland v. Purvis*[35]:

> A wife signed a guarantee to the bank in respect of a loan to a company of which she and her husband were directors. Subsequently, the bank sued both the husband and wife under the guarantee for payment of a sum of £21,635.17. The wife defended on the basis that she was in essential error at the time that she signed the document. She pointed to the following factors: (a) she signed at the request of her husband; (b) she had not read the document nor had it explained to her; (c) she was not formally educated and was unfamiliar with commercial documents; and (d) she did not realise that the document was a guarantee and would not have signed it if she had.

Lord McCluskey repelled this defence and stated:

> "The whole point of committing such obligations to writing is to avoid any inquiry into antecedent states of mind unless the whole picture is one of a signature induced by misrepresentation. I find it virtually impossible to envisage a situation in real life in which a person could repudiate a document signed by him when he was innocently, unilaterally and not negligently in ignorance of the character of the document which he was signing at the time. I think one would need to wait and see what circumstances were averred that could give rise to such a special exception to a rule upon which so much commerce depends."[36]

It is of note that Lord McCluskey distinguished the position where the error was induced. This is considered in more detail below.

Unilateral error may, however, be relevant in either of two situations. 6.19 The first is where the other party knew of the error and took unfair advantage of the situation. A person is not allowed unfairly to "snatch at a bargain". This is thought to be the ratio of *Steuart's Trs v. Hart*, where a seller sold some land believing it to be burdened with a feu-duty (annual land charge) of £9 15s.[37] The purchaser knew that the feu-duty was only three shillings and also knew of the seller's mistake. The seller was held entitled to reduce the contract since the mistake was essential and his error had been taken advantage of by the purchaser. This decision has attracted considerable controversy. Those commentators in favour of

---

[34] *Spook Erection (Northern) Ltd v. Kaye*, 1990 S.L.T. 676.
[35] 1990 S.L.T. 262.
[36] *Ibid.* at p.266; see also *McCallum v. Soudan*, 1989 S.L.T. 522 *per* Lord Morison at p.523.
[37] (1875) 3 R. 192.

the decision point to its equity in the circumstances which had occurred. It emphasises the good faith of the bargaining process. Those against the decision note the untoward consequences that a wide application of this principle would bring. A person who picked up a book or an antique "for a song" might find that the seller would seek to have the sale set aside on the basis of his own error.[38]

The ratio in *Steuart's Trs v. Hart* was considered in the more recent case of *Angus v. Bryden*[39]:

> Annbank Angling Club were the tenants of certain river fishings in the River Ayr. The river fishings were owned by Angus, who also owned sea fishings at the mouth of the river. In 1986, the club offered Angus £30,000 to purchase the fishings. This was accepted and subsequently a disposition was granted transferring the whole fishings. Angus claimed that on a true construction, all that was agreed to be transferred was the river fishings and the disposition should be corrected. As an alternative argument, he contended that if the sea fishings had been disponed, this was an error on his part known to and taken advantage of by the club. Lord Cameron of Lochbroom disposed of the action by upholding Angus' position on the principal argument. However, he went on to consider the alternative argument and stated "I consider that *Steuart's Trs. v. Hart* is still good law and is therefore binding upon me."[40]

6.20   The second way in which unilateral error may be relevant is in relation to a gratuitous transaction. It is not difficult to see the logic of this distinction. As the obligee in a gratuitous transaction is receiving something for nothing, it is thought equitable to allow the obligor to be relieved of his obligations if he can prove that he has made a mistake. Suppose that B makes a written promise to give £500 to X, believing X to be his long lost cousin. If B subsequently discovers that X is not related to him, he should be discharged from his obligation. In the case of *Hunter v. Bradford Trust Ltd*, which was discussed above with regard to force and fear, the sisters ultimately successfully set aside the contract on the basis that it had been entered gratuitously under essential error as to its effect.[41]

6.21   (b) *Common error*. Here, both parties make the same mistake. They share an assumption about the state of affairs upon which the contract is based, which turns out to be erroneous.

> *Example*: In a contract for the sale of a painting, both parties think the painting is in existence, whereas it was destroyed the day before the contract was made.

---

[38] see Gloag, *Contract* (2nd ed.,), p.438.

[39] 1992 S.L.T. 884.

[40] *Ibid.* p.887.

[41] 1970 S.L.T. 173.

In principle, common error as to some essential feature renders a contract invalid, but in practice few such cases arise. This is mainly because rules exist as to the allocation of risk. Where a house is sold, risk passes on completion of the missives. This means that if both parties believe that the house is in existence at the time the contract is made, whereas in reality it has been destroyed by fire, the risk is with the seller. But once the missives are completed, any damage to the house which occurs subsequently is the risk of the buyer. This means that each party knows the exact moment at which they should ensure that they have insurance cover in place.

(c) *Mutual error.* Where the error is mutual, the parties misapprehend each other's intention. This results in the parties being at cross purposes.   6.22

> *Example*: X believes that he is selling the 1628 "Madonna and Child", Y that he is buying the 1630 version, which X also owns.

Mutual error results in the parties not achieving agreement or consensus, but rather misunderstanding or dissensus. Normally the cases concern situations where there is potential ambiguity. The most famous case concerned the sale of a cargo of grain which was to be transported on a ship called the "*Peerless*" from Bombay to England.[42] Unknown to the parties at the time they made the contract, there were two ships of that name, one sailing in October, the other in December. The buyer thought that he was contracting in respect of the October "*Peerless*". The seller meant the December "*Peerless*". It was held that there was no contract. At no stage were the parties at one regarding the contract both had thought they had entered into. An equivalent Scottish case is *Stuart & Co. v. Kennedy*.[43] There, a quantity of stone-coping was sold at so much per foot. One party thought that the measure was the lineal foot, the other that it was the superficial foot. The charge if made by the superficial foot would be more than double what it would be if made by the lineal foot. It was held that there was no contract.

In the case of mutual error, a finding that the parties have not truly reached agreement will result in the contract being set aside. There are relatively few cases of this type and two factors account for this. First, the court will normally prefer one party's version of the contract to that of the other. For example, they will declare that it is a contract of credit sale rather than hire-purchase.[44] Secondly, where it does find that there is no consensus, a court is more likely to classify the situation as falling under the heading of offer and acceptance than of mutual error. An example is provided by *Mathieson Gee v. Quigley*, where the parties' mistaken view that they had achieved agreement was held to have arisen because the

---

[42] *Raffles v. Wichelhaus* (1864) 2 H. & C. 906.
[43] (1885) 13 R. 221.
[44] *Muirhead & Turnbull v. Dickson* (1905) 7F. 686; (1905) 13 S.L.T. 151.

offer did not meet the acceptance.[45] Accordingly, the only situation where mutual error is likely to operate occurs when there is a latent ambiguity in the contract. The two cases cited above regarding *The Peerless* and the lineal/superficial foot are examples.

An alternative analysis

6.23 It can be argued that there has been no case of error proper in the twentieth century. No case, that is, where an onerous contract has been set aside on the basis of uninduced error in intention.[46] Instead, the law uses various other principles in resolving error-type situations. As well as the two already mentioned—of offer and acceptance and passing of risk—there are two other important techniques: implied terms and personal bar. The use of implied terms converts a problem of error into a breach of contract question.

> *Example*: A person buys a pair of shoes which fall apart after two weeks' light wear. Clearly it would be possible to say that the person seeks redress because he bought the shoes under mistake—he thought they would be hard-wearing. However, such cases are invariably treated as a question of breach of the implied term of satisfactory quality under the Sale of Goods Act 1979.

The second technique is personal bar. Where performance follows on from an agreement alleged to be defective, the subsequent actions of the parties may prove decisive in determining whether the parties are bound or not. In *Morrison-Low v. Paterson*, both parties believed that the defenders had inherited the tenancy of an agricultural lease.[47] This belief arose because the solicitor, who had acted for both parties, told them that this was the position. The House of Lords accepted that the tenancy had not been validly transferred under the relevant statutory provisions. Both parties were therefore mistaken as to their legal position. Nevertheless the subsequent actions of the parties, which involved *inter alia* the defenders remaining in occupation and paying rent for six years, were only explicable on the footing that a new agreement had been entered into. Accordingly, the House of Lords held that despite the error there was a contract of lease and the landlord's action of removing must fail. He was personally barred from founding on the error.

6.24 Historically, however, the most significant change in this area of law, the one which has substantially eclipsed the role of error, has been the development of the law relating to misrepresentation. Misrepresentation means induced error. In Scots law, the shift from uninduced to induced

---

[45] 1952 S.C. (H.L.) 38.
[46] *Angus v, Bryden*, 1992 S.L.T. 884.
[47] 1985 S.L.T. 255.

error can be traced to two House of Lords' decisions in the late nineteenth century. In *Stewart v. Kennedy*[48]:

> A contract for the sale of an entailed estate was made "subject to the ratification of the court." The seller, Sir Archibald Stewart, mistakenly thought that the phrase meant that the court would determine if the price was fair and reasonable. In fact, it was a simple statutory requirement which had to be followed in the case of entailed estates. He sought to reduce the missives of sale, claiming amongst other things that he had entered the contract under essential error. In the Court of Session it was held that there was no essential error, as the person, the price and the subject-matter of the contract were clearly established. The House of Lords took an entirely different line. First, it decided that the error was an essential error. Secondly, the House of Lords decided that although there had been essential error, that of itself was not enough to set aside the contract. Essential error would only be relevant if it were induced.

This marked the beginning of a sea-change in the law. The House of Lords decided that essential error was present but then said it was not operative in the circumstances. Error, they said, would only be effective if shown to have been induced. Accordingly, the focal point was the cause of the error rather than the error itself. To demonstrate this, let us return to our two initial examples. Whether the person who bought the left-hand drive car, or the tickets to the film version of Carmen, can set aside the contract will depend on the circumstances in which his belief was formed. If his mistake was attributable to the other party then there is misrepresentation and the contract can be challenged. But if the mistake arose simply through his own uninduced error he would be unlikely to be able to set aside the contract.

The confirmation of this view is to be found in the second of the two House of Lords' cases, *Menzies v. Menzies*.[49] Lord Watson stated that: 6.25

> "Error becomes essential whenever it is shown that but for it one of the parties would have declined to contract. He cannot rescind unless his error was induced by the representations of the other contracting party, or of his agent, made in the course of negotiation, and with reference to the subject matter of the contract. If his error is proved to have been so induced, the fact that the misleading representations were made in good faith affords no defence."[50]

Two propositions can be drawn from this statement: (a) misrepresentation, rather than error, is the true ground of challenge; and

---

[48] (1890) 17 R. (H.L.) 25.
[49] (1893) 20 R. (H.L.) 108.
[50] *Ibid.* at pp.142–143.

(b) the standard required is no longer that of Bell's five categories, rather the issue is whether or not the party would have declined to contract.

Conclusion on Error

6.26 Although, as we have seen, the law on uninduced error is fairly well developed, it is of little practical importance today. The courts are reluctant to relieve people of their obligations simply because they allege that they made a mistake on entering into them. Perhaps only in the case of gratuitous obligations is it still significant.

Misrepresentation

6.27 A person who is induced to enter a contract as a result of a misleading statement has the right to be relieved of his obligations under the contract.

> *Examples*:
> (1) X buys Y's car on the faith of an assurance that the car possesses an M.O.T. certificate, Y's statement in this regard turns out to be false. X is entitled to return the car and receive back the purchase price.
> (2) B arranges for A to install new wiring in his house. B chose A because A told him that he was a qualified electrician and that he could arrange finance for B. Both statements are false. B can withdraw from the contract.

The Statement That Constitutes the Misrepresentation

6.28 To be relevant, a misrepresentation must be material and made in the course of negotiations. A trivial statement, for example, cannot be relied upon. Moreover, the misrepresentation must be an inaccurate statement of fact and not simply an expression of opinion. In one case, the seller stated that a farm would carry so many head of sheep.[51] It was known by both parties that the farm had never been used for sheep before. The statement was held not to amount to a misrepresentation. It was merely a statement of the seller's opinion which a reasonable buyer would not have relied upon. But a deliberately false statement of opinion is a representation of fact. "Trade puffs" are allowed a degree of latitude. Reasonable people are not expected to place too much reliance on the material to be found in advertisements. No one should really expect a new brand of shampoo to improve their social life. Accordingly, material which might fairly be termed "misleading" does not allow a consumer to set aside the contract. The Trade Descriptions Act 1968 and independent

---

[51] *Bisset v. Wilkinson* [1927] A.C. 177.

advertising watchdogs provide certain sanctions in the event of serious misdescriptions.

Normally there is no duty of disclosure in contract, so silence cannot constitute a misrepresentation. But silence may amount to misrepresentation in a number of situations, of which the most important class is contracts *uberrimae fidei* (of utmost good faith). The most important example of such a contract is that of insurance. Here, there is a duty to disclose all material facts. In *The Spathari*[52]:

> A vessel was registered and insured in the name of a British subject. It sank in calm waters and a claim was made under the insurance policy. The insurance company then discovered that the true owner was a Greek subject. The company refused to pay out on the policy. It was held that the company were entitled to do so. At the time, Greek ships were virtually uninsurable because they had bad risk records. Accordingly, the nationality of the owner was material in this instance. As it had not been disclosed, there had been a misrepresentation which rendered the contract voidable.

Other situations where silence may amount to misrepresentation 6.29 occur where, (a) the parties are in a fiduciary relationship, for example parent and child, trustee and beneficiary, solicitor and client; (b) where there is a half-truth that has not been completed; and (c) where a statement, true when made, is falsified by circumstances.

By Whom the Misrepresentation is Made

A contract cannot be challenged on the basis of misrepresentation unless 6.30 the misrepresentation in question was made by or on behalf of one of the contracting parties.[53]

The Degree of Misapprehension Produced

At one time it was suggested that for misrepresentation to be relevant, 6.31 there must be essential error in the sense of Bell's five categories. Although this proposition has never been expressly overruled it probably is no longer the law. It is directly counter to Lord Watson's statement in *Menzies* quoted above. The most accurate statement of the present law is probably that given by Lord Carmont:

> "It appears clear that Scots law recognises, as indicated by Bell, that when misrepresentation by a party is alleged inducing error in the other in regard to some matter, that matter need not be an essential of the contract, *but it must be material and of such a nature that not only the contracting party but any reasonable man might be moved to enter into the contract*; or put the other way, if the

---

[52] 1925 S.C. (H.L.) 6.
[53] *Universal Import Export v. Bank of Scotland* 1995 S.C. 73; 1995 S.L.T. 1318

misrepresentation had not been made, would have refrained from entering into the contract."[54]

In other words, the court is directed to look at the reasons why the person was induced to enter the contract. If they are material and pass the "reasonable man" test then the contract can be set aside, even though they do not relate to Bell's five categories.

Remedies for Misrepresentation

6.32 The remedies open to a person depend upon whether the misrepresentation is fraudulent, negligent or innocent. If the misrepresentation is innocent, the only remedy is to set aside the contract. But if negligence or fraud is present, damages may also be recovered.

6.33 (a) **Fraudulent misrepresentation.** Fraud is a "machination or contrivance to deceive."[55] Since the end of the nineteenth century, a statement has been regarded as fraudulent if, (a) the maker of the statement was aware that his representations were untrue; or (b) he made them recklessly, without knowing or caring whether they were true or not. The second proposition was established in the case of *Derry v. Peek*[56]:

> The directors of the Plymouth Devonport and District Tramways company issued a prospectus which stated that the company had the right to use steam power in its trams. The plaintiff bought shares in the company on the strength of this statement. In fact the company was only entitled to use steam power if it was issued with an appropriate certificate by the Board of Trade. The certificate was refused. It was held that the plaintiff could not succeed in his action of damages for fraud. The directors had made the statement in the honest belief that it was true.

This decision changed the law. Until that point, almost any statement which turned out to be untrue and induced a person to enter a contract grounded an action for fraud. In effect the decision in *Derry* raised the standard for civil fraud to that of criminal fraud. Damages became much more difficult to recover. It has been suggested that the judges were swayed in arriving at their decision by the argument that to call a man "fraudulent" was tantamount to expelling him from polite society. As the judges looked at the directors, Victorian gentlemen all they had a marked reluctance to place such a stain on their reputations.

6.34 The actual effect of the decision in relation to directors' liability was overturned by statute. But its general importance as a test of fraud

---

[54] *Ritchie v. Glass*, 1936 S.L.T. 591 at pp. 593–594 (emphasis added).
[55] Erskine, *Institutions*, III.i.16.
[56] (1889) 44 App.Cas. 337.

remains undiminished. In the Scottish case of *Boyd & Forrest v. Glasgow & S.W. Railway Co.*,[57] which occurred shortly after *Derry*, it was held that contractors who had built a railway line could not recover damages against the railway company in respect of wrong information which the latter had given. This was because the employee who had furnished the information had altered it honestly but mistakenly, so he could not be guilty of fraud.

(b) **Negligent misrepresentation.** A representation is negligent if the 6.35
person failed to take reasonable care in making the representation and was in the circumstances under a duty to do so. This category has only been developed in the post-war period and originated in a dissenting judgment of Lord Denning M.R.[58] His view was adopted by the House of Lords in *Hedley Byrne v. Heller & Partners*, where a bank gave information regarding the credit-worthiness of one of its customers.[59] When it was found that the information was incorrect and the bank had not exercised sufficient care in assessing the situation, it was held they could be liable to the person who had requested the information. These cases were concerned with non-contractual situations. The law has continued to develop in that field and is not considered here.

Originally it was thought that negligent misrepresentation did not apply to contracts, because the parties did not owe one another a "duty of care". However, the concept of negligent misrepresentation was extended to pre-contractual negotiations in England in *Esso Petroleum Co. v. Mardon*.[60] There an oil company was held liable in respect of statements made to a prospective tenant of a petrol filling station. An employee of the company with many years' experience had misled the tenant regarding the throughput of petrol the station could expect. Normally when parties are negotiating, each must rely on his own means of information. Because they are at arm's length neither owes a duty of care to the other. Although a false statement allows one party to withdraw from the contract it does not ground an action for damages unless there is fraud. The effect of the decision in *Esso* was to extend the right to recover damages to a situation where one party had special skill or knowledge and the other party was reasonably entitled to rely on that knowledge, which turned out to be false.

The Scottish position regarding negligent misrepresentation was 6.36
unclear. Some courts felt bound by a nineteenth century decision which decided that unless fraud was established, damages were not recoverable for statements made at the stage of negotiation between the parties. However, statute now provides that damages for negligent

---

[57] 1912 S.C. (H.L.) 93.
[58] *Candler v. Crane Christmas & Co.* [1951] 2 K.B. 164.
[59] [1964] A.C. 465.
[60] [1976] Q.B. 801.

misrepresentation are recoverable under Scots law.[61] So if a designer builds a ship which does not have the carrying capacity that he represented, he will be liable in damages. Likewise a seller who informs a buyer that the factory he is selling has been passed by the factory inspectorate and is asbestos-free.[62]

6.37 (c) **Innocent misrepresentation.** Here the representation, although inaccurate, is made with the honest belief that it is true. The only remedy is to reduce the contract. There is no additional right to damages as in the previous two categories.

Misrepresentation or a term of the contract?

6.38 A statement which is made during the course of negotiations leading up to the contract may: (1) have no legal effect; (2) amount to a misrepresentation; or (3) be a term of the contract. Whether a pre-contractual statement has legal force or not is largely a question of intention and reliance. Was it sought to induce the other party to enter the contract by means of the statement? Was it intended and understood that it became a term of the contract?

> Statements in advertisements usually have no legal effect because reasonable persons know they are exaggerated to "puff up" the product. By contrast, in many contracts for the sale of goods, statute decrees that there is a term in the contract that the goods are of satisfactory quality. Difficulties arise in cases which fall between these positions. Usually the buyer will wish to argue that the statement on which he founds his claim is a term of the contract. This is because it is easier to prove breach of contract than misrepresentation. Moreover in a breach of contract case, damages can be recovered even though fraud or negligence are not proved.

Failure to Give Advice

6.39 This new basis of challenge to a contract arose out of a recent House of Lords case, *Smith v. Bank of Scotland*[63]:

> The pursuer sought to challenge a contract she had entered into in favour of the bank. In particular, she sought to reduce a standard security she had granted over her half share of the matrimonial home. She had granted the security to the Bank in respect of sums borrowed by a firm in which her husband was a partner. Mrs Smith

---

[61] Law Reform (Miscellaneous Provisions) (Scotland) Act 1985, s.10.
[62] These examples are based upon *Kenway v. Orcantic Ltd*, 1980 S.L.T. 46 and *Foster v. Craigmillar Laundry*, 1980 S.L.T. (Sh.Ct) 100, both of which were decided before the 1985 statutory provision was in place.
[63] 1997 S.C. (H.L.) 111; 1997 S.L.T. 1061.

argued that the security was invalid because she had been induced to sign it as a result of misrepresentations made by her husband.

The House of Lords held that the security was invalid but not on the basis argued by Mrs Smith. Any misrepresentations had been made by Mrs Smith's husband and could not be said to have been made on behalf of the bank. The House of Lords then considered an English case in which a guarantee obligation given in similar circumstances had been declared to be invalid.[64] The basis for that decision was that, in the circumstances, the Bank were deemed to have notice of the wrongful acts committed by the husband in order to obtain his wife's consent to the obligation. Mrs Smith's challenge did not succeed on that basis either. Instead it was held that there was a duty on the Bank to give advice to Mrs Smith. This duty arose because the circumstances were such that the Bank might reasonably have suspected that, as a result of the relationship between the Mrs Smith and the Mr Smith, her consent was not properly given. In the circumstances, the Bank should have warned Mrs Smith of the possible consequences of the transaction and told her to get independent advice. That warning was necessary to ensure that the Bank remained in good faith.

The duty referred to in *Smith* arose because of the element of good faith required of the creditor in a transaction where one party undertakes to pay the debts of another in the event that the other party defaults.[65] It was noted in the House of Lords that there was a broad principle in the law of contract of dealing in good faith. Although this principle of good faith is of general application, it is likely that a duty to warn a party to take independent advice will be found to exist only in circumstances similar to those in *Smith*.

THE EFFECT OF A SUCCESSFUL CHALLENGE

The traditional view is that a successful challenge renders a contract 6.40 either void or voidable. A contract which is void is a complete nullity. It is treated as if it had never existed at all. There are two important consequences which flow from a contract being declared void. First, there is in theory no need to have a court decree that it is void. It is enough to notify the other party that the contract is no longer regarded as binding. If, however, he disputes that the contract is void the issue will have to be determined by a court. Secondly, no one can acquire rights under a void contract. Accordingly, a third party who has property which has been transferred under a void contract is obliged to restore it to its original owner. The court may however impose an equitable solution on the parties. For example, if goods are delivered under a void contract, the

---

[64] *Barlcays Bank plc v. O'Brien* [1994] 1 A.C. 180.
[65] This obligation is known in Scotland as caution.

courts may stipulate that the buyer must pay the appropriate market price for the goods.

A contract which is voidable is valid and effective until it is set aside. Unlike void contracts, a contract which is voidable can confer rights. Accordingly, third parties who acquire rights before the contract has been set aside are protected. There are certain requirements which must be satisfied before a voidable contract can be set aside:

(a) Restoration to the original position (*restitutio in integrum*) must be possible. In *Boyd & Forrest* this condition could not be satisfied as the contractors had gone ahead and construed the railway line.[66] It was impossible to restore the parties to their original position.

(b) There must have been no unnecessary delay in bringing the action.

(c) The rights of third parties must not be affected.

6.41   The crucial difference between void and voidable contracts concerns the rights of third parties. That difference is demonstrated by contrasting two well-known cases: *Morrisson v. Robertson*[67] and *Macleod v. Kerr*[68]:

In *Morrisson*, a man claiming to be the son of Wilson of Bonnyrigg approached Morrisson and offered to buy two cows from him. Although Morrisson did not know the man, he knew of Wilson, who was a neighbouring farmer of good financial standing. Accordingly, he let the man have the two cows on credit. In fact, the man was not the son of Wilson but a rogue called Telford. Telford sold the two cows to Robertson. When Morrisson found this out he sought to recover the cows from Robertson. The action was successful. It was held that there had been no contract between Morrisson and Telford. The purported transaction was a complete nullity. Accordingly, Telford had no rights which he could pass on to Robertson, so Morrisson was entitled to recover his cows.

Macleod v. Kerr provides a more modern setting for the same problem:

A rogue paid for a Vauxhall car with a stolen cheque. As soon as the seller discovered that the cheque had been dishonoured, he notified the police. Shortly afterwards, the car was sold by the rogue to an innocent third party. It was held that the contract between the seller and the rogue was voidable rather than void. As it had not been reduced before the rogue had sold the car, title to the car had passed. It followed that third parties could acquire good title.

---

[66] 1915 S.C. (H.L.) 20.
[67] 1908 S.C. 332.
[68] 1965 S.L.T. 358.

The distinction between the two cases is a narrow one. In *Morrisson* 6.42 it was held that the seller had never intended to contract with the person before him, Telford, but rather with Wilson. As Wilson knew nothing of the transaction there could be no contract. The seller in *Macleod*, on the other hand, was prepared to contract with the person in front of him. He did not know the identity of the person with whom he was dealing. What is important to notice is the varying results between a finding of void or voidable. In the first case, the owner was the protected party, in the second case it was the third party purchaser. It can be argued that it boils down to a question of policy. Should the law protect the seller or the innocent third party? As the seller is normally in a better position to prevent the fraud, he should take the risk. He could have taken precautions—in the first case by contacting Wilson himself; in the second by accepting only a certified cheque. This is the reason why contracts are today more often held voidable rather than void.

Reform

It may be argued that the distinction between the two types of nullity has 6.43 now become so obscure that legislative action is required to dispel confusion. The Scottish Law Commission has recommended that where a vitiating factor is present the contract should come to an end either: (a) by agreement between the parties; or (b) by judicial decree (or decree arbitral).[69] In the case of (b), the Commission recommend an accelerated annulment procedure. There ought, says the Commission, to be a swift court procedure to determine the parties' respective rights. This would be a significant improvement on the present position.

---

[69] Scot. Law Com. Memorandum No. 42.

Chapter 7

TERMS OF THE CONTRACT

The previous chapters describe the legal principles which are used to 7.1
decide whether a contract exists that is valid and enforceable. Once a
contract exists the next requirement is to determine the rights and
obligations that the parties have. Clearly, these depend on the terms of
the contract. This and the next chapter address two issues in relation to
the terms. This chapter looks at what the terms are and the next will
examine what the terms mean.

The terms of the contract may be express or implied. The former are 7.2
those that the parties are deemed to have agreed upon and made part of
their contract. Because of the many situations in which contracts may be
concluded and means by which they may be concluded it is necessary
that rules to determine the express terms are sufficiently flexible. What
has passed between the parties may not be all that finds it way into the
contract. By whatever means the contract is concluded, other terms may
be incorporated by reference. Rules are required to determine whether
terms have been validly incorporated into a contract. Even with
flexibility as to what express terms form part of the contract, it would be
unrealistic to assume that in every contract all the terms will be fully
agreed by the parties. Further rules are needed to determine how terms
may be implied into contracts.

Even once the contract terms are identified, the parties may be in
dispute as to what they mean or how they should be applied to the
situation that confronts them. Yet more rules are required to interpret the
agreed terms to translate them into practical rights and obligations.

Finally, when the contract is interpreted they may be an argument
that there has been a mistake in the wording of the contract so that it does
not reflect what the parties had agreed. Courts have a limited power to
rectify contracts when this situation occurs and it is necessary to consider
whether that is justified.

The purpose of this chapter is to consider these sets of rules that go to 7.3
determine the practical effect of the contract. The overriding principle is
the intention of the parties. Again, as before, this is subject to the
qualification that the intention is to be determined objectively—the issue
is not what a party thought he was agreeing to do but what the other party
might reasonably have thought that he was agreeing to do.

EXPRESS TERMS

7.4 As had already been noted, the range of situations in which a contract may be concluded is huge. At one end of the spectrum the parties may negotiate the terms of a written agreement for months prior to signing it. At the other end, there are everyday contracts which may be concluded with little or no exchange of words. In any situation it is necessary to determine what terms form part of the contract.

Formal Contracts

7.5 Where the contract is contained either in a formal written agreement or formal written communications passing between the parties, the documents are the starting point for the express terms of the contract. However, these documents may not tell the whole story. It may be that other agreement(s) were made between the parties at the same time and these have a bearing on the express terms.

> *Example*: Contractors building an office development enter into a written a contract with a supplier of cement for delivery of 50 tonnes of cement. The contract contains a standard clause that all terms of the contract are to be found within the written document. Three weeks later, the parties agree in a telephone conversation that, if it turns out that the development requires only 45 tonnes, the contractors will not be required to take the full 50 tonnes.

The issue that arises here is whether it is possible to rely on the agreement made orally to override the apparently clear terms of the written agreement. The Contract (Scotland) Act 1997 provides that if there is a term in the contract documents to the effect that they comprise all the express terms of the contract then such a term shall be conclusive of the matter.[1] In the example given above, the oral agreement could not contradict the written agreement. If there was no such term in the contract documents, there is a rule that where the contract documents *appear* to comprise all the express terms of a contract then it shall be presumed that this is so.[2] The reference to "appear" would mean that the presumption would apply in a situation in which the contract documents did not refer to any term(s) in another document. The presumption can be rebutted. The existence of express terms additional to the written contract may be proved by either further documents or oral evidence given by the parties.[3] The additional terms themselves may either have been written or agreed orally between the parties.

---

[1] 1997 Act, s.1(3). This section does not prevent terms from being implied. Implied terms are considered in more detail below.

[2] 1997 Act, s.1(1).

[3] 1997 Act, s.1(2).

Informal Contracts

In situations in which there is no formal written agreement, the starting 7.6
point will generally be to consider the words exchanged between the
parties prior to the contract being concluded. These may be contained in
written communications such as letters, faxes and emails or may have
been spoken by the parties in meetings and telephone calls. The rules as
to offer and acceptance may be used to identify which communications
form the contract and therefore contribute to its terms. It is in relation to
a situation in which there has been an ongoing dialogue between the
parties that it is particularly important to be able to identify the point in
time when the contract was concluded. Once the contract is concluded its
terms are fixed. The terms will remain as they were when the contract
was concluded unless the parties agree to vary them or make a new
contract. A party to a concluded contract may not unilaterally alter the
terms of that contract. An illustration of this may be found in *Thornton v.
Shoe Lane Parking Ltd*[4]:

> The owners of a carpark attempted to exclude liability not only for
> damage to property but also for personal injury to those parking their
> cars on the premises. The clause to that effect appeared on a ticket
> issued by an automatic machine at the entrance to the carpark and on
> a notice inside the carpark. The court considered that the term was
> not part of the contract. Once the customer took his ticket from the
> machine as he entered the car park the contract was formed.
> Thereafter it was too late to introduce additional terms.

Incorporation of Terms by Reference

Irrespective of the means by which the contract was concluded, terms 7.7
may be incorporated by reference rather than being spelled out in the
contract. For example, when sending out a quotation for work to be done
to repair a car, a garage will often indicate that their standard terms and
conditions will apply if the offer is accepted and tickets for travel will
often indicate on their face that they are issued subject to the terms and
conditions of the carrier. Where this is done, questions may arise as to
whether the terms have validly been incorporated into a contract.

The rules on the means by which terms may become part of a
contract may be summarised as follows. The rules are represented on a
schematic form in the diagram on page 103. It provides an indication of
how the means of interaction relate to one another but is intended only to
be indicative.

---

[4] [1971] 2 Q.B. 163.

Incorporation by Signature

7.8   Where a document has been signed and it contains either terms or a clear
      reference to terms in another document, those terms will form part of the
      contract. By signing a document a person is deemed to have assented to
      its terms and consequently to be bound by it.

> "[W]here an action is brought on a written agreement which is
> signed by the defendant, the agreement is proved by proving his
> signature and, in the absence of fraud, it is wholly immaterial that he
> has not read the agreement and does not know its contents."[5]

This principle is capable of covering situations in which an
agreement (either negotiated by the parties or pre-printed) is signed by
the parties or where there has been an exchange of correspondence. In
the latter situation the letter of acceptance which is signed will
incorporate all the terms of the contract. The principle holds even where
the clause in question is in "legible, but regrettably small print"[6] but not
where the writing is illegible, or where the effect of the clause has been
misrepresented. This rule may operate particularly harshly where one
party is required to sign a pre-printed contract prepared by the other
party.[7] Dissatisfaction with this rule has frequently been expressed:

> "If it were possible for your Lordships to escape from the world of
> make-believe which the law has created into the real world in which
> transactions of this sort are actually done, the answer would be short
> and simple. It [signature] should make no difference whatsoever.
> This document is not meant to be read, still less to be understood. Its
> signature is in truth about as significant as a handshake that marks
> the formal conclusion of a bargain."[8]

7.9   There is force in this contention. Even contract lawyers are unlikely
      to pore over the fine print of every holiday booking form, car hire
      document and receipt which they sign. Like Homer, their heads may nod.
      Nevertheless signature is the outward and visible sign of assent to the
      terms of an agreement. It remains an important factor in determining
      whether or not a contract term has been incorporated.

      A recent Scottish case appears to cast doubt over the principle that
      signature is sufficient to incorporate a term. In *Montgomery Litho Ltd v.
      Maxwell*[9]:

> Mr Maxwell was a director of a company. He signed an agreement
> for the supply of printing services to that company. His company
> went into liquidation. The printers sought to recover sums owing to

---

[5] *Parker v. S. E. Railway Co.* (1877) 2 C.P.D. 416, *per* Mellish L.J., at p.421.
[6] *L'Estrange v. Graucob* [1934] 2 K.B. 394.
[7] Measures to prevent the unfairness that may result are considered in Chapter 9.
[8] *McCutcheon v. MacBrayne*, 1964 S.C. (H.L.) 28, 39–40 *per* Lord Devlin.
[9] 1999 S.L.T. 1431.

them from Mr Maxwell personally. They relied on the fact that Mr Maxwell had signed a credit application which said that he had read the printers' standard terms and conditions. There was a clause in those conditions to the effect that the director of a company was liable along with the company for any amount owing to the printers.

The court considered that Mr Maxwell was not liable. The basis for the decision is curious. The court might have analysed the situation as being one of offer and acceptance—that Mr Maxwell has accepted the terms on behalf of the company and there was no acceptance by him personally to be bound. Instead they decided that the clause making Mr Maxwell liable had not been properly drawn to his attention. They considered the judgments in the English case of *Interfoto Picture Library Ltd v. Stiletto Visual Programmes Ltd*[10] and concluded

> "we see no reason to doubt that the general principle on which they both proceeded, viz that the failure by a proferens fairly to draw attention to a particularly onerous and unusual provision may disable him from effectually founding on it, represents also the law of Scotland."

If this does represent the law of Scotland it is a bold innovation in applying the test of reasonable notice even where a contract has been signed. The decision in *Interfoto* was concerned with the quite different situation in which the term was contained in a document that had not been signed. That decision and the tests of reasonable notice in such a situation are considered below. Time will tell whether the avenue opened up by the judges in *Montgomery Litho* leads somewhere interesting or turns out to have been a wrong turning and a dead end. 7.10

Incorporation by Express Assent

Where no document is actually signed, one party may, at the time of contracting, point out an exemption clause and say "I am contracting on the basis of this term being part of our contract, do you agree?" Following the signature principle, the term will be held to be part of the contract if the other party does expressly agree. If the agreement to be bound by the term is not clear, it may be necessary to consider whether the term has been incorporated by notice. 7.11

Incorporation by express consent may prove to be particularly useful in relation to contracts concluded by means of computer. There is at present no means of obtaining signature to these terms. However, where a notice is brought to the attention of customer and he or she clicks on an "I agree" box on screen, this would appear to amount to an express assent to that term being part of the contract.

---

[10] [1989] Q.B. 433; [1988] 2 W.L.R. 615; [1988] 1 All E.R. 348.

Incorporation by Notice

7.12   A party seeking to incorporate a term may rely upon a notice. Many
terms incorporated in this way have the intention of restricting the
liability of the contracting party providing goods or services. The notice
may itself contain the term, such as those one sees on dry-cleaners'
counters. Alternatively it may refer to another document which actually
contains the term. Bus tickets often refer to terms and conditions of
carriage which are printed elsewhere. These notices may be used in
situations where there is no writing to constitute the contract and little if
any oral exchange. Over the years the courts have had to consider the
question of incorporation in relation to such notices many times.

   In answering the question whether such a reference is effective the
courts have had regard to the nature of the document in which the
reference is made. The issue is whether the document containing the
reference is a core element of the contract and might therefore reasonably
have been expected to contain contract terms. For example, in *Thompson
v. London Midland & Scottish Railway Company*[11]:

>   Mrs Thompson had sustained injuries as a result of the railway
>   company's negligence. It was held that the railway company had
>   incorporated an exemption clause into the contract. This was despite
>   the following: Mrs Thompson could not read; the ticket had been
>   bought for her by her niece; and the relevant exemption clause
>   referred to in the ticket was contained on page 552 of a separate
>   timetable which itself cost 6d. Lord Hamworth M.R. based his
>   decision on the fact that the contract in question was a contract of
>   carriage in which the ticket was required to get onto the platform and
>   thence the train. The issue of a railway ticket accordingly ought to
>   indicate to a reasonable person that there were conditions to be
>   found upon it. This could be distinguished from a contract of deposit
>   where no written document was required where the customer would
>   treat the ticket as a mere voucher.

7.13   A similar distinction between reference in a mere voucher and
reference in a document fundamental to the contract was made in *Taylor
v. Glasgow Corporation*[12]:

>   Mrs Taylor went weekly for a hot bath to her local public baths in
>   Glasgow. On one such occasion she fell down a stair and suffered
>   serious injury. The corporation sought to rely on an exemption
>   clause. This clause appeared on the ticket with which all bathers
>   were issued when they entered the building and paid the price for the
>   facility they sought. On the front of the ticket it said, "For conditions
>   see other side" and on the reverse were words to the effect that the

---

[11] [1930] 1 K.B. 41.
[12] 1952 S.C. 440.

corporation accepted no liability for an injury which was caused to anyone using the establishment.

Lord Justice-Clerk Thomson said that the ticket performed the following functions: (a) it was a domestic check on the running of the establishment; (b) it was a receipt for the price; and (c) it was a voucher, indicating what facility had been paid for. He regarded the voucher aspect as the significant one. A person would not regard a voucher as containing contractual conditions, unlike a railway ticket where it was accepted that the ticket was a contractual document.

Where the reference is in a document which would *not* be expected to contain terms of the contract, the court will examine whether the party knew there was writing that contained conditions or, if they did not, whether enough had been done to bring the reference to the term to their attention. In the English case of *Parker v. S.E. Railway Company*[13]: 7.14

> Mr Parker deposited a bag worth £24 10s, in a railway cloakroom. He was charged 2d. and received in return for his money a ticket which bore on its face the opening hours of the cloakroom and the words "see back." On the reverse it stated that the company would not be responsible for any bag worth more than £10. A notice to the same effect hung in the cloakroom. Although Parker admitted that he knew there was writing on the ticket he denied that he had read either it or the notice. He said that he imagined that the ticket was a receipt for the bag.

By a majority, the court held that if the plaintiff knew that there was writing and also knew that it was the other party's intention that these constituted terms of the contract he would be bound. But if he had not read the term, nor knew that the intention was to constitute contractual terms, then the correct question to ask was "whether the railway company did what was reasonably sufficient to give the plaintiff notice of the condition."[14] The point is illustrated by *Taylor v. Glasgow Corporation.*[15] Mrs Taylor said that she knew there was writing on the ticket but not that it referred to contractual terms. It was held that the corporation had not sufficiently brought the clause to Mrs Taylor's notice. The term was therefore not incorporated into the contract.

What is meant by reasonable notice? In deciding this a court will consider the nature of the term that is to be incorporated. In *Thornton v. Shoe Lane Parking Ltd,*[16] the term in dispute excluded liability of car park owners for damage to property and personal injury. As noted above, the attempt to have a notice on the ticket issued by the car parking machine came too late. In relation to the notice on a board inside the car 7.15

---

[13] (1877) 2 C.P.D. 416.
[14] *Ibid. per* Mellish L.J. at p.424.
[15] *Ibid.*
[16] *Ibid.*

park the Court of Appeal held that no reasonable notice of the clause had
been given. To see the notice the customer would have to leave his car at
the entrance and enter the carpark. No one was likely to follow this
course of action. Lord Denning M.R. suggested that to exempt liability
for personal injury as well as damage to property the notice would have
to be "in red ink with a red hand pointing to it".[17] The approach which
underlies Lord Denning's view has been accepted by other judges in the
Court of Appeal. In the case of *Interfoto Picture Library Ltd v. Stiletto
Visual Programmes Ltd*[18] referred to above in relation to incorporation by
signature:

> The defendants asked the plaintiffs whether they had photographs
> that would be of use to them in preparing a presentation. The
> plaintiffs sent negatives to the defendants together with a set of
> terms that provided for a very high charge to be levied if the
> negatives were retained for more than 14 days. The defendants
> telephoned the plaintiffs acknowledging receipt of the negatives but
> not referring to the terms. The defendants said that they might be
> interested in using some of the images. The negatives were returned
> late. The plaintiffs sought to rely on the terms for payment of the late
> return sum. The terms were not contained in a signed document.

The court held that the claim failed as the term relating to payment
for late return was not part of the contract. This was because the
plaintiffs had done insufficient to bring the term to the defendants'
attention. The judges referred to the term as "very onerous" and
"unreasonable and extortionate". Dillon L.J. concluded:

> "It is in my judgment a logical development of the common law into
> modern conditions that it should be held, as it was in *Thornton v.
> Shoe Lane Parking Ltd*, that, if one condition in a set of printed
> conditions is particularly onerous or unusual, the party seeking to
> enforce it must show that that particular condition was fairly brought
> to the attention of the other party."[19]

Incorporation by Course of Dealing

7.16   Even though no notice is given, a person may nevertheless be bound by
an exemption clause because he knows of it as a result of a course of
dealing. In each case the question to be asked is whether or not the
circumstances yield the inference that both parties proceeded on the basis

---

[17] *Ibid.* at p.170.
[18] [1989] Q.B. 433; [1988] 2 W.L.R. 615; [1988] 1 All E.R. 348.
[19] p.352.

that the exemption clause was a term of the contract.[20] The most famous case on this topic is *McCutcheon v. MacBrayne*[21]:

> The pursuer sought damages in respect of his car which had been lost when the defenders' ferry sank on a trip from Islay to Tarbert. His brother-in-law had arranged the shipment of the car and both men had transferred items on the ferry in the past. In principle the defenders required shippers to sign a risk note exempting them from liability, but the pursuer and his brother-in-law had sometimes, but not always, signed such a note. Inadvertently no such note had been signed on this occasion. Notices containing the exemption clause were also displayed in the defenders' office and on the pier but the pursuer had never read them.

The House of Lords first distinguished *Parker* on the ground that there was no contractual document such as a ticket or receipt seeking to import conditions. Further as the notices had not been read they could not bind the pursuer. On the question of the prior dealings of the parties, the House held that while a consistent course of dealing could in principle bind the parties, there had been no consistent course here. The risk note had sometimes been signed, sometimes not. Accordingly the defenders had also failed to establish that the clause had been inserted on the basis of notice by means of course of dealing. Mr McCutcheon was accordingly entitled to full compensation in respect of his car.

Surprisingly few examples of a course of dealing leading to 7.17 incorporation can be given. One case where a parallel principle was successfully invoked occurred when a crane was hired under an oral contract made by telephone.[22] Both the companies concerned were engaged in the business of hiring cranes and both used the standard industry conditions of contract when hiring out cranes. The standard conditions contained an exemption clause. Although there was not strictly a course of dealing between the parties, both ought to have reasonably assumed that the term in question would be part of the contract. Long usage of the term by both parties indicated that it was to be incorporated. A contrasting case is *Grayston Plant Ltd v. Plean Precast Ltd.*[23] Over a period of four years there were 12 instances in which the pursuers followed up an oral contract by sending an "acknowledgement of order form" which referred to the general conditions upon which they traded. It was held that the general conditions were not incorporated into the contract because it could not be proved that the defenders were aware of the conditions.

---

[20] *Continental Tyre & Rubber Co. Ltd v. Trunk Trailer Co. Ltd*, 1987 S.L.T. 58; *Wm. Teacher & Sons Ltd v. Bell Lines Ltd*, 1991 S.L.T. 876.

[21] 1964 S.C. (H.L.) 28.

[22] *British Crane Hire Corp. Ltd v. Ipswich Plant Hire Ltd* [1975] Q.B. 303; [1976] 1 All E.R. 1059.

[23] 1976 S.C. 206.

IMPLIED TERMS

7.18 The parties can never provide for every contingency that may arise under the contract. Accordingly, they will leave some terms to be implied. If it is a typical contract in a familiar context, few difficulties will arise. Over the years the incidents of these contracts have been fully worked out. Originally the courts were most willing to imply terms in contracts of everyday occurrence, such as sale, hire and lease. Implication would usually be based upon the custom which had grown up regarding such transactions. Many of these individual instances of implication of terms eventually found their way into statute. The contract of sale of goods provides the classic example of this process. By the end of the nineteenth century the implied terms of this contract had been so well worked out by judicial decisions that it was possible to codify the law. This was done by the Sale of Goods Act 1893. Over the years various amendments were made to the 1893 Act and the law was consolidated in the Sale of Goods Act 1979.

> *Example*: Fred paid £600 for a chair which was described in the catalogue as "a reclining chair". Shortly after taking delivery Fred discovers that the chair can only remain in a fixed position and cannot recline. In a sale by description there is an implied term that the goods correspond with that description. Fred is entitled to return the chair to the seller and to recover his money.

In other instances implied terms have originated directly with Parliament rather than having been developed by the courts. Statutes may imply certain terms to give effect to some economic or social policy. For instance, the Consumer Protection (Distance Selling) Regulations 2000 which were discussed in Chapter 2 require that the supplier perform the contract within a period of 30 days.

7.19 In contracts of less common occurrence two general principles may be stated regarding implication of terms by the courts. First, no term will be implied which is directly contradictory to an express term. Secondly, a term will more easily be implied in a verbal than in a written and formal contract.[24] Beyond those two principles it becomes more difficult to state the law with precision. The classic statement on this branch of contract law was made by Lord McLaren:

> "The conception of an implied condition is one with which we are familiar in relation to contracts of every description, and if we seek to trace any such implied conditions to their source it will be found in almost every instance that they are founded either on universal custom or in the nature of the contract itself. If the condition is such that every reasonable man on the one part would desire for his own

---

[24] Gloag, *Contract* (2nd ed.,) pp. 288–289. Approved in *Crawford v. Bruce*, 1992 S.L.T. 524, *per* L.P. Hope at 531G.

protection to stipulate for the condition, and that no reasonable man on the other would refuse to accede to it, then it is not unnatural that the condition should be taken for granted in all contracts of this class without the necessity of giving it formal expression."[25]

It is worth noting that in this passage, Lord McLaren flirts with two different bases for the implication of terms. The first basis is that of "universal custom or the nature of the contract itself". We have already seen that this applies perfectly to everyday contracts such as sale, hire or lease. It is assumed in such cases that the parties simply did not trouble to express the term. The passage goes on to discuss terms being implied by reference to the test of the "reasonable man". However, it should be noted that it is not suggested that the fact that a reasonable man would imply such a term is enough. The second part of Lord McLaren's dictum is still referring to terms that might be implied into certain *classes* of contract. It adds an additional test that no reasonable person on either side would refuse the term sought.

Lord McLaren's approach has recently been approved and adopted in   7.20
the Inner House.[26] In *G.M. Shepherd v. North West Securities Ltd*[27]:

Retail chemists hired a compact processor to develop films on their premises at Cults. As is so frequently the case today, the equipment was supplied by one company, Photosystems (U.K.) Ltd, but the actual contract of hire was with the defenders, a finance company. Clause six of the hire agreement stated that the hirers had inspected and approved the equipment and that the defenders would not be subject to any implied terms. The processor failed to work satisfactorily and the chemists purported to reject it and rescind the contract. They claimed that they were entitled to do so because the contract included an implied term that the equipment was hireworthy. At issue was whether or not such a term fell to be implied into the contract. It was held that no such term fell to be implied. The Second Division recognised that typical contracts of hire were subject to the item being hireworthy. However, they found that this contract was atypical in that "the owner never had possession of the compact printer processor, and he only purchased it from the supplier at the special request of the hirer who acknowledged that he, the hirer, had inspected and approved the equipment." With no implied term, the chemists were nit entitled to reject the processor.[28]

---

[25] *Morton & Co. v. Muir Bros.*, 1907 S.C. 1211 at p.1224.
[26] *G.M. Shepherd v. North West Securities Ltd*, 1991 S.L.T. 499; *Crawford v. Bruce*, 1992 S.L.T. 524.
[27] 1991 S.L.T. 499.
[28] *G.M. Shepherd v. North West Securities Ltd*, *supra per* L.J.C. Ross at p.507A; see also Lord Murray at p.511C and Lord McCluskey at p.513G–514B.

This demonstrates that even where a contract falls within a class in respect of which a particular term is implied, the facts may be such as to take the case out of the class and therefore prevent the terms from being implied.

7.21   In *Crawford v. Bruce*, shop premises were leased for an initial period of ten years.[29] It was provided that the rent should be reviewed every three years, but no mechanism was provided to determine how that rent should be assessed. The landlord contended that a term fell to be implied into the lease that the rent should be market rent at each three year review. The First Division rejected this contention. Delivering the opinion of the court, Lord President Hope stated that:

> "The hypothesis on which we are asked to say the rent should be fixed is that the rent should be a market rent, and that the duration on the expiry of each three year period is to be the same as the initial duration of the lease. But both points could be said to be likely to operate to the disadvantage of the tenant, and it is far from clear that the hypothesis is one which satisfies the test which Lord McLaren described in *Morton & Co. v. Muir Bros.*, namely that the implied condition is such that no reasonable man in the tenant's position would have refused to accede to it."[30]

By considering the matter from the position of the tenant, the court was able to reject the idea that a term fell to be implied. The second part of Lord McLaren's dictum was used to define a situation in which a term should not be implied.

English Law

7.22   In arriving at their views on implied terms, the Scottish courts have carefully considered the English cases on this subject. Various tests have been adopted by the English judiciary to determine whether or not a term should be implied into a particular contract and these were summarised by Lord Wilberforce in *Liverpool City Council v. Irwin*[31] when he said,

> "there are varieties of implications which the courts think fit to make and they do not necessarily involve the same process. Where there is, on the face of it, a complete, bilateral contract, the courts are sometimes willing to add terms to it, as implied terms; this is very common in mercantile contracts where there is an established usage; in that case the courts are spelling out what both parties know and would, if asked, unhesitatingly agree to be part of the bargain. In other cases, where there is an apparently complete bargain, the courts are willing to add a term on the ground that without it the

---

[29] 1992 S.L.T. 524.
[30] *Ibid.* at p.532I.
[31] [1977] A.C. 239, [1976] 2 All E.R. 39.

contract will not work - this is the case, if not of *The Moorcock* itself on its facts, at least of the doctrine of *The Moorcock* as usually applied. This is, as was pointed out by the majority in the Court of Appeal, a strict test—though the degree of strictness seems to vary with the current legal trend, and I think that they were right not to accept it as applicable here. There is a third variety of implication, that which I think Lord Denning M.R. favours, or at least did favour in this case, and that is the implication of reasonable terms. But though I agree with many of his instances, which in fact fall under one or other of the preceding heads, I cannot go so far as to endorse his principle; indeed, it seems to me, with respect, to extend a long, and undesirable, way beyond sound authority.

The present case, in my opinion, represents a fourth category or, I would rather say, a fourth shade on a continuous spectrum. The court here is simply concerned to establish what the contract is, the parties not having themselves fully stated the terms. In this sense the court is searching for what must be implied."

This part of Lord Wilberforce's speech contains four alternative bases   7.23 on which a term might be implied. For the sake of convenience, these may be considered separately, but in practice it is not always easy to differentiate them.

Established Usage

The first basis for implication—established usage in mercantile   7.24 contracts—is similar to the implication of terms into contracts of a particular class referred to by Lord Maclaren in *Morton & Co*. In each instance the rationale for implying the term is that it is something that the parties would have clearly agreed to had they been asked. Where this happens the term is being implied on the assumption that it was intended by the parties. Contracts for services provide an example of this. In these contracts, terms are implied to the effect that the work will be done in reasonable time and to a reasonable standard.

Necessity

The second suggested basis for implication relates to a situation in which   7.25 it is necessary to make the contract work. In this regard Lord Wilberforce refers to the case of *The Moorcock*.[32] There, the court approached the question from the angle of "efficacy".

A vessel had arranged to discharge its cargo at a pier on the River Thames. At low tide the keel of the vessel was damaged when it grounded on the bed of the river. There was held to be an implied term in the contract between the owner of the vessel and the

---

[32] (1889) 14 P.D. 64.

wharfingers that the latter had taken reasonable steps to ensure that it was safe anchorage. In awarding damages against the wharfingers, Bowen L.J. framed the test for implying terms as follows: "I believe if one were to take all the cases, and they are many, it will be found that in all of them the law is raising an implication from the presumed intention of the parties with the object of giving to the transaction such efficacy as both parties must have intended that in all events it should have."[33]

This indicates that terms are implied on this basis not because they themselves were intended by the parties but because they are necessary to reach a result that the court is satisfied was intended by the parties.

Reasonableness

7.26   Lord Wilberforce's third basis for implication of terms is that the term in question is reasonable. This is rejected as a test for determining whether a term should be implied. To imply a term merely because it is reasonable without considering what the parties actually intended would be an usurpation of the function of the parties and would be making their agreement for them.

Spelling Out the Contract the Parties Have Made

7.27   The fourth basis on which Lord Wilberforce said that terms might be implied is the need to spell out the terms of a contract that is incomplete. An example of this type of implication in Scotland is found in *City of Aberdeen Council v. Clark*[34]:

> The pursuers were landlords of property that had been let to the defender for a period of 99 years. There was a clause in the lease for review of the rent after every 21 years. Although the lease specified that failing agreement as to the reviewed rent it was to be determined by an arbiter, it did not state on what basis the arbiter was to set the new rent. The tenants claimed that in the absence of such provision the review provisions were void for uncertainty. The landlords claimed that it was possible to imply that the rent fixed by the arbiter should be a fair rent.

The court considered the circumstances of the case made it appropriate to "amplify the contested clause by implication". The court concluded that the circumstances made it possible to imply that the rent should be fixed, "on the basis of what was fair and reasonable between the parties to the lease".

---

[33] at p.68.
[34] 1999 S.L.T. 613.

Lord Wilberforce characterised this basis of implication as being a   7.28
search to "establish what the contract is". Once again the focus is on the
aim of the contract—the objective intention of the parties as to what the
contract should achieve. The reliance on the intention means that this
basis of implication has a lot in common with construction of the
contract. In some situations the desired result may be achieved by either
means. For example, in *Staffordshire Area Health Authority v. South
Staffordshire Waterworks Co.*,[35] the issue was whether the defendants
were entitled to terminate an agreement in which they were obliged to
supply water free of charge or at a low cost "at all times hereafter". Lord
Denning M.R. held that they were on the basis of a proper construction
of the agreement. Goff and Cumming-Bruce L.JJ. also held that they
were but on the basis that the court should infer a term that the contract
was terminable on reasonable notice.

Implying Terms in Practice

It can be difficult to decide whether a term falls to be implied in a   7.29
particular case. In *Lothian v. Jenolite,* a company sought to terminate its
contract with an agent which sold industrial chemicals on its behalf.[36]
The company claimed that the agent had sold a competitor's products.
They argued that this breached an implied term of the agreement that the
agent would work exclusively for them. It was held that there was no
implied term to that effect. The company had not stipulated that the
agency was to be an exclusive one in the written contract.

By contrast in *North American Continental Sales Inc. v. Bepi
Electronics Ltd*, an American company gave a Scottish company sole
rights to distribute its software in the United Kingdom.[37] Under the
contract, the Scottish company was to pay the American company a
proportion of the value of the sales it achieved. The Scottish company
failed to market the software, alleging that it did not work. In
consequence the American company raised an action claiming that there
was an implied term in the contract that the Scottish company would use
its best endeavours to sell the process. It was held that business efficacy
did require such a term to be implied into the contract.

More recently, in *Scottish Power plc v. Kvaerner Construction*   7.30
(Regions) Limited,[38] the issue was whether terms could be implied in a
contract between sub-contractors and main contractors. Lord MacFadyen
expressed reservations about the analysis used by Lord Wilberforce in
Liverpool City Council. He expressed the view that if it was to be argued
that the term was one that would be implied in all contracts of a
particular class, one would expect to find instances where that conclusion

---

[35] [1978] 1 W.L.R. 1387; 3 All E.R. 769.
[36] 1969 S.C. 111.
[37] 1982 S.L.T. 47.
[38] 1999 S.L.T. 931.

had been reached in the past. If there were no such past examples, one would have to consider the other bases for implication. As to them, he considered that if the business efficacy test could not be met, it was doubtful that the term could be implied as an ordinary incident of the contract (that is on Lord Wilberforce's fourth basis). He expressed the view that "the court should be slow to accept that a term that fails the business efficacy test, is implied on any other basis".

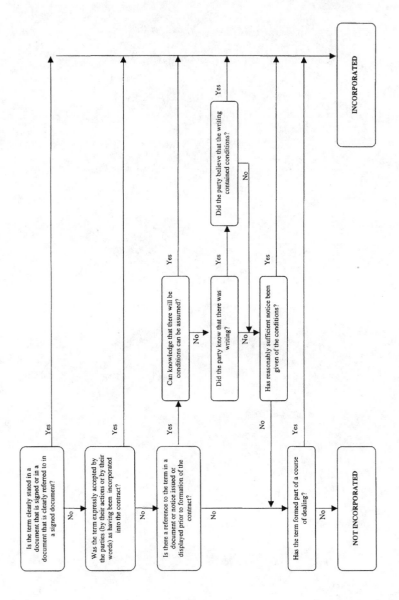

CHAPTER 8

CONSTRUCTION OF THE CONTRACT

Having determined what the terms of the contract are, it is necessary to 8.1
determine what effect they have. To do this requires both that the terms
of the contract are interpreted and that they are applied to the facts in
question. These two matters together may be referred to as construction
of the contract.

When interpreting a contract, the court is seeking to determine the
intention of the parties at the time the contract was made. In one sense
this is an artificial exercise. If the parties are in dispute as to their rights
and obligations there will be no longer be any common intention.
However, the same rule applies here as applied to formation of contract.
The relevant question is not what the parties' subjective intentions.
Rather it is what the parties must be deemed to have intended when the
matter is examined objectively. In a recent English House of Lords case,[1]
Lord Hoffman considered the developments that had taken place in the
law relating to interpretation of contracts. He offered a summary of the
process of interpretation:

> "Interpretation is the ascertainment of the meaning which the
> document would convey to a reasonable person having all the
> background knowledge which would reasonably have been available
> to the parties in the situation that they were at the time of the
> contract."

There is more than one approach that courts can take to the problem
of interpreting a contract. This is demonstrated by the leading Scottish
case on this issue, *Bank of Scotland v. Dunedin Property Investment
Company Ltd.*[2] The facts of this case are considered later in this Chapter.
For now it is enough to note while all three of the Inner House judges
reached the same conclusion as to the meaning of the contract, they took
different routes. The Lord President adopted the approach that the
starting point should be to consider the ordinary meaning of the words
but that the court was entitled to examine the circumstances in which the
words were used. Lord Kirkwood and Lord Caplan both referred to Lord

---

[1] *Investors Compensation Scheme v. West Bromwich Building Society* [1998] 1
W.L.R. 896; [1998] 1 All E.R. 98.
[2] 1998 S.C. 657; 1999 S.L.T. 470.

Hoffmans's *dictum* quoted above. They took the view it was necessary to consider the knowledge that the parties would have had at the time that they made the contract and the result that they must have intended.

To reflect the two approaches found in *Dunedin*, this Chapter first considers the use to be made of the wording of the contract and then the relevance of surrounding circumstances. Finally, some other legal principles which may have bearing on interpretation are noted.

Wording of the Contract

8.2   Consideration must be given to the words that are actually used in the contract. In *Bank of Scotland*,[3] the Lord President adopted the approach taken in an English case[4] that most expressions have a natural meaning and that the search for the meaning of a contract "will start, and usually finish, by asking what is the ordinary meaning of the words used". Where the words do have an ordinary and natural meaning then it may be presumed that the parties intended that meaning to take effect. In *Investors Compensation Scheme v. West Bromwich Building Society*,[5] Lord Hoffman noted that this was on the basis that we do not easily accept that parties have made a mistake. More recently, he has described the words used as "the primary source for understanding what the parties meant".[6]

Considering the meaning of words involves examining not only the words that are directly in dispute but also the remainder of contract.

> *Example*: In a contract for repairs to be carried out to a house there might be a clause whereby the builder is liable for any water damage arising while he is working on the house. The builder works for a week in January, stops for a fortnight and then resumes work at the start of February. When he restarts he discovers that a pipe has frozen and burst during the fortnight causing damage. The issue would be whether the expression "while he is working" includes the period when the builder was off site. If the contract provided that, from the start of the works until they were completely finished, the householders were to leave the house solely in his possession, that he would be responsible for heating the house and that he was to insure the house against damage caused by water the conclusion might be that he was liable. However, if the contract said that the householders would continue to live in the house and that the "work" could be carried out only between the hours of 9.30am and 16.30, the outcome might be different.

---

[3] 1998 S.C. 657; 1999 S.L.T. 470.
[4] *Charter Reinsurance Co. Ltd v. Fagan* [1997] A.C. 313.
[5] [1998] 1 W.L.R. 896; [1998] 1 All E.R. 98.
[6] *Bank of Credit of Commerce International SA v. Ali* [2001] 1 All E.R. 961 at para. 39.

Sometimes the words will be ones used in everyday conversation and will need no explanation. Sometimes, however, specialist terms or expressions may be used. If this is so it will be necessary to consider that special meaning.

Surrounding Circumstances

In some situations the meaning of the words may be affected by the   8.3
context in which the words were used. In *Reardon Smith Line Limited v. Yngvar Hangsen-Tangen,*[7] Lord Wilberforce stated:

> "No contracts are made in a vacuum; there is always a setting in which they have to be placed. The nature of what is legitimate to have regard to is usually described as "the surrounding circumstances" but the phrase is imprecise: it can be illustrated but hardly defined. In a commercial contract it is certainly right that the court should know the commercial purpose of the contract and this in turn presupposes knowledge of the genesis of the transaction, the background, the context, the market in which the parties are operating."[8]

Courts are therefore willing to consider these surrounding circumstances—often referred to as the "factual matrix"[9]—for the purpose of deciding what the parties meant when they used certain words or forms of words for their agreement. This may involve inquiry as to the aim or purpose of the contract. However, this is done for a limited purpose. The courts do not determine the aim and then attempt to make the wording meet that aim. They determine what the aim was and consider it as something that the parties had in mind when they used the words in question. It is therefore only a means to a proper understanding of the words that have been used. This can be illustrated by the English case of *Prenn v. Simmonds*[10]:

> Simmonds was employed by a subsidiary of RTT as its managing director. He was entitled to purchase part of the share capital of RTT provided that "the aggregate profits of RTT earned during the four years ending 19 August 1963...shall have amounted to £300,000". The parties were in dispute as to whether the reference to the aggregate profits of RTT meant that company alone or the group of companies consisting of RTT and its subsidiary.

After examining the background, the House of Lords took the view that Simmonds was engaged to generate profits at the subsidiary and was to receive an incentive for that purpose. On that basis they concluded that

---

[7] [1976] 1 W.L.R. 989; 3 All E.R. 570.
[8] p.995H; p.574.
[9] *per* Lord Wilberforce at p.997C, p.575.
[10] [1971] 3 All E.R. 237.

the reference to profits of RTT only made commercial sense if it was construed to mean the aggregate profits of both RTT and its subsidiary.

8.4   In addition to the purpose of the contract, the courts will also consider all the facts that are known to the parties at the time that the agreement was concluded. Again, this is not with the intention of deciding what the agreement *ought* to have been. It is simply that the circumstances may indicate what the parties meant when they used the particular words in the contract. The point is illustrated by *Bank of Scotland v. Dunedin Property Management Company Limited*[11]:

> Dunedin converted a number of bank loans into one consolidated loan of £10 million. The interest of the loan was a fixed rate. The borrowing was intended to last for ten years. There was a term in the loan agreement which gave the company a right to terminate the borrowing prior to the ten years. That was subject to the Bank, "being reimbursed for all costs, charges and expenses incurred by it in connection with the stock". In order to lend to the company, the Bank in turn borrowed £10 million from another institution. The money that the bank borrowed was at a fluctuating rate of interest. To protect itself against the possibility that the fluctuating interest that it was paying would rise above the fixed interest it was receiving, the Bank entered into an interest rate swap contract. Dunedin terminated the borrowing from the Bank prior to the ten-year-term. The Bank also terminated its borrowing and the interest swap agreement and thereby became liable to pay termination charges. The dispute between Dunedin and the Bank was whether these termination charges for which the Bank had become liable were costs "in connection with" the loan stock.

It was established Dunedin were aware that, in order for the Bank to lend to them, it would require to borrow money and to take steps to protect itself from interest rate fluctuations. They were also aware that if the loan was terminated prior to the ten-year-period, the Bank would incur costs in terminating the agreements that it would enter into. Against that background the court considered that the expression "costs...in connection with the stock", was wide enough to include the costs of terminating those arrangements.

8.5   As was noted by Lord Wilberforce in his dictum from *Reardon Smith Line* the expression "surrounding circumstances" is imprecise and there can be considerable difficulty in deciding where a court should draw the line in relation to what it will consider and what it will not consider. The following principles may be drawn from the cases.

> (1) For the courts to refer to any facts that existed at the time that the contract was concluded in order to interpret it, those facts

---

[11] 1998 S.C. 657.

must have been known to all the contracting parties.[12] This may be justified by the rationale that the contract is the product of agreement between two (or more) parties and what the court is doing is attempting to discover the presumed common intention of those parties. If the facts were known to only one of the parties they could not have a bearing on the common intention.

(2) The details of and terms of prior negotiations of the parties may be looked at only for the purpose of determining what facts were known to the parties at the time they concluded their agreement.[13] It is not permissible to examine the terms of the prior negotiations and argue that the words used at that stage provide any guidance to the words in the final agreement. This is referred to as the prior communings rule. The justification for the rule is easily apparent. When the parties are negotiating their intentions are not fixed. There may be considerable change between their intention at that time and their intention when agreement is concluded.

(3) It is not possible to have regard to subjective declarations of intent by the parties. This is justified on the basis that the exercise of interpretation is to determine the objective intention of the parties. The issue is not what parties think they have undertaken, but what they said.

Legal principles

There are some other legal principles that may influence interpretation of 8.6 a term.

Contra Proferentem

Where a clause is ambiguous, it is construed against the interest of the 8.7 party who seeks to rely upon it. This is known as interpretation *contra proferentem*. It applies only when there is an ambiguity—it may not be used to create any ambiguity. In many circumstances where it might apply both parties to the dispute will be relying on the same clause so that there is no obvious party against whom it may be construed.

Application of the principle may be illustrated by a case in which an insurance company stipulated in a contract of life insurance that the contract would be void should any of the statements made by the proposer turn out to be untrue.[14] A lady made statements on the proposal form indicating that she was not suffering from any malady. Unknown to

---

[12] *Scottish Power plc v. Britoil (Exploration) Limited* [1997] T.L.R. 616, referred to in *Bank of Scotland v. Dunedin Property Investment Co Ltd*, 1998 S.C. 657.

[13] *Bank of Scotland v. Dunedin Property Investment Co Ltd*, 1998 S.C. 657 *per* Lord President Rodger at p.665F.

[14] *Life Association of Scotland v. Foster* (1873) 11 M. 351.

her, at the time of filling out the form, she was already suffering from the disease which was to cause her death some months later. The company initially refused to pay out on the policy. The court held that the company was bound to do so. Construing the clause *contra proferentem* it meant that the proposer required to disclose any illness known to her; it did not apply where she did not know of her true medical condition.

8.8   A particular manifestation of the *contra proferentem* rule exists in relation to exemption clauses. These are clauses whereby a party seeks to restrict his legal liability to the other party. Such clauses are known as exemption clauses. They may seek to either totally or partially exclude liability on the part of one party. Where they seek merely to impose a cap on the maximum liability of a part they are often referred to as limitation clauses. Here are some familiar examples of exemption and limitation clauses: "The management accepts no liability for any article lost on the premises"; "In the event of any damage occurring to this item when in the control of the company, the company shall not be liable for any loss in excess of £100"; and "Persons enter these premises at their own risk".

These clauses can have much to commend them. By allocating the risk of a particular event, the liability of the parties is determined in advance. This avoids unnecessary litigation, indicates who is to bear the cost of insurance and enables the value of goods and services to be accurately priced.

> *Example*: Blunt Ltd, supplies widgets to Klim Ltd. In their contract it is stipulated that Blunt shall not be liable if a widget is defective and causes loss to Klim. Should, accordingly, a widget prove defective, the parties know their legal position. Klim can insure against loss if it wishes while Blunt can keep the price of the widgets down, because it does not have to pass on the cost of insurance premiums to its customers.

8.9   Statutory regulation of these clauses is considered the next chapter. However, apart from such regulation the courts have traditionally been hostile to such terms. In particular, the strong presumption of the law is that one party will not agree to release the other from liability for his own negligence. Such a course is regarded as "inherently improbable."[15] So in a series of cases it has been established that unless the draftsman is particularly precise, actually uses the term "negligence" or some synonym and exempts from all other forms of liability, the defender might still be liable. An example illustrates the rigour with which the courts follow this approach[16]:

---

[15] *Gillespie Bros. & Co. Ltd v. Roy Bowles Transport Ltd* [1973] Q.B. 400, *per* Buckley L.J. at p.419.
[16] *Graham v. The Shore Porter's Society*, 1979 S.L.T. 119; see also *Golden Sea Produce Ltd v. Scottish Nuclear plc*, 1992 S.L.T. 942.

A clause in a contract for the carriage of household goods from Aberdeen to Glasgow stated: "The contractors shall not be responsible for loss and damage to furniture and effects caused by or incidental to fire or aircraft but will endeavour to effect insurance on behalf of the customer on receipt of instructions." The goods were destroyed by fire and the owners sought compensation from the transport company. It was held that the clause did not exempt the carriers from liability.

This apparently surprising result was reached because the clause could be construed to refer both to the carrier's liability under contract and also to its liability under statute. The Mercantile Law Amendment Act (Scotland) 1856 makes carriers of goods liable for loss caused by fire while the goods are in their possession. Construing the clause strictly, the court decided that it only exempted the carriers from their statutory liability.[17] What the decision shows is the willingness of the courts to prevent a contracting party from relying on an exemption clause by adopting a strict construction of the contract. However, that willingness was apparent most in situations where the courts considered it necessary to "protect" one party to the contract. Statutory controls now exist for that purpose. There may therefore be less need to a strict construction.

The *contra proferentem* rule has a further incarnation in the Unfair Terms in Consumer Contracts Regulations 1999. These Regulations are considered in the following Chapter.

Commercially Sensible Results

The courts interpret commercial agreements, as far as possible, so as to produce commercially sensible results. In *R & J Dempster Ltd v. Motherwell Bridge Engineering Co Ltd*, Lord Guthrie stated: 8.10

"The object of our law of contract is to facilitate the transactions of commercial men and not to create obstacles in the way of solving practical problems arising out of circumstances confronting them, or to expose them to unnecessary pitfalls."[18]

The rationale behind this policy has been stated to be that the "commercial construction is more likely to give effect to the intention of the parties."[19] Thus presumed intention is once more at play.

---

[17] The same strict approach applies in relation to limitation clauses but not with the some rigour. See *Bovis Construction (Scotland) Ltd v. Whatlings Construction Ltd,* 1995 S.C. (H.L.) 19, 1995 S.L.T. 1339.

[18] 1964 S.C. 308.

[19] *Mannai Investment Co Ltd v. Eagle Star Life Assurance Co Limited* [1997] 3 All E.R. 352 *per* Lord Steyn at 372. See also the opinion of the Lord President in *Bank of Scotland v. Dunedin Property Investment,* 1998 S.C. 657; 1989 S.L.T. 470.

Legality

8.11   "[A]...presumption of legality...exists where a contract is
            reasonable susceptible of two meanings."[20]

            Thus if the possible means of interpretation throw up two alternatives
            and one of them would be unlawful and therefore unenforceable, the
            courts will prefer the interpretation that give the contract some effect.

RECTIFICATION OF THE CONTRACT

8.12   On occasions the parties may have reached agreement but the terms of
        that agreement are then incorrectly recorded. This is sometimes referred
        to as an "error in expression". But error is not the appropriate term to use
        since the error is not as to the parties' intention. Rather, it is a defect in
        its expression. There is a discrepancy between what A and B have agreed
        and the terms of the document expressing the agreement.

        At common law in Scotland there was an equitable power to deal
        with such situations. This can be seen from the case of *Krupp v.
        Menzies*.[21] There, a clerk had been instructed to record an agreement
        whereby a hotel manageress was to receive one twentieth of the annual
        profits of the hotel. By mixing up percentages and fractions, the clerk
        recorded that the manageress was entitled to one fifth of the profits. The
        court rectified the error. Likewise the court intervened where there was a
        discrepancy between the missives of sale and the disposition as to the
        ambit of the subjects to be sold.[22]

8.13   The courts have now been granted a wide power under statute to
        rectify documents that are defectively expressed.[23] Where the need for
        rectification occurs, parties generally rely on this power rather than the
        old rules. The power applies where in the situation in which "a document
        intended to express or give effect to an agreement fails to express
        accurately the common intention of the parties to the agreement at the
        date when it was made". The court may rectify the document to give
        effect to that intention. The court may not order rectification if it would
        adversely affect the interests of a party who has (a) not known (or ought
        to have been aware) of the defective expression; (b) has placed reliance
        upon the deed; with the result that his position has been affected to a
        material extent; and (c) does not consent to the proposed rectification.

        It is of note that the document in question must fail to give effect to a
        common intention of the parties. The party seeking rectification must
        prove that there was an underlying agreement and establish the common

---

[20] *Neilson v. Stewart*, 1991 S.L.T. 523, *per* Lord Jauncey at p.525.
[21] 1907 S.C. 903.
[22] *Anderson v. Lambie*, 1954 S.C. (H.L.) 43.
[23] Law Reform (Miscellaneous Provisions) (Scotland) Act 1985, ss. 8, 9.

intention that lay behind it. That agreement and common intention must be proved by objective means in the same way as *consensus in idem* would be established for proving any contract.[24] It is not enough for a party seeking rectification to demonstrate that it does not meet their intention.

---

[24] *Rehman v. Ahmed* 1993 S.L.T. 741.

CHAPTER 9

STATUTORY CONTROL OF CONTRACT TERMS

Suppose all contracts were the product of negotiations between two 9.1
parties of equal bargaining strength. Then the offer/acceptance analysis
would then truly identify the intention of the parties. Each party would
have secured the best arrangement available, having regard to their own
respective best interests. In the real world, however, the majority of
contracts are not freely negotiated between parties. In many situations
one party is in a position to impose the terms that he wants on the
relationship between himself and the other party. For example, an
individual who wishes to hire a car cannot discuss and revise all the
terms of the hire agreement and a person taking clothes to a dry cleaner
cannot haggle about the cleaner's liability in the event that the clothes are
damaged. Often this is a good thing. If it was necessary to negotiate and
agree all the terms every time one sought to hire a car it would be quicker
to take the bus. Another advantage of a standardised contract is that the
party offering the product or service is in a position to know exactly
where they stand in concluding agreements that make up their business.
This degree of certainty is necessary to permit business to set their
prices—if each customer hiring a car demanded different contract terms,
it would be necessary to charge different rates.

    With the advantages of standardised contract terms there also come
disadvantages. The freedom to determine the conditions under which a
person is willing to enter into a contract may be quite illusory where they
are used. This problem has been recognised by the courts.[1] As noted
previously, the intention of the parties underlies many aspects of the law
of contract. Where standard form contracts are concerned, any approach
based on intention is, at best, artificial.

    The problems that can arise were considered by the Law 9.2
Commissions in relation to exemption clauses.[2] The legislation that
followed is in the Unfair Contract Terms Act 1977 ("the 1977 Act").
More recently, there have been harmonisation measures across the
European Union. This has resulted in controls which are now contained
in the Unfair Terms in Consumer Contracts Regulation 1999. These are

---

[1] *McCutcheon v. MacBrayne* 1964 S.C. (H.L.) 28 referred to in Chap. 7.
[2] (1969) Law Com. No. 24; Scot. Law Com. No. 12, (1975) Law Com. No. 69;
Scot. Law Com. No. 39.

the two principal sources of legislative control of contract terms. Other legislation applies controls in certain areas. For example, the Road Traffic Act 1988 provides that the user of a road vehicle may not exclude liability for negligence which results in personal injury or death to a passenger in the vehicle.[3] The 1977 Act and the 1999 Regulations provide a more general scheme of control and our discussion therefore focuses on them.

THE UNFAIR CONTRACT TERMS ACT 1977

9.3 It should be emphasised at the outset that the title of the 1977 Act is a misnomer. It does not cover all unfair contract terms, only exemption clauses. Some exemption clauses are declared void; others are subject to a "fair and reasonable" test before they can be given effect. The 1977 Act does not prohibit such clauses being inserted into contracts. It simply provides that they cannot be relied upon in the event of a claim for damages arising.

The Scope of the Act

9.4 The provisions of the 1977 Act apply to a variety of contracts: contracts for the sale and supply of goods, contracts to enter upon land, employment contracts and contracts for services.[4] These contracts are the most common ones in which exemption clauses appear. To take some examples, the 1977 Act covers contracts to (i) park a car; (ii) attend a sporting venue; (iii) have an item repaired; and (iv) deposit luggage. But the 1977 Act does not apply to contracts of insurance, nor to contracts relating to the formation or dissolution of a company or partnership.

> The 1977 Act not only covers clauses which actually appear in a written document, but also to notices.[5] Such notices are commonly found on walls and counters in restaurants, hotels and drycleaners. Non-contractual notices are also within the ambit of the 1977 Act.[6] Such notices may accompany information or professional advice. For example, a surveyor providing a house report to a building society has no contract with the prospective purchaser. However, the purchaser will usually learn of the contents of the report and rely upon it in determining whether or not to buy the house. An attempt

---

[3] Road Traffic Act 1972, s.148(3).
[4] Unfair Contract Terms Act 1977 (hereinafter "1977 Act"), s.15.
[5] 1977 Act, ss. 25(3)(d) and (4).
[6] Law Reform (Miscellaneous Provisions) (Scotland) Act 1990, s.68.

by the surveyor to exclude liability is capable of being struck down under the 1977 Act.[7]

The commonest exemption clauses are those which expressly seek to exclude or restrict liability. To ensure that other devices are not used to circumvent the 1977 Act, its scope is widened to include other attempts to hinder or prevent one party's right to pursue his normal legal remedies[8]: 9.5

- "Refunds must be accompanied by a receipt."
- "The purchaser's claim shall be restricted to damages and he shall not be entitled to sue for delivery."
- "Any claim relating to this contract must be made within fourteen days of the date hereof."

The 1977 Act only applies to the attempted exclusion of liability by businesses. For the purpose of the Act, "business" covers most forms of enterprise: companies, firms, professionals, sole traders as well as government and local authority departments.[9] The only clear exception is individuals acting in a personal capacity.

Control (1)—Liability for "Negligence"

The 1977 Act talks about "breach of duty". That term is designed to refer to one party's liability for breach of a contractual term and for delictual liability. What does this mean? Let us take an example. An architect may be commissioned to prepare plans for a loft extension. The extension as planned turns out to be dangerous. The architect could be sued for negligence. This encompasses breach of contract and delict. The expression used is, however, rather unwieldy and in most instances simply means "negligence". We shall use "negligence" in preference to "breach of duty" in our discussion of the Act's provisions. The extent of the control applied depends on whether the clause seeks to exclude liability for death or personal injury or for economic loss. 9.6

Death or Personal Injury

Parliament took the view that there was no justification for allowing businesses to avoid liability where their negligence had occasioned death or personal injury.[10] Such terms are void and of no effect. 9.7

It is a complete defence to a delictual action if the injured person voluntarily assumed the risk of the harm that occurred.[11] To take an

---

[7] *Smith v. Eric S. Bush* [1990] 1 A.C. 831; [1989] 2 W.L.R. 790; *cf. Robbie v. Graham & Sibbald*, 1989 S.L.T. 870; 1989 S.C.L.R. 578 (decided prior to the amendment to the Act).

[8] 1977 Act, ss. 25(3)(a), (b) and (c).

[9] 1977 Act, s.25(1).

[10] 1977 Act, s.16.

extreme example, suppose that Dean asks his friend to drive him to work but insists on travelling on the roof of his car. The risk is obvious and Dean will be taken to have accepted the risk. If he is injured in the course of his journey, his friend would have a complete defence to any action of negligence that Dean might bring. An argument might be made that the negligence provisions of the 1977 Act would not apply where a person had his attention specifically drawn to the exemption clause at the time of contracting and consented to assume a particular risk. In order to guard against such an argument, the 1977 Act specifically provides that the fact that a person agreed to, or was aware of, the term would not of itself be sufficient evidence of voluntary assumption of risk.[12] Something more is required. As yet this provision has not been the subject of judicial scrutiny and it remains to be seen just how it will be construed.

Economic Loss

9.8   Negligence on the part of one party will often give rise to financial loss rather than to death or personal injury. This is particularly true of contracts for services. If drycleaners negligently clean your garment it is more likely that you will suffer financial loss because your garment is ruined, rather than that you will be injured by getting a skin inflammation. Similarly, if a solicitor or architect does not take reasonable care, the loss sustained by a client will normally be financial rather than physical. Under the 1977 Act clauses which attempt to evade liability for financial loss are not automatically void. Rather they are subject to a "fair and reasonable" test. If the court thinks they are justified in the circumstances, such clauses will be upheld. Otherwise they will be denied effect. It has, for example, been held that it is not reasonable for a photographic developing company to exclude liability in respect of films deposited with it for processing which are lost or damaged as a result of its negligence.[13]

Control (2)—Liability for Breach of Contract Not Involving Negligence

9.9   Many breaches of contract are not concerned with "negligence". A builder does not complete a house extension on time, a coach tour goes to a different destination from that advertised, a wedding photographer fails to turn up at the church, a plumber uses different fittings from those specified in his estimate. In each of these cases one party has failed to fulfil his contractual obligations, but the breach has not necessarily occurred as a result of negligence. There may be no duty of care between

---

[11] This defence is called *volenti non fit injuria* (to he who consents no wrong is done).

[12] 1977 Act, s.16(3).

[13] *Woodman v. Photo Trade Processing Ltd*, noted in (1981) Scolag 281.

the parties. The controls in the 1977 Act here apply to exemption clauses in two types of contract: consumer contracts and standard form contracts.[14] In both cases the test of fairness and reasonableness is used.

Consumer Contracts

The term "consumer contract" is defined in the 1977 Act.[15] It is a contract 9.10
where (a) one party deals in the course of a business; and (b) the other does not; and (c) in contracts involving the transfer of ownership or possession of goods, the goods are of a type ordinarily supplied for private use or consumption.

> *Example*: When Oswald moves into his new flat he hires a washing machine from a shop nearby. Tow weeks after it is delivered, a pipe in it bursts and his flat is flooded. When Oswald complains, the shop assistant points out a term of the rental agreement that says the hirer is liable only for damage to the machine itself and not to other property. This clause will be subject to the "fair and reasonable test".

Standard Form Contracts

Common features of standard form contracts are that they are 9.11
prearranged, not subject to negotiation and offered to everyone with whom the business deals.[16] Such contracts are not, however, defined in the 1977 Act. It was thought that, however the definition was drawn, there would always be a danger of evasion. Clever draftsmen would draft around the definition. In the debate in Parliament it was suggested that judges recognised such contracts when they saw them. Where a transaction is made using a standard form contract the provisions of the 1977 Act apply. This applies even where the recipient of the standard form is itself a business.

> *Example*: Easiclean Windows arrange to clean the windows of a large office building owned by Bright Ltd. Easiclean make the contract with Bright on its own standard form in which it seeks to exempt liability for any damage to the windows and the stonework of the building. If damage does occur and Easiclean seek to rely on the clause, Bright can challenge its validity under the 1977 Act. It will then be subject to the fair and reasonable test.

In the case of consumer and standard form contracts, the fair and reasonable test applies not only to exemption clauses but also to clauses which allow a party (a) to render no performance or (b) to render a performance substantially different from that which the other party

---

[14] 1977 Act, s.17.
[15] 1977 Act, s.25(1).
[16] See *McCrone v. Boots Farm Sales*, 1981 S.L.T. 103.

reasonably expected from the contract.[17] So in the example above, an attempt by Easiclean to evade liability for breach if it fails to turn up to clean the office windows, or to use automatic sprinklers instead of trained window cleaners, would be caught under the 1977 Act.

Control (3)—Statutory Implied Terms

9.12   As noted in Chapter 7 in certain common contracts the implied terms have been codified and are contained in statute. In the past it had become common for sellers in contracts for the sale of goods to exempt themselves from the standard terms implied into such contracts by the Sale of Goods legislation. Controls were necessary to prevent this and it was also thought desirable that the law relating to hire-purchase was brought into line with that of sale of goods.

A term seeking to exclude an implied term as to title to goods sold or hired is void. A term seeking to exclude implied terms as to conformity of goods with descriptions or samples, quality or fitness for purpose are void in consumer contracts and are of no effect in other contracts if they are not fair and reasonable.[18]

> *Example*: Font Ltd supply bathroom suites to both private and trade customers. Font sells a bath to Alf and six bidets to Alf's brother-in-law Sid, who is a builder currently involved in converting a large house into flats. The bidets do not belong to Font and the bath delivered to Alf has a large crack in it. Any attempt by Font Ltd to exempt its liability to Alf and Sid is void. If the bath had been supplied to Sid the question would be whether it was fair and reasonable for any term excluding liability for defective products to be inserted.

The Fair and Reasonable Test

9.13   Clearly the "fair and reasonable test" is of key significance in applying the 1977 Act. A number of points can be made about it:

(a)   The onus is on the party seeking to rely upon the clause to show that it is fair and reasonable[19];

(b)   whether the clause was fair and reasonable is determined at the time the contract was made, not with regard to the subsequent events which have occurred[20];

(c)   in the case of limitation clauses the court must have regard to,

     (i)   the resources open to the party seeking to rely on the term;

---

[17] 1977 Act, s.17(1)(b).
[18] 1977 Act, s.20.
[19] 1977 Act, s.24(4).
[20] 1977 Act, s.24(4).

(ii)   how far he can cover himself by insurance.[21]

So far as exemptions from the implied terms in sale and supply of goods are concerned, the fair and reasonable test is elaborated even further.[22] In such cases the courts are directed to consider:

(1) the parties' relative bargaining positions;
(2) whether an inducement was offered to accept the exemption clause or other offending term;
(3) whether the customer knew or ought to have known of the term;
(4) in the case of conditional terms, the likelihood of the condition not being complied with; and
(5) whether in the case of supply of goods, the goods were specially made for the customer.

These factors may also be relevant in other situations in which the "fair and reasonable" test is to be applied.

Four illustrations of the test can be provided. First, a power boat was supplied which was a total loss within 27 hours of delivery as a result of electrical defects.[23] A clause seeking to exempt the sellers was held not to be fair and reasonable. Secondly, a man who had deposited a suitcase worth over £300 was held entitled to recover full compensation from British Rail when the suitcase disappeared, despite a limitation clause which attempted to restrict their liability to £7.[24] This clause was held not to be reasonable since the suitcase had disappeared whilst in British Rail's control. The third illustration provides an example of a clause which was held to be fair and reasonable.[25] It was a clause inserted into a contract for the repair of a ship designed to exempt the shipowners from various types of loss. It was decided that their attempt to exclude liability for loss was not unfair or unreasonable given that the two parties were of equal bargaining strength. Finally, a clause putting a ceiling on damages that could be claimed where a computer program has been at fault was considered not to be fair and reasonable.[26] The court took account of the facts that the defendants were a large company who held insurance for the risk in question and that they were the only company that could meet the plaintiff's requirements. They also considered that all the defendants' competitors dealt in similar terms. The defenders were therefore in a very strong bargaining position.

9.14

---

[21] 1977 Act, s.24(3).

[22] 1977 Act, s.24(2) and Sched. 2.

[23] *Rasbora v. UCL Marine* [1977] 1 Lloyd's Rep. 645.

[24] *Waldron-Kelly v. British Rail*, 1981 C.L.Y. 303.

[25] *The Zinnia* [1984] 2 Lloyd's Rep. 211.

[26] *St Alban's City and D.C. v. International Computers plc* [1995] F.S.R. 686. This case was appealed on an issue other than the applicability of the clause.

Further Controls

9.15 In order to prevent draftsmen using devices to avoid the implication of
the 1977 Act controls, the Act itself specifies that it is not possible to
evade its provisions by means of a secondary contract. Nor is it possible
to attempt to avoid the negligence provisions of the 1977 Act by defining
the obligations undertaken rather than exempting liability for breach of
duty.[27] Suppose the owner of a sports stadium sought to exempt himself
from liability to spectators using the premises. Instead of inserting an
exemption clause in respect of negligent acts by himself and his
employees, he might state that his sole obligation under the contract was
to provide a spectator with a seat with a reasonable view of the event.
Under the 1977 Act this would not exempt him from his liabilities.
Neither is it possible to use a "choice of law" clause to evade the
operation of the 1977 Act.[28] This prevents parties from inserting a clause
such as "this contract shall be subject to the law of Burkina Faso as
administered by the courts in Ouagadougou" to circumvent the Act.
Manufacturers' guarantees and indemnity clauses are also regulated.[29]

THE UNFAIR TERMS IN CONSUMER CONTRACTS
REGULATIONS 1999

9.16 The ambit of the 1977 Act is relatively narrow. The Unfair Contract
Terms in Consumer Contract Regulations 1999[30] provide a far more
general protection for consumers from clauses in certain contracts that
work to their disadvantage. They identify classes of contract terms where
the consent of the weaker part to the contract is not real and then apply a
test of fairness. The Regulations were made in pursuance of a European
Union Council Directive.[31] The Directive seeks to harmonise the rules on
unfair contracts throughout the European Union.

Scope of Application

9.17 The Regulations apply in relation to unfair terms in contracts concluded
between a seller or a supplier and a consumer.[32] What is a "consumer"? It
is defined in a different way from the 1977 Act as, "any natural person
who...is acting for purposes which are outside his trade, business or
profession."[33] This excludes companies and partnerships as well as any

---

[27] 1977 Act, s.25(5).

[28] 1977 Act, s.27.

[29] 1977 Act, ss. 18, 19.

[30] S.I. 1999 No. 2083. These replace the 1994 Regulations of the same name (S.I.
1994 No. 3159).

[31] Directive 93/13 [1993] O.J. L95/29 on unfair terms in consumer contracts.

[32] reg. 4(1).

[33] reg. 3.

individual who enters into a contract for business purposes. On the other side of the contract, the expression "seller or supplier" is defined as, "any natural or legal person who…is acting for purposes relating to his trade, business or profession, whether publicly owned or privately owned."[34] Accordingly, if a sole trader buys or sells office equipment or a car for use in his business, he would appear to be acting for a purpose relating to his business and therefore would not be a "consumer' in terms of the Regulations.

Terms to Which the Regulations Apply

What contracts are covered? The Regulations do not spell this out. The use of the expression "seller or supplier" would appear to limit it to contracts for sale and supply. In contrast to the 1977 Act this would exclude a contract of employment but would include a contract of insurance. There are also references within the Regulations to "goods" and "services".[35] This appears to exclude contracts for sale or lease of heritable property. However, in the parts of the Regulations which actually set out their scope of application, there is no such limitation. 9.18

The Regulations do not apply to every contract term. They apply only to terms which have "not been individually negotiated."[36] The onus of showing that a term was individually negotiated rests on the seller or supplier.[37] What is meant by "individually negotiated"? The Regulations provide some guidance:

> "A term shall always be regarded as not having been individually negotiated where it has been drafted in advance and the consumer has therefore not been able to influence the substance of the term."[38]

There is a further limitation on which clauses are subject to the fairness test that is much less clear[39]: 9.19

> "In so far as it in plain intelligible language, the assessment of fairness of a term shall not relate—
> (a) to the definition of the main subject matter of the contract, or
> (b) to the adequacy of the price or remuneration, as against the goods or services supplied in exchange."

Read literally this would mean that reference could not be made to the definition of the subject matter or the price in assessing the fairness of any term. This would be absurd. Consider the sale of a car. Assessing

---

[34] reg. 3.

[35] reg. 6(2) and Sched. 2.

[36] reg. 5(1).

[37] reg. 5(4).

[38] reg. 5(2). These terms mirror exactly the terms of the directive on which the Regulations are based.

[39] reg. 6(2).

a term dealing with defects, the court would be required to ignore whether it cost £5,000 or £50,000. Reference to the preamble to the Directive, however, may assist.

> "assessment of unfair character shall not be made of terms which describe the main subject matter of the contract nor the quality/price ratio of the goods or services supplied;…the main subject matter of the contract and the price/quality ration may nevertheless be taken into account in assessing the fairness of other terms."

In other words, the court may not assess fairness of a clause which defines the subject matter or contains the price.[40] This second interpretation makes sense. To strike down these terms at the core of the contract as unfair would amount to making the contract for the parties rather than ensuring that a contract as unfair would amount to making the contract for the parties rather than ensuring that a contract they had made was fair. This second interpretation has been adopted in practice.[41] Of course, if the term *defining price or subject matter* is not in plain intelligible language, it is *still* subject to the test of unfairness. This makes it ironic that the Regulation itself is expressed in such language.

The Test of Unfairness

9.20
> "A contractual term…shall be regarded as unfair if, contrary to the requirement of good faith, it causes a significant imbalance in the parties' rights and obligations arising under the contract, to the detriment of the consumer."[42]

The Regulations provide a lengthy list of the types of terms that may be regarded as unfair.[43] Essentially, the terms "caught" by the Regulations include features which may be summarised as follows:

(1) Restrictions on the rights that the consumer might have against the supplier. These restrictions may take the form of exclusion of liability, limitation of liability or barriers in the way of taking proceedings to enforce rights. An example would be a term in a contract for sale of a computer printer stating, "The seller will not be liable for any damage caused to other computer equipment caused by the use of this product."

(2) Granting the supplier a wide discretion as to whether, when or for how long his obligations under the contract should exist. An example would be a clause in the same contract saying,

---

[40] It should be noted that Art. 4(2) within the Directive appears to confirm the literal reading.
[41] *Director General of Fair Trading v. First National Bank plc* [2000] 2 All E.R. 759.
[42] reg. 5(1).
[43] reg. 5(5), Sched. 2.

"Delivery of the goods ordered will be made at a time determined by the supplier".

(3) An inability of the consumer to complain if his obligations under the contract are made more onerous or those of the supplier are made less onerous. Suppose, for example, that an insurance contract provided that the policyholder must make a claim within 14 days of an accident and that the insurer had to make payment on a valid claim within two months of the accident. A clause saying, "The insurer reserves the right to vary the period in which claims must be intimated and/or the period in which payments will be made" would be unfair.

(4) The imposition of a financial burden on the consumer upon termination of the contract that is excessive or not matched by similar burdens on the supplier. Take, for example, a contract for hire of a television and video in which there is a clause saying that either party may terminate the contract on 30 day's notice. If there is another clause that says that if the consumer exercises his option to terminate he will have to pay a termination charge equivalent to 6 month's rental it will be caught.

(5) Requirements that the consumer be irrevocably bound to terms without having given a real opportunity to become acquainted with them prior to the conclusion of the contract. For example, a person wishes to hire a car. When he arrives at the garage to collect it, he is given a contract with a term that states, "Our standard terms and conditions of hire apply. A copy of these terms may be obtained by writing to our head office."

In respect of some of the sample unfair terms there are special exceptions to take account of situations in which they might operate too widely.[44] For example, terms which have the effect of providing for the price of goods to be determined at the time of delivery are in the list. Without an exception this would catch a contracts for a broker to buy shares or a contract in which a bank was to supply foreign currency travellers cheques to a customers.

The list in the Regulations is said to be indicative. In other words, 9.21 inclusion in the list does not automatically mean that the term is unfair. The fact a term falls within the schedule would, however, carry a party most of the way in any argument as to whether it was unfair. Equally it is note an exhaustive list.

The issue of whether a term was unfair was considered by the Court 9.22 of Appeal in *Director General of Fair Trading v. First National Bank*[45]:

---

[44] Sched. 2(2).
[45] [2000] 2 All E.R. 759. At the time of writing, this case is under appeal to the House of Lords.

The Bank carried on a consumer credit business. They lent money on the basis of a standard form of agreement. One of the terms of that agreement was to the effect that, where the borrower defaulted in making repayment of an instalment of the loan, the bank could demand repayment of the whole sum of principal and interest then outstanding and could charge additional interest on this whole sum until it was paid.

The court required to consider whether the term in question was unfair under regulation 4(1) of the 1994 Regulations which is in substantially the same terms as regulation 5(1) of the 1999 Regulations. In interpreting the Regulations, the court referred to the Directive which they were intended to implement. The court noted that there were three tests for unfairness all of which had to be met; there must be (1) an absence of good faith, (2) a significant imbalance in the parties rights and obligations and (3) detriment to the consumer. In construing what was meant by the concept of "good faith" the court had regard to an earlier decision which stated,

> "its effect is perhaps most aptly conveyed by such metaphorical colloquialisms as 'playing fair', 'coming clean' or 'putting one's cards face upwards on the table'. It is in essence a principle of fair and open dealing"[46]

In attempting to apply this the court referred to a number of factors. It referred to the reasonable expectations of the consumer and the desire to prevent unfair surprises. It was relevant to consider whether it has been brought to the attention of the consumer. It might be necessary for the seller or supplier to consider the interests of the consumer. The court considered factors such as the absence of choice. On the facts before them, they considered that the requirement of good faith had been breached. They concluded that the clause had the effect in practice of defeating protection to which borrowers might be entitled and that this was something that the borrowers were not aware of when entering the contract. The bank had therefore not adequately considered the interests of the consumer and it came an unfair surprise to the consumers.

The court did not consider the other two tests in detail but some help in interpreting them is available from the 1999 Regulations themselves. The list of the features that may be regarded as being unfair may provide guidance as to the considerations that may be taken into account. It is apparent that all these features create an imbalance in the parties' rights and obligations and would be to the detriment of the consumer.

9.23   Within the thicket of the Regulations, there is another thorny branch to get past. It goes by the name "preformulated standard contract". The Regulations state:

---

[46] *Interfoto Picture Library Limited v. Stiletto Visual Programmes Limited* [1988] 1 All E.R. 348.

"Notwithstanding that a specific term or certain aspects of it in a contract has been individually negotiated, these regulations shall apply to the rest of the contract if an overall assessment of it indicates that it is a preformulated standard contract."[47]

As we have seen above, the test of unfairness from the Regulations applies to, "[a] contract term which has not been individually negotiated".[48] If a term has not been individually negotiated, it should not matter that other parts of the contract have been negotiated. There appears to be no need for this additional provision as to "a preformulated standard contract". The purpose of the Regulations is to provide further assistance to consumers. It can therefore hardly be supposed that it was intended to add a barrier to invoking them.

The Effect of Unfairness

If a term is found to be unfair, it shall not be binding on the consumer.[49]   9.24
The contract shall continue to bind the parties if it is capable of continuing in existence without the unfair term.[50]

One of the types of terms that is indicated in Schedule 2 as being unfair is that which binds the consumer to terms which he has had no real chance of considering. This might apply to a term which seeks to incorporate standard terms and conditions contained in another document which the consumer has not had a chance to consider. If this clause is struck at as being unfair, the effect would be that *all* the other standard terms and conditions would cease to bind the consumer irrespective of whether individually they were unfair.

Written Contracts

There is a requirement that any written term of a contract be expressed in   9.25
plain, intelligible language.[51] There is no sanction applied for failure to comply with this requirement.

Where there is a doubt about the meaning of a written term, the interpretation most favourable to the consumer shall prevail.[52] In some situations this would function as a modification of the *contra proferentem* rule referred to in Chapter 8.

---

[47] reg. 5(3).
[48] reg. 5(1). See para. 9.18.
[49] reg. 8(1).
[50] reg. 8(2).
[51] reg. 7.
[52] reg. 7(2).

Further Controls

9.26 There are two further controls which we wish to mention. The first is an anti avoidance measure. As with the 1977 Act, the Regulations prevent a seller or supplier from circumventing the protection to consumers by means of a choice of law clause.[53]

The second control provides a vetting procedure. Certain public bodies may seek to apply to a court to prevent a seller or supplier from using a term that is unfair.[54]

---

[53] reg. 9.
[54] regs. 10–15.

CHAPTER 10

BREACH OF CONTRACT

The terms of the contract determine the obligations owed by the parties 10.1
to one another. Breach of contract occurs when a party breaks one or
more of those terms. Breach can occur in a number of ways:

> *Example*: A gas fitter, Mr A, contracts to install a central heating
> system in Mrs B's house.
> (1) A telephones B a week before the work is due to begin and
>   informs B that he will not do the job because he has found more
>   profitable work elsewhere. (Anticipatory breach.)
> (2) A fails to turn up on the due date. (Failure to perform.)
> (3) A installs the system in such a manner that seriously damages
>   the fabric of B's house. Moreover, the system itself does not
>   work. (Defective performance.)
> (4) A takes an unreasonably long time to complete the job. (Failure
>   to perform timeously.)

In each instance, A fails to fulfil his obligations under the contract.
For the sake of convenience, throughout this chapter we shall refer to the
party faced by a breach of contract (in the example, B) as the innocent
party.

When there is a breach of contract the innocent party will have a 10.2
remedy. Sometimes the remedy is stipulated in the contract itself. Others
are provided by the general law of contract, such as damages.

GENERAL LEGAL REMEDIES FOR BREACH

Two Basic Principles

Mutuality

The obligations under the contract are reciprocal in nature. This is known 10.3
as the principal of mutuality. Either both the parties are bound or neither
is bound. This is relevant when considering the remedies that the law
grants to the innocent party. Lord Justice Clerk Moncreiff provided the
classic statement on this branch of the law:

"I understand the law of Scotland in regard to mutual contracts to be quite clear—first, that the stipulations on either side are the counterparts and the consideration given for each other; second, that a failure to perform any material or substantial part of the contract on the part of one will prevent him from suing the other for performance; and, third, that where one party has refused or failed to perform his part of the contract in any material respect the other is entitled either to insist for implement, claiming damages for the breach, or to rescind the contract altogether—except so far as it has been performed."[1]

10.4   The party seeking a contractual remedy should therefore demonstrate that he himself is not in breach of a material part of his obligations. He can only insist on performance by the other party if he himself has fulfilled his side of the bargain. In the case of *Graham v. United Turkey Red Company Ltd*[2]:

Graham entered into an agency contract in 1914, in terms of which he was to sell cotton goods manufactured by the United Turkey Red Company Ltd. Payment for his services was to be made on a commission basis. It was stipulated in the contract that he was not to sell other manufacturers' goods. From 1916 onwards, Graham was in breach of that term. In 1918, after a dispute, Graham terminated the agreement and sued for the balance of his commission for the whole period of the contract.

The court held that he was only entitled to commission up to the time when he himself was still adhering to the agreement. The moment he began selling goods for other manufacturers, he lost his right to insist on performance by the United Turkey Red Company. After 1916 he was not fulfilling his side of the bargain so he could not require them to fulfil theirs. The mutuality of their bargain had ceased.

Materiality

10.5 The other factor that influences the remedies available to the innocent party is the materiality of the breach. Materiality means the degree of importance or seriousness of the breach.

"It is familiar law, and quite settled by decision, that in any contract which contains multifarious stipulations there are some which go so to the root of the contract that a breach of those stipulations entitles the party pleading the breach to declare that the contract is at an end. There are others which do not go to the root of the contract, but

---

[1] *Turnbull v. McLean & Co.* (1874) 1 R. 730 at p.738.
[2] 1922 S.C. 533.

which are part of the contract, and which would give rise, if broken, to an action of damages."[3]

The more serious the breach which has occurred, the greater the range of remedies open to the innocent party. It is one thing to deliver a Ford Fiesta instead of a Porsche, it is quite another to deliver a Porsche with a slight scratch on the bonnet. Where a breach goes to the root or core of the contract it is said that the party in breach has repudiated the contract. What constitutes the core of the contract must be determined by examining the whole contract. Alternatively, the parties may choose to stipulate that a term is material or of the essence.[4]

Rescission

A person faced by a breach of contract may wish to be released from the contract. Suppose a florist fails to deliver flowers to a hotel on time. The hotel may wish to rescind (that is, cancel) the agreement and obtain the flowers elsewhere. By rescinding the contract, the innocent party accepts that neither party requires to fulfil the contract.[5] The florist no longer needs to send the flowers, the hotel does not require to pay the price. However, the contract may remain alive for some purposes. For example, certain debts may have accrued or a right to damages in respect of the breach may exist. Further, there may be an arbitration clause or a liquidate damage clause to regulate any dispute which has arisen. Accordingly, it is more correct to say that the effect of rescission is to terminate the innocent party's future obligations under the contract.

The innocent party may only rescind the contract if faced by a breach which is so material as to amount to repudiation of the contract. Courts are slow to hold that there has been repudiation,

> "it is a drastic conclusion which should only be held to arise in clear cases of a refusal, in a matter going to the root of the contract, to perform contractual obligations."[6]

It is important to note that repudiation of itself does not terminate the contract. It is not open to one party unilaterally to declare the contract terminated. When repudiation occurs, the contract will only be terminated if the innocent party responds by rescinding it. There is a narrow line between rescission and repudiation. In the case of *Wade v. Waldron*[7]:

10.6

10.7

---

[3] *Wade v. Waldon*, 1909 S.C. 571 *per* L.P. Dunedin at p.576.
[4] This is common in insurance contracts. See *Dawsons Limited v. Bonnin,* 1922 S.C. (H.L.) 156.
[5] *G.L. Group Plc v. Ash Gupta Advertising Ltd*, 1987 S.C.L.R. 149.
[6] *Woodar Investment Development Ltd v Wimpey Construction (U.K.) Ltd* [1980] 1 All E.R. 571 *per* Lord Wilberforce at p.576; [1980] 1 W.L.R. 277.
[7] 1909 S.C. 571.

George Robey, a famous comedian of the time, contracted to appear a year later at two Glasgow theatres, the Palace and the Pavilion, for a one-week engagement. Shortly before his performances were due to take place, Robey looked in vain for advertisements for his show. He contacted the management. They informed him that the booking was cancelled. They referred to clause six of his contract which stated: "All artistes engaged...must give fourteen days' notice prior to such engagements, such notice to be accompanied by bill matter [publicity material]." He had omitted to provide such material. Robey offered to fulfil his engagement but the management refused. He pointed out that he had not given notice or "bill matter" for his last engagement, and sued them for £300. The defenders argued that breach of clause six was a serious one and they were entitled to rescind the contract. The court held that the failure to provide bill matter did not go to the root of the contract and found against the management. By refusing to allow Robey to appear, the management itself had repudiated the contract, thereby giving him a claim for damages.

Some writers have argued that this is a hard decision. Why should the management be forced to accept Robey without proper notice or advertising material? The answer may be that his fame was such that the theatre simply had to put up his name for an audience to appear so that the failure to provide bill matter was not material. Further, the management had waived the requirement for bill matter in the past. It therefore seems that justice was done.

10.8   Two further cases underline the difficulties of determining who has repudiated the contract. In *Blyth v. Scottish Liberal Club* an employee refused to perform certain duties which he believed formed no part of the scope of his employment.[8] Although it was accepted that his belief was an honest one, it was held to be mistaken. Accordingly, his employers were entitled to terminate the employment as a result of his breach. His belief was unjustifiable in the circumstances. In *G.L. Group plc v. Ash Gupta Advertising*, an advertising company became concerned about the financial position of their clients.[9] They wrote seeking payment of all their work to date, together with a sum in respect of future work. The letter also stated that if payment was not received within 24 hours they "would have no alternative to resile from the contract." This was held to amount to repudiation.

Before moving on from rescission it is necessary to note the confusion that can exist regarding terminology. One needs to be clear about the terms, "rescission" and "repudiation". Repudiation is the act by the guilty person in breach of the contract. Rescission is the response by the innocent party who, in response to the repudiation, wishes to bring

---

[8] 1983 S.L.T. 260; see now *Ghaznavi v. B.P. Oil (U.K.) Ltd*, 1992 S.L.T. 924.
[9] 1987 S.C.L.R. 149.

the contract to an end. The scope for confusion is extended by the term, "resile". This applies when a party withdraws from a contract. A party may have a right in terms of the contract to withdraw on the occurrence of certain events. These events may themselves be a breach of contract. For instance, missives for the sale of property may stipulate that, if the purchase price is not paid within 14 days of the due date, the innocent party shall be entitled to resile seven days after having given notice of their intention to do so.

Two further points about terminology need to be made. First, in the case of sale of goods, a buyer faced by the seller's material breach may "reject the goods and treat the contract as repudiated."[10] Accordingly, should Charlie receive a washing machine which fails to work, he is entitled to return it to the shop (rejection) and to claim his money back (rescission). The Act appears to equate repudiation and cancellation. However, the seller's breach may still be seen as a repudiation of the contract and the rejection of the goods by the buyer would amount to rescission. Secondly, "rescission" is sometimes used in a different sense. In the context of misrepresentation, a person induced to enter the contract through error may "rescind" the contract. It is preferable to avoid using the term "rescission" in this second sense. A person who decides not to go ahead with a contract because of the other party's misrepresentation should be said to have withdrawn (or resiled) from the contract. The term "reduction" is appropriate in the case of a contract judicially set aside on the ground of misrepresentation.   10.9

Retention and Lien

A breach may not be sufficiently material to justify rescission. In *Linn v. Shields*, a purchaser requested 12 stacks of corn to be delivered, payment on delivery.[11] He received three stacks but made no payment. In an action by him for the remaining nine stacks, the seller was held entitled to withhold delivery, although it was observed that the breach was not sufficiently material to justify the seller rescinding. Alternatively it may be disadvantageous to the innocent party to rescind. Contracts of lease furnish a useful illustration. The tenant may wish to withhold payment of the rent until the landlord fulfils his obligation to keep the premises in good repair. He will often not wish to terminate the lease.   10.10

Faced by breach, a person may withhold performance of his own obligations under the contract (retention) or retain possession of the other party's goods (lien). Retention and lien are ways of exerting pressure on the other party to perform his side of the bargain. If a solicitor is carrying out work for a client and is faced by a refusal to pay interim fees that are due, he may refuse to carry out the remainder of the work that he had agreed to do until he is paid. Commonly, retention takes the form of a

---

[10] Sale of Goods Act 1979, s.11(5).

[11] (1863) 2 M. 88.

refusal to make a payment due under the contract because the other party is in breach of their obligations. For payment to be retained in this way it is necessary that the breach existed when the payment fell due.[12]

10.11   In the example given above, in addition to the right to do further work the solicitor may exercise a lien by holding on to documents such as title deeds or share certificates which belong to the client. Lien is really a particular type of retention. It takes the form of holding on to property which should otherwise be delivered to the other party. A special lien arises when a person is employed to do work on specific goods belonging to another. For example, a garage may hold on to a car until the repairs that have been carried out have been paid for. Certain persons such as solicitors have a general lien over all documents in their hands against the balance of their account.

Action for Payment

10.12   The most common action which arises out of contract is a simple action for the payment of money. Where the contract price is not paid, the creditor will seek payment by way of an action to recover his debt. The creditor will be entitled to interest on the sum due. The date and rate from which interest will run will depend on the terms of the contract. If the contract does not specify a rate, interest at the judicial rate can be claimed.

Specific Implement and Interdict

10.13   A person faced by breach may apply to the court to require the other party to fulfil his obligations under the contract. In the case of a positive obligation, the remedy is specific implement.[13] Suppose D purchases an antique bureau at auction. Subsequently, the seller decides that she no longer wishes to sell the bureau and refuses to deliver it to D. D can raise an action concluding for specific implement of the contract of sale. In the case of a negative obligation the remedy is interdict. Take an example drawn from the law of options: E pays G £10,000 in return for an option to purchase G's factory on or before a date three years from the date of payment. Should G attempt to sell the factory to L before the time limit has expired, E may seek an interdict to prevent him from doing so. Failure to obey an interlocutor (*i.e.* decree) pronouncing specific implement or interdict may amount to contempt of court and be visited by a fine or imprisonment. Because of this there is a requirement that a decree of specific implement or interdict must be expressed in clear terms that leave the defender in no doubt as to what he has to do.

---

[12] *Redpath Dorman Long v. Cummings Engine Co. Ltd*, 1982 S.C. 370, S.L.T.489.

[13] The type of decree sought is often referred to in the cases as, "decree *ad factum praestandum*".

The laws of Scotland and England are different in relation to these remedies.[14] In the Scottish House of Lords case of *Stewart v. Kennedy*,[15] Lord Watson said:

> "I do not think that upon this matter any assistance can be derived from English decisions; because the laws of the two countries regard the right to specific performance from different standpoints. In England the only legal right arising from a breach of contract is a claim of damages; specific performance is not matter [*sic*] of legal right, but a purely equitable remedy, which the Court can withhold when there are sufficient reasons of conscience or expediency against it. But in Scotland the breach of a contract for the sale of a specific subject such as landed estate gives the party aggrieved the legal right to sue for implement, and although he may elect to do so, he cannot be compelled to resort to the alternative of an action of damages, unless implement is shewn to be impossible, in which case *loco facti subit damnum et interesse*. Even where implement is possible, I do not doubt that the Court of Session has inherent power to refuse the legal remedy upon equitable grounds, although I know of no instance in which it has done so. It is quite conceivable that circumstances might occur which would make it inconvenient and unjust to enforce specific performance of contract of sale, but I do not think that any such case is presented in this appeal."

The difference can be illustrated by cases, two in Scotland[16] and one in England,[17] where the facts were similar but the result reached could not have been more different: 10.14

> Each case was an action brought by a landlord of a shopping centre against a tenant of the centre. In each case, the lease between the landlord and the tenant contained a clause that required the tenant to remain in the property and conduct business from the property. In each case the tenant did not wish to continue to conduct business from the property but was content to pay the rent stipulated in the lease and to observe their other obligations. There is a value to landlords of shopping centres in having the units occupied so that the centre is popular and attracts shoppers. The landlords applied to the courts for orders that would require the tenants to conduct business from the premises.

---

[14] In England the terms are specific performance and injunction respectively.
[15] (1890) 17 R. (H.L.) 1.
[16] *Retail Parks Investments Ltd v. The Royal Bank of Scotland plc (No. 2)*, 1996 S.C. 227, 1996 S.L.T. 669 and *Highland and Universal Properties Ltd v. Safeway Properties Ltd*, 2000 S.C. 297, 2000 S.L.T. 414.
[17] *Co-operative Insurance Society Ltd v. Argyll Stores (Holdings) Ltd* [1998] AC 1, [1997] 3 All E.R. 297.

In each of the Scottish cases the order was granted. In the English case it was not. The Scottish cases adopted and relied upon Lord Watson's dictum to the effect that the innocent party was entitled to insist that the contract that they had made be performed. In the English case, Lord Hoffman re-stated the position there and noted that:

> "Specific performance is traditionally regarded in English law as an exceptional remedy, as opposed to the common law damages to which a successful plaintiff is entitled as of right...[B]y the nineteenth century it was orthodox doctrine that the power to decree specific performance was part of the discretionary jurisdiction of the Court of Chancery to do justice in cases in which the remedies available at common law were inadequate. This is the basis of the general principle that specific performance will not be ordered when damages are an adequate remedy."

10.15   Although specific implement is the primary remedy in Scotland, the courts retain an equitable power to refuse the remedy:

> "It appears to me that a superior court, having equitable jurisdiction, must also have a discretion, in certain exceptional cases, to withhold from parties applying for it that remedy to which, in ordinary circumstances, they would be entitled as a matter of course. In order to justify the exercise of such a discretionary power there must be some very cogent reason for depriving litigants of the ordinary means of enforcing their legal rights."[18]

Lord Watson's dictum indicates that the discretion is a narrow one. On one case it was noted that, "Considerations of what is or is not reasonable are quite irrelevant."[19] The circumstances in which it might apply have been variously described as those where the decree would be "inconvenient and unjust"[20] or where the innocent party had "no legitimate interest, financial or otherwise, in performing the contract rather than claiming damages."[21] It is apparent that whatever test is applied, it is one that is difficult to satisfy.

In addition to the general equitable power to withhold the remedy there are a number of situations where it is recognised that the innocent party has no right to implement:

(a) A decree of specific implement cannot be obtained to enforce an obligation to pay money. Otherwise a debtor would be in

---

[18] *Grahame v. Magistrates of Kirkcaldy* (1882) 9 R. (H.L.) 91.
[19] *Salaried Staff London Loan Co Ltd v. Swears and Wells Ltd,* 1985 S.C. 189; S.L.T. 326, *per* Lord President Emslie.
[20] *Ibid. per* Lord President Emslie at p.xx/329.
[21] *White and Carter (Councils) Ltd v. McGregor*, 1962 S.C. (H.L.) 1, 1962 S.L.T. 9.

      contempt of court for defaulting in payment and liable to imprisonment.

(b) The courts will not enforce contracts involving a personal relationship. It would be an undue restraint on personal liberty to compel persons to work together. The manager of the pop group "The Troggs" could not keep his post when the group members lost faith in him and sacked him.[22] Similarly, where the boxer Nigel Benn changed management and his original manager sought to prevent the new manager from inducing a breach of the original contract.[23]

(c) The court will not grant decree if a decree could not be enforced, or if it is impossible for the party to fulfil performance under the contract.

Damages

Every breach of contract gives rise to a claim for damages: 10.16

> "The contract and the breach of it are established. That leads of necessity to an award of damages. It is impossible to say that a contract can be broken even in respect of time without the party being entitled to claim damages - at the lowest, nominal damages."[24]

It was formerly the case that in contracts of sale, the buyer could not retain the property sold to him *and* claim damages.[25] This rule was abolished by the Contract (Scotland) Act 1997.[26]

Despite this general right to damages, in the case of minor breaches, parties will rarely wish to undergo the financial (and sometimes emotional) outlay involved in vindicating their rights in a court of law. Suppose a customer has a complaint which is not satisfactorily dealt with by personal representation at the shop. He may well seek help from a newspaper consumer column or a trade association, rather than raise an action in the sheriff court.[27]

Causation

Before an award of damages can be made it must be established not only 10.17
that there has been a breach, but that there is a direct causal link between

---

[22] *Page One Records Ltd v. Britton (t/a The Troggs)* [1967] 3 All E.R. 822; *cf.* Employment Protection (Consolidation) Act 1978, s.69.

[23] *Warren v. Mendy* [1989] 1 W.L.R. 853; [1989] 3 All E.R. 103.

[24] *Webster v. Cramond Iron Co.* (1875) 2 R. 752 *per* L.P. Inglis at p.754.

[25] *e.g. Fortune v. Fraser*, 1996 S.L.T. 878.

[26] s.2.

[27] Although there are simplified forms of procedure to deal with small claims in the sheriff court.

the breach and the loss which has occurred. In *A/B Karlhamns Oljefabriker v. Monarch Steamship Co.*[28]:

> A charterparty was entered into for the transport of soya beans from Manchuria to Sweden. The contract included two clauses which provided (a) that the ship should be seaworthy, and (b) that it would not be a breach if the ship deviated, if required to do so by an order of the British Government. This second clause was inserted because the parties recognised the risk of war and thought there was a real chance that the ship might be requisitioned during the course of its voyage. Unknown to the shipowners, the ship was unseaworthy when it left port and it was delayed in both Colombo and Port Said to effect repairs. When it reached Britain it was detained by the government, war having broken out. The characters sought to recover from the owners the extra cost of transhipment of the soya beans from Glasgow to Sweden. The owners defended the action on the basis that the real cause of the extra cost was the act of the British government in requisitioning the ship. As the contract stated the government action was not to be a breach, no claim for damages could succeed.

The House of Lords rejected this argument and found that the dominant cause of the loss was the initial unseaworthiness of the ship. Without that, the ship would in all likelihood have arrived on time and avoided requisition by the government. Accordingly, the pursuers had established the link between their loss and the defenders' breach of contract and were entitled to damages.

The Measure of Damages

10.18   Every day, courts assess damages. However, "the assessment of damages is not an exact science."[29] It is easier to state the general principles than to determine the exact level of award in a particular case.

> "the broad general rule of the law of damages [is] that a party injured by the other party's breach of contract is entitled to such money compensation as will put him in the position in which he would have been but for the breach."[30]

In general, damages are measured according to the loss suffered by the innocent party, not by reference to the gain made in consequence of the breach by the contract-breaker. In *Teacher v. Calder*[31]:

---

[28] 1949 S.C. (H.L.) 1.
[29] *The Heron II* [1969] 1 A.C. 350, *per* Lord Upjohn at p.425.
[30] *Ibid. per* Lord Wright at p.18.
[31] (1898) 25 R. 661; (aff'd on this point (1899) 1 F. (H.L.) 39).

A agreed to lend £15,000 to B to use in his business as a timber-merchant under an agreement which was to last five years. B agreed to keep at least £15,000 of his own money in the business during that period. B broke the contract and withdrew sums which he invested in a distillery where they earned lucrative profits. Damages were assessed by reference to A's loss, not by reference to the profits made by B.

Recently, two English cases have adopted different basses for 10.19 measuring damages. First, in *Ruxley Electronics and Construction Limited v. Forsyth*[32]:

The defendant had contracted with the plaintiffs for them to install a swimming pool in his garden. The contract said that at the deep end the pool should be 7 feet 6 inches deep. When it was complete it was discovered that it was only 6 feet 9 inches deep. This change in depth had not diminished the value of the pool. If that was the only measure of damages, the defendant would have got nothing despite the fact that there was clearly a breach of contract. The defendant argued that in order to reflect his loss the damages would have to be the sum it would cost to dig up the pool and reconstruct it.

The House of Lords were unanimous in rejecting the defendant's claim. They did so on the basis that the cost of reinstatement would be excessive when compared to the benefit that would result, this did not mean that, because there was no diminution in value, there was no award of damages. They said that apart from diminution in value and the cost of re-doing the works, there was a third means of assessing damages. This was to examine the loss of amenity that had occurred. The defendant had been denied a pleasurable amenity for which he contracted and should be compensated for that loss.

The second development occurred in *Attorney-General v. Blake*[33]: 10.20

The defendant was employed in the security and intelligence services from 1944 to 1961. During that period he became an agent for the Soviet Union and supplied secret information to them secret information. In 1961 he was convicted of treason and sentenced to 42 years imprisonment. In 1966 he escaped and fled to the Soviet Union. In the late 1980s he wrote his autobiography. He earned substantial royalties. The Attorney General raised proceedings against him which ultimately came to include a claim for damages for having breached a contractual undertaking not to divulge information learned in the course of his employment. Although there had been a breach of the contractual undertaking, it could not be said that the United Kingdom government had suffered any loss. The

---

[32] [1995] 3 All E.R. 268.
[33] [2001] 1 A.C. 268; [2000] 4 All E.R. 385.

issue became whether the damages could be assessed by reference to what the defendant had gained—the royalties on his book. This would be achieved by requiring him to account to the government for the profits he had made.

By a majority of four to one the House of Lords held that the government were entitled to an accounting for profits. This is a substantial departure from the rule noted in *Teacher*. The circumstances in which the new rule might apply are not clear. Lord Nichols indicated that two conditions would have to be satisfied. The first was that the plaintiff could demonstrate a "legitimate interest in preventing the defendant's profit-making activity and, hence, in depriving him of his profit". The second was that the legitimate interest made it "just and equitable that the defendant should retain no benefit from his breach of contract". It is clear that this measure of damages will be applied only in exceptional circumstances.

Remoteness

10.21 Some breaches of contract gave rise to many consequences. The contract-breaker will not be held liable for all that flows from the breach:

> *Example*: Mr A, a businessman, hires a taxi to go to the airport. The taxi fails to turn up, A misses his flight and loses the opportunity to make an important business deal at his proposed destination. Subsequently A's business goes bankrupt, his wife leaves him and so on.

The policy decision for the law to answer is, how far should the contract-breaker be responsible for the consequences of his breach? In general, a defender is not liable when the loss is "too remote". What is remoteness? Bankton said compensation was payable in respect of loss which "proceeds immediately from the thing itself."[34] The leading Scottish case is *Balfour Beatty Construction (Scotland) Limited v. Scottish Power plc*[35]:

> In 1985 Balfour Beatty were engaged in constructing a bypass road to the west of Edinburgh. The works included the construction of an aqueduct to carry the Union canal across the bypass. Both the roadway and the aqueduct were made of concrete. In order to mix the concrete a site was obtained nearby at a quarry near Ratho. The South of Scotland Electricity Board (SSEB) supplied electricity to the site. Subsequently Scottish Power inherited SSEB's liabilities. The aqueduct required a long continuous pour of concrete for the first stage of its construction. When the stage was almost complete, the electricity supply was interrupted. In consequence, the first stage

---

[34] *Institutions*, I.xi.15.
[35] 1994 S.C. (H.L.) 20, 1994 S.L.T. 807.

had to be demolished and reconstructed. Balfour Beatty sued for breach of contract and concluded for payment of damages of £229,102.53. At first instance, Lord Clyde held (a) that SSEB were in breach of contract; but (b) that the loss claimed was too remote. SSEB were not informed nor could they have been otherwise aware that a continuous pour of concrete was required for a particular operation and that reconstruction would be required if the electricity supply failed. Lord Clyde therefore made no award. On appeal that decision was reversed by the Second Division. They held that it was not necessary for SSEB to forsee the precise damage which occurred. It was enough that the type of consequence was within their contemplation. Scottish Power appealed to the House of Lords.

In deciding the case, the House of Lords referred to the classic nineteenth century statement on this matter—a dictum of Alderson B. in *Hadley v. Baxendale*: 10.22

"The damages...should be such as may fairly and reasonably be considered either arising naturally, ie, according to the usual course of things, from such breach of contract itself, or such as may reasonably be supposed to have been in the contemplation of both parties at the time they made the contract as the probable result of the breach."[36]

Note the two branches of the test:

(1) it was a normal result, one involving knowledge imputed to everyone;
(2) the parties were aware of special circumstances which made it a probable result.

In the *Balfour Beatty* case the House of Lords concluded that the requirement to demolish and re-build the aqueduct were not matters within the reasonable contemplation of the electricity board. Balfour Beatty were therefore not entitled to damages reflecting the cost of these works. In deciding what could be said to have been within the contemplation of the parties, Lord Jauncey referred to a dictum of Lord Reid in *Czarnikow Ltd v. Koufos*[37]:

"I would agree...that it is generally sufficient that that event would have appeared to the defendant as not unlikely to occur. It is hardly ever possible in this matter to assess probabilities with any degree of mathematical accuracy. But I do not find in [earlier cases] any warrant for regarding as within the contemplation of the parties any

---

[36] (1854) 9 Exch. 341 at p.354.
[37] [1969] 1 A.C. 350 at p.388E.

event which would not have appeared to the defendant, had he thought about it, to have a very substantial degree of probability."

10.23　This indicates that the second alternative within the *Hadley* is a hard test to meet. A case which clearly illustrates the two branches of the test is *Victoria Laundry (Windsor) Ltd v. Newman Industries Ltd*[1]:

> A boiler was ordered by the plaintiffs who operated a laundering and cleaning business. It was delivered 20 weeks late. The plaintiffs sought to recover damages in respect of lost business profits for the period during which they should have had the use of the boiler. The defendants knew the purpose for which the boiler was to be used. They also knew it was required as soon as possible. They were not informed specifically, however, regarding the loss of profits which might occur if there was a delay in delivery. These comprised (a) a large amount of profits drawn from the new business "the demand for laundry services at that time being insatiable", valued at £16 per week, and (b) highly lucrative government dyeing contracts valued at £262 per week.

The trial judge held that the loss of profits was not recoverable. This decision was overturned by the Court of Appeal only to be reinstated on a further appeal to the House of Lords. This indicates the difficulty in applying this test.

Type of Loss Suffered

10.24　Breach of contract normally involves loss measurable in money terms (pecuniary loss). The innocent party is hit in the pocket. As contracts are concerned with economic transactions, it was for a long time impossible to obtain damages for non-pecuniary loss. So if an employee was wrongfully dismissed in humiliating circumstances he could not recover compensation in respect of the injured feelings which he suffered.[2] Such loss was said to be too remote. He could only recover in respect of his lost wages.

　　In some contracts, however, the only or main loss which results is non-pecuniary. In certain circumstances such loss can be recovered. A wedding photographer who fails to turn up at the wedding to take the official photographs is liable in damages for the disappointment this causes.[3] Likewise when a holiday completely fails to live up to the claims made for it in the brochure and ruins the pleasure of the holidaymaker.[4] The principle is that where a purpose of the contract is to raise

---

[1] [1949] 2 K.B. 528; [1949] 1 All E.R. 997.
[2] *Addis v. Gramophone Co. Ltd* [1909] A.C. 488.
[3] *Diesen v. Samson*, 1971 S.L.T. (Sh.Ct) 49.
[4] *Jarvis v. Swan's Tours Ltd* [1973] 2 Q.B. 233; [1973] 1 All E.R. 71. This was approved by the House of Lords in *Ruxley Electronics and Construction Ltd v. Forsyth* [1995] 3 All E.R. 257.

expectations of a non-pecuniary nature and breach occurs, damages may be recoverable for the disappointment and injured feelings which result. It has been extended to cover situations where it is a direct consequence of the breach that the innocent party will suffer trouble, distress and inconvenience. Many cases for professional negligence brought against solicitors include such a claim. Take the example of a client who alleges that her solicitor has been negligent in respect of conveyancing on her new house. One head of damage will relate to trouble, distress and inconvenience in respect of matters such as not getting into a new house on time.[5]

Mitigation of loss

Faced by a breach of contract, the innocent party is expected to take whatever steps are available to him to minimise the loss. He should act like a prudent person following the dictates of common sense. If possible he must attempt to stem the loss. He does not, however, have to go to great or extraordinary lengths; the onus of proof is on the contract-breaker to show that the other party has not mitigated his loss. So a person who breached a contract to ship goods to Canada was liable to pay the costs of shipping by another route at four times the cost unless he could show that another, cheaper method was available.[6] The legal principle is that the innocent party cannot recover a greater sum by way of damages than if he had taken those steps. In a contract for sale of goods, for example, if a buyer wrongfully refuses the goods then the measure of damages is, *prima facie*, to be ascertained by the difference between the contract price and the market or current price at the time or times when the goods ought to have been accepted.[7] So a grain merchant must attempt to sell the goods to another buyer if the original buyer under the contract refuses to pay for the goods. If the price the merchant achieves is the same or higher, only nominal damages are recoverable. 10.25

The Measure of Damages Seen from a Different Viewpoint

Some writers believe that damages can be more appropriately analysed by breaking down a party's loss into three types: restitution, reliance and expectation of loss. The case of *McRae v. Commonwealth Disposals Commission*, illustrates these three types of loss[8]: 10.26

> After the Second World War, McRae bought from the defendants the wreck of an oil tanker which was said to lie beside the Jourmaund Reef. He fitted out a vessel to salvage the wreck, hired a crew and proceeded to the supposed location of the wreck. No wreck

---

[5] *Curran v. Docherty* 1995 S.L.T. 716.
[6] *Connal Connal & Co. v. Fisher Renwick & Co.* (1883) 10 R. 824.
[7] Sale of Goods Act 1979, s.50 (3).
[8] (1951) 84 C.L.R. 377.

was found. McRae sought damages in respect of the following losses he had sustained.

(1) The cost of purchasing the wreck from the defendants—£ 285 (restitution loss).

(2) The cost of arranging a vessel and crew for salvage—£10,000 (reliance loss).

(3) The profit he would have made if the wreck had been there and he had successfully salvaged it—£250,000 (expectation loss).

The court decided that the expectation loss was too speculative. Instead, it awarded McRae compensation in respect of his restitution and reliance interests. On the evidence, it decided that his actual expenditure was in the region of £3,000 rather than £10,000, and he received £3,285. Accordingly, he was not being put in the position which he would have been if the contract had been performed—only expectation loss would have done that. Instead, he was compensated for the loss to his pocket— the financial outlay he had sustained on the faith of the bargain. There has been no judicial recognition of this analysis in the Scottish courts, but it does perhaps provide a cross check against which the conventional method can be tested.

REMEDIES PROVIDED BY THE CONTRACT

10.27   The parties may insert terms into the contract expressly providing what should happen in the event of breach. This provides much more certainty about the consequences of breach of that contract. One party may seek to limit his liability by means of an exemption clause as discussed above. A second device which is commonly used by contracting parties is to stipulate that a determinate amount should be payable by way of damages in the event of breach. Such clauses are perfectly legitimate and enforceable so long as they constitute a genuine pre-estimate of loss. They are then referred to as liquidate damage clauses. But if the clause is intended to punish the party in breach then it is invalid and unenforceable. A clause of that type is known as a penalty clause. The general tendency of the court is not to find that the clause is penal unless it is clearly exorbitant.

Penalty and Liquidate Damage Clauses

10.28   In distinguishing between penalty clauses and liquidate damage clauses, the courts have recourse to principles which were authoritatively set out in *Dunlop Pneumatic Tyre Co. v. New Garage & Motor Co.* by Lord Dunedin.[9] The principles can be summarised as follows:

---

[9] [1915] A.C. 79 at p.86.

(1) The use of the term "penalty" or "liquidated damages" is not conclusive. In each case the court must determine whether the payment stipulated is in truth a penalty or liquidated damages.

(2) A penalty is in essence designed to punish the offending party; the essence of liquidated damages is that the sum payable is a genuine pre-estimate of loss.

(3) Whether a sum stipulated is a penalty or liquidated damages is a question judged at the time of the making of the contract, not at the time of the breach.

(4) Various tests of interpretation are used by the courts in their task:

(a) A clause will be held to be penal if the sum in question is extravagant and unconscionable.

(b) A clause will be penal if the breach consists only in not paying a sum of money, and the clause stipulates for a sum greater than the sum which ought to have been paid.

(c) A clause is presumed penal when "a single lump sum is made payable by way of compensation, on the occurrence of one or more or all of several events, some of which may occasion serious and other, but trifling, damage."

(d) A sum will not be penal simply because the consequences of the breach cannot be estimated. Indeed "that is just the situation when it is probable that pre-estimated damage was the true bargain between the parties."

An unusual illustration of the application of these principles is provided by *Clydebank Engineering & Shipbuilding Co. Ltd v. Castaneda*:[10]

Four torpedo boat destroyers were ordered by the Spanish government from a Scottish shipyard. Substantial sums were to be paid by way of damages in the event of the vessels being delivered late. The ships were delivered many months late but the shipyard declined to pay the sum stipulated. It alleged that the sum was penal and unenforceable because (a) Navy ships were not profit-making assets and accordingly there was no loss to the Spanish government, and (b) the remainder of the fleet had been sunk by the American Navy off Cuba shortly after the delivery date set in the contract. Accordingly, it was contended, no loss had been suffered.

Both these arguments were swiftly despatched by the court and the 10.29
Spanish government awarded the sums claimed. Two matters were noted.
First, the clause itself had been inserted precisely because the quantification of loss was so difficult. Secondly, the shipyard had fixed

---

[10] (1904) 7 F. (H.L.) 77; (1903) 5 F. 1016.

the terms as a means of attracting the order for the vessels. It was also stated that if the destroyers had been delivered on time, the fleet might not have sunk.

Liquidate damage clauses may have the effect of limiting the liability of one party. This happens where the actual loss suffered is greater than that stipulated for in the contract. But there is a difference in the two types of clause. In a limitation clause, the sum specified operates as a ceiling on damages. If the actual loss is lower, the sum recoverable is lower. Where there is a liquidate damage clause, the same amount is recoverable irrespective of whether the actual loss is greater or less than the sum specified in the clause.

10.30   Where a clause is held to be a penalty, there is Scottish authority that the actual loss is recoverable even when it is greater than the sum stipulated for in the penalty.[11] Here, the paradox is that the penalty clause is invalid because it "terrorises" the other party, yet the loss suffered is greater than that sum.

Other Contractual Clauses

10.31   Several other devices can be used to provide in advance what the remedy should be on the occurrence of a certain event. Examples are (1) acceleration clauses, where if one instalment is not paid time, the whole price becomes immediately payable; (2) forfeiture clauses, where if there is a breach the injured party forfeits his deposit[12]; (3) non-breach clauses, where sums are stipulated to be payable otherwise than on the occurrence of breach[13]; and (4) retention clauses, where a percentage of the price is retained for a specified period to cover the cost of remedying any defective performance. In these cases, neither the rules as to penalty clauses nor the provisions of the Unfair Contract Terms Act 1977 apply. However, if the contract is a consumer contract, compatibility with the Unfair Terms in Consumer Contracts Regulations 1999 will have to be considered if the term is to be enforceable.

A common clause in leases is an irritancy clause. It provides that the landlord is entitled to irritate (*i.e.* terminate) the lease in the event of specified breaches by the other party. In a lease for a term of years, for example, it might be provided that if the tenant should default in his payment of the rent, the landlord should be able to irritate the lease. It is now provided by statute that the landlord's right to terminate depends upon his issuing a notice of default to the tenant.[14]

---

[11] *Dingwall v. Burnett*, 1912 S.C. 1097.
[12] *Cf. Zemhunt Holdings Ltd v. Control Securities plc*, 1991 S.L.T. 653.
[13] *E.F.T. Commercial Ltd v. Security Change Ltd*, 1992 S.C.L.R. 706.
[14] Law Reform (Miscellaneous Provisions) (Scotland) Act 1985, ss. 4–7.

ANTICIPATORY BREACH

In many of the examples considered above, the breach has occurred 10.32
where one party does not fulfil their obligations at the time that they
become due. In contracts where performance is due to take place at some
future date, one party may indicate in advance that he is not going to
fulfil his side of the bargain. He thus repudiates the contract before the
time for performance arrives. This is known as anticipatory breach. It
leaves the innocent party with three options:

(1) To rescind the contract and immediately sue for damages.
(2) To wait until the time for performance has arrived (in case the
other party changes his mind) then sue for damages.
(3) To perform his side of the bargain and claim the contract price.

The third of these options has proved the most controversial. It is
worth stressing that it is only a viable option in a limited number of
cases. This is because firstly, contracts normally require the co-operation
of both parties in order for performance to take place. If, for example, X
repudiates a contract to have an extension built on to his house, the
builder cannot enter on to the land and commence construction without
X's permission. Secondly, few parties will wish to render a performance
which is no longer desired. The builder will be unlikely to try to build the
extension in the teeth of X's opposition. Exceptionally, however, the
innocent party will not require the co-operation of the other party to fulfil
his side of the bargain and will ignore the fact that performance is no
longer required. The leading authority on this issue is *White & Carter
(Councils) Ltd v. McGregor*[15]:

A representative from an advertising agency called at a garage to
arrange a new advertising contract which was to last for three years.
Terms were agreed with the manager and the contract completed.
Later the same day, the owner of the garage telephoned the agency
to cancel the contract. The agency ignored the purported
cancellation, continued with the contract and sued for the full
contract price. On behalf of the garage, it was argued that the agency
should have sued for damages (if any) when the cancellation was
notified. By suing for a debt (the contract price) rather than for
damages, the agency were thus able to avoid having to show that
they had mitigated their loss.

An earlier Scottish case had held that the proper test in such 10.33
situations was: what was the "reasonable and proper course" for the
pursuer to take?[16] By a narrow three to two majority, the House of Lords

---

[15] 1962 S.C. (H.L.) 1; [1961] 3 All E.R. 1178.
[16] *Langford v. Dutch*, 1952 S.C. 15.

overruled this view and held that the agency were entitled to succeed in this claim:

> "It might be, but it never has been, the law that a person is only entitled to enforce his contractual rights in a reasonable way and that a court will not support an attempt to enforce them in an unreasonable way. One reason why this is the law is no doubt because it was thought that it would create too much uncertainty to require the court to decide whether it is reasonable or equitable to allow a party to enforce his full rights under a contract."

This is an area of law in which the approach differs in Scotland and England. This is because this third option, noted above, will, in many situations, involve the innocent party compelling the party in breach to perform their obligations under the contract. This requires either an action for payment, where money is sought, or an action of specific implement, where performance of some other obligation is sought. The differences between the Scottish and English courts in this field have been noted above.[17] The result is that in Scotland, provided that the contract is such that the innocent party can seek decree of specific implement or payment, the option of insisting on the contract will be open.

---

[17] See para. 10.14.

CHAPTER 11

TITLE TO SUE

Each party to a contract acquires legal rights against the other. Persons 11.1
who are not parties to the contract do not acquire rights or duties under it.
In this respect a contract can be regarded as a private legislative
arrangement between the parties. And this indeed is the general principle
of the law—a transaction between certain parties cannot advantage or
injure those who are not parties to that transaction (*res inter alios acta
aliis nec nocet nec prodest*). Let us take an example: A is owed £100 by
B who in turn is owed £100 by C; A cannot sue C for the £100 because
he has no rights under the contract between B and C. It is not possible to
sue one's debtor's debtor.[1] There are several important exceptions to this
principle—agency, assignation, *jus quaesitum tertio* and contracts
transferred by operation of law.

AGENCY

Agency describes the relationship which arises when one person (the 11.2
agent) is appointed to act as the representative of another (the principal).
A variety of examples come to mind. The owners of a house instruct a
solicitor to sell their house for them. A woman going to live abroad
appoints her daughter to conduct her affairs in Scotland during her
absence. A foreign manufacturer retains a Scottish firm to sell its goods
in the United Kingdom. In each of these cases, two different aspects of
agency arise. First, the contract of agency is created between the
principal and the agent. Secondly, the agent can make contracts which
bind his principal. This second aspect means that the principal acquires
rights and duties under a contract which he himself has not made. In
other words, he becomes a party to the contract, even though he took no
direct part in its formation. For this to occur, the agent must act within
the four corners of the authority vested in him. If he acts without
authority, then he alone is liable on the contract, unless the principal
subsequently ratifies his act.

---

[1] See *Henderson v. Robb* (1889) 16 R. 341.

Example: Joe, Don and Fay are partners in an architects' firm. Fay agrees to purchase three sports cars for herself and her partners. If the partnership deed grants Fay authority to do this, then the partnership must pay for the cars. Otherwise Fay alone is liable to pay the purchase price of the cars, unless Joe and Don held Fay out as having the necessary authority or they are prepared to ratify the purchase.

Where the agent is acting with authority, then normally only the principal acquires rights and duties under the contract. It is presumed that the other party intends to contract with the principal rather than the agent. The seller of a house intends to contract with the prospective purchasers, not the solicitor who has drafted and sent the formal offer. If the purchaser defaults in paying the price, the seller will sue him, not his solicitor. In two situations, however, the agent himself may be bound by the contract. This occurs where the agent either (a) does not disclose that he has a principal, or (b) does not divulge his principal's identity. In both cases the third party has a right of election—to sue the agent personally or to sue the principal (assuming that the latter's identity is disclosed). A bidder at an auction, for example, might refuse to state the identity of the client for whom he is bidding. If the bid is successful but the price is not paid within a reasonable time, the seller might opt to sue the bidder. The bidder will be personally liable on the contract of sale, although he has a right of recourse against his principal.

ASSIGNATION

11.3 Assignation is the process by which contractual rights, and arguably contractual obligations, are transferred to a third party. For instance, a person who orders a boat to be built might assign the right to receive the boat to another person or the boat builder might assign his right to make payment. The transferor is known as the assignor (or cedent), while the transferee is known as the assignee.

Assignation of Rights

11.4 Most contractual rights are assignable when consent is given. The question of whether or not one party can assign his rights without the consent of the other party is more difficult. Some contracts prohibit assignation. In other cases the nature of the right may make it apparent that it is not capable of being assigned. Simple debts are, however, generally assignable. Debt collection companies rely on this principle. It enables them to purchase bad debts from other businesses to pursue against the debtors.

Assignation of Obligations

This is less straightforward. When a party seeks to assign a right, the 11.5
other party must perform exactly the same obligation but to a different
person. Generally, this will make little difference to the party performing
the obligation. If, on the other hand, a party seeks to assign his
obligations, the effect on the other party can be considerable. A person
who had concluded a contract with a bespoke tailor in Saville Row for a
suit would be justifiably unhappy if the obligation to make and deliver
the suit was assigned to a theatrical costumier.

To deal with this, it is possible for the contracting parties to include a
term that assignation shall not be allowed. Even without such a term, it
will not be possible to assign an obligation where it is clear that there has
been a choice of person (*delectus personae*). This will be so where the
identity of the contracting party subject to the obligation is of
importance. That will depend on the obligation in question. Factors that
mean that *delectus personae* is more likely to exist include the
importance of any qualities of personal service within the obligation and
a degree of skill of craftsmanship being required to complete the work.[2]
If, on the other hand, the obligation is to supply materials or do work of a
stipulated standard it is less likely. For example, the obligation of the
Saville Row tailor could not be assigned but an obligation to supply five
metres of a specified cloth might be capable of assignation.

The issue of whether it is possible to assign obligations at all remains 11.6
a contentious one. A party who has undertaken an obligation and wishes
to transfer it to a third party may do so by novation[3] or sub-contracting.
The former requires the consent of the other contracting party. The latter
means leaves the other contracting party with his rights against the
person with whom he contracted. Assignation of obligations removes
these protections. In England, the House of Lords have stated recently
that the burden of a contract cannot be assigned.[4] In Scotland, support for
the proposition that assignation of obligations is permissible is derived
from *Cole v. Handasyde & Co.*[5] In that case, however, the competency of
assigning an obligation was not the principal issue. That was whether
delectus personae existed. Despite these doubts, modern support for the
proposition that assignation of obligations is possible may be derived
from *Scottish Homes v. Inverclyde District Council*:

> "If on a sound construction of its terms, express or implied, a
> contract entitles a contracting party to substitute another in his place

---

[2] *Cole v. Handasyde & Co.*, 1910 S.C. 68, *Scottish Homes v. Inverclyde D.C.*,
1997 S.L.T. 829.
[3] Considered in Chapter 13.
[4] *Linden Garden Trust Ltd v. Lenesta Sludge Disposals Ltd* [1994] 1 A.C. 85;
[1993] 3 W.L.R. 408; [1993] 3 All E.R. 417.
[5] 1910 S.C. 68.

both as regards performance and the benefits of the contract, there is, in my opinion, no rule of Scots law which would prevent that from having effect."[6]

Form of Assignation

11.7 No particular form of words is required to assign a right.[7] It is enough that words are used which show that the assignor intended to transfer his particular rights under the contract to another person. Although assignation takes place between the assignor and assignee, intimation to the other party to the contract may be extremely important in perfecting the assignee's right. If, for example, a debtor pays his debt to the original creditor because he has not been informed that the debt has been assigned, he will be held to have discharged his obligation.

What is the Assignee's Right?

11.8 He stands in the shoes of the cedent. All pleas available against the assignor are thus available against the assignee. The relevant Latin tag here is *assignatur utitur jure auctoris* (an assignee exercises the right of his cedent). Where an insured allegedly made false statements in his proposal form for life assurance and then assigned the benefit of the policy, the insurance company was entitled to seek to reduce the insurance contract.[8] The assignees had no better right to the proceeds of the policy than the insured himself. If his statements were false, he (and in consequence the assignees) had no entitlement to benefit under the policy.

> "It appears to me to be long ago settled in the law of Scotland—and I have never heard of any attempt to disturb the doctrine—that in a personal obligation, whether contained in a unilateral deed or in a mutual contract, if the creditor's right is sold to an assignee for value, and the assignee purchases in good faith, he is nevertheless subject to all the exceptions and pleas pleadable against the original creditor."[9]

One of the legal effects of death and bankruptcy is to transfer all assignable rights and duties automatically to the executor or the permanent trustee in bankruptcy respectively. Accordingly, when a party to a contract dies, his rights pass to his representatives.

---

[6] 1997 S.L.T. 829 *per* Lord Penrose at 835.
[7] *Brownlee v. Robb*, 1907 S.C. 1302.
[8] *Scottish Widows' Fund v. Buist* (1876) 3 R. 1078.
[9] *Ibid. per* L.P. Inglis at p.1082.

JUS QUAESITUM TERTIO

Jus quaesitum tertio is a right required by a third party, literally "the 11.9
third party has acquired a right". Scots law allows two parties to confer
an enforceable right upon a third party who is not a party to the contract.
The basis of the doctrine is to be found in a passage in Stair's
Institutions:

> "It is likewise the opinion of Molina, cap. 263 and it quadrats to our
> Customs, that when Parties Contract, if there be any Article in
> favour of a third Party, at any time, *est jus quaesitum tertio*, which
> cannot be recalled by both the Contractors, but he may compel either
> of them to exhibit the Contract, and thereupon the obliged may be
> compelled to perform."[10]

Read literally, this passage implies that the third party's right is
complete as soon as there is a provision in his favour in the contract. He
can sue upon the contract as soon as it is made. It will also be seen that
Stair identifies three aspects to this right:

(1) the contracting parties cannot revoke the agreement;
(2) the third party can compel the contracting parties to display the
    contract to him; and
(3) the third party can enforce the provision in his favour.

The courts have been somewhat reluctant to allow the third party such 11.10
extensive rights. They will only do so where that is the manifest intention
of the contracting parties. This reluctance is understandable. In most
instances of *jus quaesitum tertio*, the third party will be receiving a gift
and there is a strong presumption against donation. The leading case is
Carmichael v. Carmichael's Executor[11]:

> A father took out an insurance policy for £1,000 on the life of his
> eight-year-old son. The policy provided that the sum assured was to
> be paid on death to the son's executor's, providing he attained the
> age of 21 years and continued to pay the premiums. If the son died
> before attaining 21, however, the premiums were to be repaid by the
> insurance company to the father. Alternatively, he could surrender
> the policy for whatever value it had. The father duly paid the
> premiums and kept the policy in his possession, never delivering it
> to the son. Between his 21st and 22nd birthday and before the first
> premium payable by him was due, the son was killed in an air
> accident. He left a will leaving all his property to his aunt. In an
> action to determine whether the father or the aunt was entitled to the
> benefit of the policy, the father claimed that the son had not acquired
> a right to the proceeds of the policy. The contract, he said, was

---

[10] *Institutions,* I.x.5.
[11] 1920 S.C. (H.L.) 195.

between him and the insurance company. The son would only acquire a right after he had paid the first premium due by him, or if the father had delivered or formally intimated that policy to the son. None of these things had happened. Despite these considerations, the House of Lords found in favour of the aunt.

The decision might suggest that the court adopted a broad view of the doctrine. In fact, the reverse occurred, the speech of Lord Dunedin considerably narrowed the doctrine. He suggested that in Stair's statement, the phrase "*est jus quaesitum tertio*" should be transposed with the words "which cannot be recalled by both the contractors." In other words, the insertion of the clause in the third party's favour was of itself not enough. In addition, it had to be shown that the contracting parties could not revoke their agreement. Delivery or intimation to the other party would be ways of evincing this intention, but in other cases it would be a question of interpretation. Here, the whole circumstances of the case pointed to an irrevocable intention having been formed. The terms of the policy clearly envisaged that the father's rights ceased after the son reached majority. Thereafter, the son could elect to continue the policy, or convert it into a different type of policy, or receive a cash benefit. Irrevocability, however, was no longer a consequence of the agreement, as Stair had stipulated, but rather a condition of the establishment of the right.

11.11   The right to revoke may not be an absolute bar to establishing the existence of a *jus quaesitum tertio*. In *Love v. Amalgamated Society of Lithographic Printers of Great Britain & Ireland*, a widow claimed sickness benefit in terms of her husband's trade union membership.[12] Although the right to benefit was revocable (the union rules could be altered at any time) it had not been so revoked at the time of his death. The widow was successful in her claim. This case is difficult to reconcile with *Carmichael* and is perhaps an apt illustration of the saying that hard cases make bad law, or at least law which is more difficult to state with certainty and precision. In any event it does seem just to hold that the wife's right would only have been defeated if the union rules had been altered before her entitlement arose.

What, then, are the criteria to be satisfied to establish a *jus quaesitum tertio*? The parties must expressly state that the third party is to benefit. In *Morton's Trs v. The Aged Christian Friend Society of Scotland*, the agreement was made between a benefactor and a provisional committee charged with the duty of setting up a charitable society.[13] The contract specifically stipulated that the benefactor was to pay annual instalments to the society, rather than to the provisional committee. This was described as "a clear instance of our doctrine of *jus quaesitum tertio*".

---

[12] 1912 S.C. 1078.
[13] (1899) 2 F. 82.

Accordingly, the society was entitled to enforce its right to payment of the instalments outstanding on the benefactor's death.

It is not enough for the third party to show merely that a benefit was 11.12 incidentally conferred upon him. There must be an express provision in her favour (*pactum in favorem tertii*). In *Finnie v. Glasgow & South-Western Railway Co.*, two railway companies agreed to fix the freight rate for the carriage of coal along a certain railway line.[14] When the railway companies varied the rate upwards, a person who transported freight along the line sought to enforce the companies' agreement. The action was unsuccessful. It was not a contract made for his benefit so he had no *jus quaesitum tertio*. Whether the requisite intention is present or not can be evinced in several ways:

(1) by the nature of the original contract;
(2) by the whole circumstances of the case;
(3) by intimation or delivery of the contract.

In *Carmichael*, the son and indeed the whole family knew of the policy. Before joining the air force, he had contacted the insurers to check that military service was not inconsistent with the policy and he had spoken to his lawyer about it in relation to his will.

Rights of Enforcement

A *jus quaesitum tertio* can be enforced even if the original contracting 11.13 parties no longer have an interest to sue. In *Morton's Trs*, the provisional committee had become defunct once the charitable society had been founded. The third party may enforce the right even where one of the contracting parties can also sue on the contract. In *Lamont v. Burnett*, the purchaser of a hotel in Crieff, in addition to the purchase price of £7,000, offered to pay to the seller's wife "not less than one hundred pounds as some compensation for the annoyance and worry of the past few days, and for her kindness and attention to me on my several visits to Crieff".[15] This was accepted by the seller. It was held that this extra provision could be enforced by the wife and the view was expressed that the husband might also enforce the provision.

A doubt existed as to whether the tertius could sue for defective performance or only for total failure to perform.[16] That question was considered in *Scott Lithgow v. G.E.C. Electrical Products Ltd*[17]:

The Ministry of Defence commissioned Scott Lithgow's predecessors to build a new naval vessel, H.M.S. Challenger. The electrical work was sub-contracted to G.E.C. Electrical Products Ltd,

---

[14] (1857) 3 Macq. 75.
[15] (1901) 3 F. 797.
[16] See Gloag on *Contract* (2nd ed.), p.239; *cf. Cullen v. McMenamin*, 1928 S.L.T. (Sh.Ct) 2.
[17] 1992 S.L.T. 244.

which in turn sub-contracted some of the work to other sub-contractors. Defects developed in the wiring of the electrical equipment. The Ministry claimed that they had a *jus quaesitum tertio* arising out of the contracts between G.E.C. and the sub-contractors as they were expressly mentioned in those sub-contracts. They also claimed that they were entitled to seek damages from the "sub-sub-contractors" for defective performance.

11.14   After debate, Lord Clyde held that such a claim could exist and allowed the averments on this branch of the case to go to proof before answer. He stated:

> "In general I can see no reason why a third party should not be entitled to sue for damages for negligent performance of a contract under the principle of *jus quaesitum tertio*, but whether he is so entitled must be a matter of the intention of the contracting parties. That has to be ascertained from the terms of the contract."

The Status of Jus Quaesitum Tertio

11.15   There have been relatively few cases of late dealing with *jus quaesitum tertio*. However, that does not mean it is without significance in Scots law. There is good sense in giving effect to contracting parties' intention to benefit a third party, if they make that intention sufficiently clear. In England a similar right has been introduced by statute.[18]

TRANSFER BY OPERATION OF LAW

11.16   In some instances a legal entity which has entered into contracts will cease to exist and be replaced by a new entity. An example of this occurs where local government or other public bodies are reorganised. In such a situation there is often legislation intended to transfer the rights and obligations of the body to be abolished to its successor.

    In addition to these special situations which are the subject of particular rules there is at least one set of general set of rules which has the effect of transferring contracts of employment where a business of purchased—the Transfer of Undertakings (Protection of Employment) Regulations 1981. The circumstances in which these Regulations operate and the detailed rules that have evolved as to how they are applied are not matters within the scope of this book. It is relevant here simply to note that when the regulations apply, the effect is that one employer may be substituted for another in the contract of employment.[19]

---

[18] Contract (Rights of Third Parties) Act 1999.
[19] For example, see *Morris Angel and Son Ltd v. Hollande* [1993] 3 All E.R. 569.

JOINT AND SEVERAL LIABILITY

We have been examining circumstances where someone other than the   11.17
parties themselves can sue upon the contract. It is convenient to discuss
here the principles to be applied where more than one party is liable
under a contract. A contract may involve undertakings by more than two
parties. For example, if a man and woman jointly contract to purchase a
flat, they will both be liable to the seller. In the event of default, the seller
may choose to sue both prospective purchasers. However, suppose that
the man has gone missing and cannot be traced. The seller is entitled to
sue the woman alone for the whole account. This is referred to as joint
and several liability. The liability is "joint", in the sense that each
obligant is liable for the whole amount to the creditor. It is "several", in
the sense that each has a right to seek to recover the contribution from
the co-obligant. Accordingly, should the woman in the example pay the
whole purchase price, she has a right of action against the man for his
share, should he re-appear.[20]

In many situations in Scots law, joint and several liability will be
expressed by the parties or be implied by law.[21] This occurs where, for
example, the words "joint and several liability" are actually used, in
guarantees, in partnership obligations, and in relation to bills of
exchange.

> *Example*: Lender X lends money to Y after receiving an undertaking
> that Z will guarantee the sum. Should Y default in payment, Z is
> bound to repay the whole £100 to X and Z would then be entitled to
> recover any such payment from Y.

If the liability of the obligants is not joint and several, each co-
obligant is only bound to the extent of his own proportionate (*pro rata*)
share.

---

[20] *Moss v. Penman*, 1993 S.C.L.R. 374; *McGillivray v. Davidson*, 1993 S.L.T.
693.
[21] See *Wright v. Tennant Caledonian Breweries Ltd*, 1991 S.L.T. 823

CHAPTER 12

THE REQUIREMENT OF LEGALITY

A contract must be lawful both in its object and in its mode of 12.1
performance. If either of these requirements is not satisfied, then the
courts will decline to enforce the contract. Such contracts are referred to
as illegal contracts (*pacta illicita*). The reference to illegality is
misleading as it tends to suggest the commission of a crime, whereas the
principle of contractual legality extends over a much wider field. A
contract of slavery would not be enforced by the courts, but the mere
making of the agreement is not a criminal offence. Indeed one of the
curiosities of contract law is that the most important type of agreement
classified under this heading, a restrictive covenant, is one which is
frequently seen as laudable and enforced rather than illegal and invalid.

The general principle is that no action arises out of an immoral
situation (*ex turpi causa non oritur actio*). Neither party can enforce or
claim damages for breach of an unlawful agreement. The unlawfulness
does not need to be pleaded by the parties; it is the duty of the judge to
take notice of an unlawful transaction.

> *Example*: A householder engages a plumber to carry out the
> replacement of the lead pipes and tank in his house. The works are
> eligible for grant assistance from the local authority. The parties
> agree that the plumber shall carry out various other repair works at
> the house and that he will artificially inflate the estimate for the lead
> replacement work in order to attract the maximum council grant. If a
> dispute arises and either party seeks to enforce the contract, they run
> the risk that the court will refuse to adjudicate on the matter. Both
> parties seek to defraud the local authority. Accordingly their contract
> is tainted by illegality.[1] The sheriff may even direct that the papers
> be sent to the Procurator Fiscal's office to consider whether a
> prosecution should be brought.

---

[1] Since this example was first used in this book it has become a reality; *Taylor v.
Bhail, The Independent*, November 20, 1995.

WHAT CONSTITUTES UNLAWFULNESS?

12.2   Some contracts are forbidden by statute. Others are illegal at common law. The most important categories of unlawful contracts are as follows:

Contracts to Commit a Crime or Delict

12.3   An agreement to commit a crime is not enforceable. It may also amount to conspiracy and be punishable under the provisions of the criminal law. Contracts to commit a delict are likewise unenforceable. It is clearly against public policy to uphold such bargains.

Contracts Promoting Sexual Immorality

12.4   Contracts tending to promote sexual immorality are not upheld. It is thought undesirable to associate the law with such transactions. This can be illustrated by reference to a case beloved of generations of law students, *Hamilton v. Main*[2]:

> Hamilton sought to set aside a promissory note for £60 which he had granted to Main. Hamilton gave the note in payment of his account in respect of his sojourn at Main's public house. The evidence disclosed that Hamilton had resided there for seven days, together with a prostitute. During his stay they had purchased 113 bottles of "port and Madeira, besides a large quantity of spiritous and malt liquors." Hamilton claimed that he had granted the promissory note when he was intoxicated and that it had been induced by fraud and circumvention.

> The First Division held that the promissory note could not be enforced. No reasons for the decision are given in the somewhat cryptic report of the case. It is probable that the bill was not enforced because such transactions were not to receive the approbation of the court. By depriving the landlord of his normal right to enforce the bill, the decision of the court deterred other landlords from countenancing such immoral arrangements. The dignity of the law should not be soiled by adjudicating upon disputes of this nature.

> If there is an immoral purpose known to both parties, the courts will refuse to allow the parties to sue on the contract even where the bargain itself is perfectly legitimate. In *Pearce v. Brooks*:[3]

> A firm of coachbuilders agreed to hire a brougham carriage of "intriguing design" to a prostitute. They knew she was going to use the carriage to ply her trade. She failed to pay the hire and the firm sued on the contract.

---

[2] (1823) 2 S. 356.
[3] (1866) L.R. 1 Ex. 213.

It was held that they could not succeed. The contract indirectly promoted sexual immorality and was therefore illegal. What constitutes immorality is changing. In a recent English Court of Appeal case, a contract to place advertisements for telephone sex chat lines was held not to be void on grounds of public policy.[4]

Contingency Fees

It has always been the law of Scotland that lawyers are not entitled to 12.5 accept contingency fees (*pacta de quota litis*) for their services. In other words, lawyers cannot agree to act in a case in return for a percentage of any sums successfully recovered for their clients. It is, however, possible for lawyers to agree to act on the basis that the fees will be paid only if there is a successful outcome to the case. Such cases are referred to as speculative actions. There is no restriction on parties other than solicitors and advocates entering into contracts whereby they will be paid contingency fees.[5]

Contracts Against Public Arrangements and Justice

Arrangements which involve any element of corruption will be held 12.6 unlawful. These include the purchase of honours such as knighthoods, together with contracts attempting to interfere with the processes of justice, such as an agreement to bribe a witness. When war breaks out, contracts with individuals or companies in the opposing state are in general invalidated. The foreign national is then deemed to be an enemy alien and it is against public policy to assist such persons.

Contracts in Restraint of Trade

This is the most important type of contract presumed to be unlawful. It 12.7 will be discussed later in the chapter.

DECLARING CONTRACTS UNLAWFUL

The courts have long asserted a power to declare contracts illegal at 12.8 common law. Underlying the courts' intervention in this area is the notion of public policy. Is it in the interest of the community that a particular contract be struck down? Obviously, the greater the intervention of the courts, the more they will be seen to be legislating and thereby usurping the function of Parliament. After a lengthy period of judicial creativity, particularly in the nineteenth century, there has been a tendency for the courts to avoid inventing new heads of public policy.

---

[4] *Armhouse Lee Ltd v. Chappell, The Times*, August 7, 1996.
[5] *Quantum Claims Compensation Specialists Ltd v. Powell*, 1998 S.L.T. 228.

But, as always, there are supporters and opponents of this view. For those who believe that there are no new grounds on which courts can declare contracts to be against public policy and hence unlawful, the following quotation of Burroughs J. is apt:

> "Public policy is a very unruly horse and when you once get astride it you never know where it will carry you."[6]

But with typical bravado, Lord Denning adopted a more adventurous approach:

> "With a good man in the saddle, the unruly horse can be kept in control. He can jump over obstacles."[7]

Perhaps the wisest words on this matter came from Sir George Jessel[8]:

> "It must not be forgotten that you are not to extend arbitrarily those rules which say that a given contract is void as being against public policy, because if there is one thing more than another public policy requires it is that men of full age and competent understanding shall have the utmost liberty of contracting and that when their contracts are entered into freely and voluntarily shall be held sacred and shall be enforced by Courts of Justice. Therefore, you have this permanent public policy to consider—that you are not lightly to interfere with this freedom of contract."

12.9   This statement is often cited as the embodiment of the doctrine of freedom of contract. That doctrine accepts that public policy requires that certain contracts should not be enforced, but indicates that it is of the first importance that those powers be exercised sparingly. Accordingly, it is the legislature which has had a more important role in relation to unlawful contracts in recent times.

Many statutes contain provisions affecting the validity of particular contracts. Early Scottish statutes provided that contracts of usury (money laundering), where the interest stipulated was above the legal rate, were annulled. When applying these provisions to individual circumstances today, the judges emphasise that their task is to construe the provision in the context of the whole Act in question and the mischief at which it was directed. Readers will also recall that when interpreting a contract if two meanings are possible, it will be presumed that the parties intended that the contract would be legal.

12.10   Where a contract is not directly prohibited by statute, it may still be alleged that it is illegal and unenforceable. This may occur, for example, if a statute imposes a penalty a particular type of conduct. This can occur

---

[6] *Richardson v. Mellish* (1824) 2 Bing. 229 at p.252.
[7] *Enderby Town F.C. v. F.A.* [1971] Ch. 591 at p.606.
[8] *Printing and Numerical Registering Co. v. Sampson* (1875) L.R. 19 Eq. 462 at p.465.

where a contract is performed in an illegal manner. In *St John Shipping Corp. v. Joseph Rank*[9]:

> A charterparty was entered into for the carriage of grain from America to Britain. Contrary to the Merchant Shipping Acts, the master overloaded the ship 11 inches beyond what was legal on the "Plimsoll marks". He was fined £1,200 for the offence. The charterer refused to pay part of the costs of carriage, claiming that it should not be bound when its cargo had been put at risk. So when the shipowners brought action for recovery of these sums, the defence was that the contract was illegal.

Justice Devlin held that the sums were recoverable. Upon a true construction, he said that the statute was directed toward the prevention of overloading, not the prohibition of contracts. Accordingly, the mere fact that there had been an illegal manner of performance did not debar the shipowners from recovering. The intention of the legislature was to create a statutory offence for overloading, not to declare particular types of contract illegal.

THE CONSEQUENCES OF ILLEGALITY

If an action could never be brought on an illegal contract, injustice could result. A rogue could engage in an unlawful contract with an innocent party and thereby obtain money or property. If no action were allowed, then he would reap the advantage of his own pernicious dealings. **12.11**

> *Example*: X agrees to supply Mongolian widgets to Y. After Y pays the price, X discloses that it is illegal to import Mongolian widgets into this country. If no action for recovery of the price was available to Y—as suggested by the maxim *ex turpi causa non oritur actio*—the rogue X would have successfully duped Y.

Accordingly, the law has devised a series of principles to deal with the consequences of illegal contracts. The difficulty is that these principles have never been fitted into a coherent scheme and that the two leading cases on the topic are conflicting. Let us begin by trying to identify the general approach of the law.

Parties Equally Blameworthy

If the parties are equally at fault (*in pari delicto*), the principle is that the position of the possessor is the better one (*in turpi causa melior est conditio possidentis*). To put it another way, the loss is allowed to lie where it falls. So if a person pays money for an illegal drug, he cannot **12.12**

---

[9] [1957] 1 Q.B. 267.

recover the money from the supplier, even if the drugs were never given
to him. An illustration of this point is provided by *Barr v. Crawford*[10]:

> A woman was informed that her chances of taking over the licence
> of a public house from her deceased husband were slender. On the
> strength of certain representations made to her, she made an initial
> payment of £8,000 to two individuals. She understood that a
> payment of £10,000 would secure the transfer of the licence at the
> next meeting of the district licensing board. Later, she sought to
> recover the money from the two individuals.

It was held that the payment was a bribe and the transaction was an
illegal one. The pursuer did not offer to prove that she was not *in pari
delicto* and accordingly the judge dismissed the action.

Parties not Equally Blameworthy

12.13   Where parties are not equally blameworthy, a distinction is drawn
between the rights of the guilty party and the rights of the innocent party.
By "innocent party" in this context we mean a person who has been
induced to enter the unlawful contract as the result of some unfair
advantage having been taken of him by the other party. The courts do not
weigh the relative turpitude of two guilty parties against one another.

(a) The Guilty Party

12.14   The guilty party can never sue on the contract. "No court will lend its aid
to a man who founds his cause of action upon an immoral or an illegal
act," said Lord Mansfield. It should, however, be remembered that where
there has been an illegality in performance and not in the object of the
contract, the party who has transgressed the statute may recover.

(b) The Innocent Party

12.15   The innocent party can enforce the contract if he has made a mistake
regarding the illegality alleged to taint it. In *Archbolds (Freightage) Ltd
v. Spanglett Ltd*[11]:

> The defendants contracted to carry the plaintiff's whisky in their
> van. Unknown to the plaintiffs, the van was not licensed to carry
> goods by the defendants and the carriage therefore amounted to an
> offence. The whisky was stolen. The plaintiff's action for recovery
> of the value of the whisky was defended on the ground of illegality.
> The Court of Appeal held the plaintiffs entitled to recover the value
> of the whisky as the measure of damages for breach of contract. A
> mistake as to the existence of the licence did not deprive the

---

[10] 1983 S.L.T. 481.
[11] [1961] 1 Q.B. 374; [1961] 1 All E.R. 417.

plaintiffs of the right to enforce the contract. It was only the method of performance which was illegal rather than the making of the contract itself.

Apart from mistake, two other grounds which may protect the innocent party have been developed in English law.

(1) If the contract itself is illegal, the innocent party may enforce a collateral warranty.
(2) If there has been fraud then, even though the contract cannot be enforced there may be damages for fraud.

It is difficult to know how far such grounds might be accepted in Scotland. Scots law has, arguable, a more fully developed concept of unjust enrichment than English law. There are, accordingly, circumstances where a party may recover when a contract has failed through illegality. In addition, there may be recovery upon a *quantum meruit* basis (payment for work done). If it is shown that a statute was designed to protect a particular class, and an innocent party has been prejudiced as a result of an illegal contract, then he may be granted a remedy. Accordingly, where a contract of loan was made with an unregistered moneylender, the borrower could recover property deposited with the moneylender. This was because the Act which required the moneylender to be registered was for the benefit of borrowers as a class.[12]   **12.16**

There are two leading Scottish authorities on the consequences of statutory illegality. In *Cuthbertson v. Lowes*[13]:

> Two fields of potatoes, were sold by the Scots acre. This was contrary to the Weights and Measure Act, which declared null and void any contract using local or customary measures. It was held that the seller was entitled to recover the market value of the potatoes.

Lord President Inglis said that the seller was not suing upon the contract but was in effect pursuing a claim for recompense under the principles of unjust enrichment. The decision was distinguished in the subsequent case of *Jamieson v. Watt's Trs*,[14] where a joiner did work in excess of the amount he was authorised to do by licence under the Defence Regulations. It was held that the proprietor did not have to pay for the excess. There has been a tendency to regard *Cuthbertson* as wrongly decided or, at best, to be binding only on its own special facts. For instance, Gloag draws a distinction between agreements which the law will not allow to operate as contracts and contracts which are contrary to law.[15] That is a difficult distinction to understand or apply. It   **12.17**

---

[12] *Phillips v. Blackhurst*, 1912 2 S.L.T. 254.
[13] (1870) 8 M. 1073.
[14] 1950 S.C. 265.
[15] at p.550.

seems rather that the consequences of illegality depend on two factors: the degree of turpitude involved and the requirements of public policy. It was not particularly heinous to sell potatoes according to an old measure. But there were strong grounds of public policy for preventing joiners from doing work without a licence shortly after the Second World War, when a number of economic restrictions were in force.

It may be the case that the courts reserve the right to deal with illegality on an equitable basis depending on the particular circumstances which have occurred. An example is provided by a recent decision of the Court of Appeal in England[16]:

> S agreed to pay H £25,000 to remove an aircraft from Nigerian airspace. The sum was to be paid in two instalments. In Nigeria, H feared there was a threat to his life. Without obtaining the necessary permission, he flew the aircraft to the Ivory Coast chased by a Nigerian fighter. The aircraft was impounded and returned to Nigeria. S sought the return of the first instalment of £12,500 which had been paid. H sought payment of the balance. He was held entitled to the full sum. His side of the bargain was fulfilled when he flew the plane out of Nigeria. The breach of air traffic control regulations was committed to escape imminent danger. It was therefore not against public policy to allow him to recover the sum from S.

RESTRICTIVE COVENANTS

12.18 Restrictive covenants are clauses which limit a party's liberty to practice his or her trade or profession. They are sometimes referred to as clauses in restraint of trade. Such clauses are frequently found in contracts of employment, partnership, and sale.

> *Examples*:
> (1) Chop agrees to buy Loin's butcher shop. In terms of the agreement, Loin undertakes not to set up in business as a butcher within five miles of the shop for a three-year period.
> (2) Amp works for the Plug Electric Co. His contract of employment stipulates that if Amp leaves the company he shall not join a rival company within the U.K. for 12 months after his employment with Plug ceases.

Courts dealing with restrictive covenants have a difficult balance to strike. On the one hand, they wish to uphold contracts. They are reluctant to release a party from an obligation freely entered into. To do so destroys the security of contractual engagements. It tends to make parties less likely to abide by their contracts in future. However, the courts also

---

[16] *Howard v. Shirlstar Container Transport* [1990] 1 W.L.R. 1292.

wish to uphold individual liberty. A person ought to have the right to earn a livelihood. It is in the public interest that competition be encouraged. Persons should not be allowed to abuse a superior bargaining position to secure an unfair trading advantage. Accordingly, the balance is between:

Freedom of Contract *v.* Freedom of Trade

The Right to Bargain *v.* the Right to Work or Trade

The Ground Rules

Over the years, a number of principles have been developed to determine 12.19 whether or not a restrictive covenant is valid. The principles are essentially five in number:

(1) Restrictive covenants are prima facie void and unenforceable.
(2) Restrictive covenants will only be upheld if they are reasonable (i) as between the parties, and (ii) in the public interest.
(3) Restrictive covenants are most readily enforced in contracts of sale of a business.
(4) In employment cases, an employer cannot protect himself against competition alone. He must demonstrate some exceptional proprietorial interest, *e.g.* a trade connection or trade secret.
(5) The restriction must go no further than is reasonably required.

The classic statement of the law occurs in the speech of Lord Macnaghten in *Nordenfelt v. Maxim Nordenfelt Guns and Ammunition Co. Ltd*[17]:

"The public have an interest in every person's carrying on his trade freely: so has the individual. All interference with individual liberty of action in trading, and all restraints of trade of themselves, if there is nothing more, are contrary to public policy, and therefore void. That is the general rule. But there are exceptions: restraints of trade and interference with individual liberty of action may be justified by the special circumstances of a particular case. It is sufficient justification, and indeed it is the only justification, if the restriction is reasonable - reasonable, that is, in reference to the interests of the parties concerned and reasonable in reference to the interests of the public, so framed and so guarded as to afford adequate protection to the party in whose favour it is imposed, while at the same time it is in no way injurious to the public."

In determining reasonableness, regard will be had to a number of 12.20 factors, including the nature of the restriction imposed, its duration, and the spatial area over which it is imposed. At one time it was thought that

---

[17] [1894] A.C. 535.

a general restraint, which prevented a person from working anywhere in the world, was unenforceable. This was considered in *Nordenfelt*:

> In 1886, Nordenfelt sold his arms business to a limited company which was formed for the purpose of purchasing it. He received a large sum for the sale and it was agreed he would act as the new company's managing director for five years after its formation. Two years later, the company amalgamated with another company. At the time of the transfer Nordenfelt entered into a restrictive covenant with the company similar in terms to one he had agreed to on the sale of the business in 1886. It was stipulated that for a 25-year period he should not "engage except on behalf of the company either directly or indirectly in the trade or business of a manufacturer of guns, gun-mountings or gun powder explosives or ammunition."

When he attempted to breach this undertaking, the company sought to enforce the covenant by way of injunction. Nordenfelt contended that the restraint was wider than was required to protect the company's legitimate interests and that: "It cannot be the law that a man should be prevented from earning his living in any part of the wide world." The House of Lords rejected this contention and upheld the covenant. In view of the fact that it was a worldwide business ("He had upon his books almost every monarch and almost every State of any note in the habitable globe") and that he had received a very good price for his transfer, the restraint was reasonable.

Contracts of Sale of a Business

12.21 When a business is sold as a going concern, one part of the purchase price will be in respect of the goodwill of the business. The goodwill comprises the customers and reputation of the seller, in other words, the seller's trade connection. If the purchaser could not insert a restrictive covenant into the contract to restrict competition by the seller, the goodwill would be valueless. The seller could immediately set up in the same business again and attract his customers to the new premises. Accordingly, such restrictions will be enforced when they provide protection to the purchaser's legitimate interests. In one case, the Privy Council stated that such clauses do not come within the operation of the doctrine of restraint of trade "provided that the degree of interference does not exceed the accepted standard."[18] This is another way of saying that in contracts of sale of a business, the presumption has shifted in favour of such covenants being upheld. The power of the court to intervene is still present, but it will only be exercised when the restraint is demonstrably excessive or against the public interest.[19]

---

[18] *Deacons v. Bridge* [1984] 2 All E.R. 19.
[19] See *George Walker & Co. v. Jann*, 1991 S.L.T. 771.

While it is open to the purchaser to restrict competition by the seller, the converse proposition does not hold. In one case, the seller of a men's hairdressing business sought to prevent the buyer from engaging in ladies' hairdressing in competition with the seller.[20] The restriction sought was refused. The reason given by the sheriff in this novel situation was that the restraint was not designed to protect the seller's legitimate interest, but simply to stifle competition.

Contracts of Partnership

Where a restrictive covenant is inserted in a partnership deed, the question will again turn on the legitimate interests of those who rely upon the term for protection. In the first reported Scots decision on restrictive covenants, the court upheld a covenant involving a bookselling partnership in Glasgow.[21] If all the partners accept the same restriction there is a definite presumption that the term is enforceable. Otherwise it is impossible to give a precise guide to which covenants will and which will not be enforced. Two cases will suffice as illustrations. Interdict has been granted to prevent a doctor from exercising the profession of a general practitioner in a small country town on the basis of covenant. No argument seems to have been led regarding the public interest in securing the best possible medical provision in the particular area.[22] But public interest was a factor of some importance when a large Hong Kong firm of solicitors sought to enforce a covenant against a partner who had left the firm.[23] The firm was departmentalised, which meant that the covenant went well beyond the individual partner's role in the firm. Nevertheless, the public interest in facilitating the assumption of new partners by established solicitors' firms was accepted by the Privy Council. If a partner was not bound by such a provision, it would deter firms from assuming partners, because once the partner had acquired clients through the firm, he might set up on his own taking the clients with him. However, if the restriction sought is too wide, it will be struck down. A covenant which sought to prevent a solicitor from practising within twenty miles of Glasgow Cross was thought to be excessive and interim interdict refused.[24] Council for the respondent had submitted that the area probably included about half the law firms in Scotland.

12.22

---

[20] *Giblin v. Murdoch*, 1979 S.L.T. (Sh.Ct) 5.

[21] *Stalker v. Carmichael* (1735) Mor. 9455.

[22] *Anthony v. Rennie*, 1981 S.L.T. (Notes) 11.

[23] *Deacons v. Bridge* [1984] 2 All E.R. 19.

[24] *Dallas McMillan & Sinclair v. Simpson*, 1989 S.L.T. 454.

"Solus" Agreements

12.23   A more specialised category of restrictive covenants involves attempts by
        oil companies to regulate the trading of petrol stations. In these
        situations, the contract between the parties may include various elements
        of the relationships of landlord and tenant, seller and buyer or licensor
        and licensee. Such agreements contain restrictions intended to apply
        during the trading relationship between the parties rather than only when
        it is at an end. They are known as "solus" agreements and usually
        involve three elements:

    (1) an obligation upon the retailer to purchase all his products from
         the company;
    (2) an obligation to keep the garage open during stipulated hours;
         and
    (3) an obligation to ensure that any subsequent purchaser enters a
         similar agreement with the oil company.

        The novelty of such agreements is that they restrict the trading use of
        a particular piece of land, rather than the future exercise of a trade or
        profession by an individual. On that basis, it was argued that the doctrine
        of restraint of trade did not apply. That approach has been rejected by the
        House of Lords. In the leading case on the issue, a solus agreement of
        four years, five months was held reasonable, but one for 26 years
        unreasonable. The latter restriction was held to be too long and against
        the public interest.[25]

Cartels etc.

12.24   Apart from covenants involving individuals, freedom of trade can also be
        prejudiced where manufacturers or traders combine together to regulate
        the availability of certain commodities, or to fix prices. Suppose, for
        example, all the manufacturers of widgets agreed together to fix a price
        for widgets well in excess of production costs. That would greatly
        enhance their profits to the detriment of the public interest. This area is
        now largely covered by statute and the competition laws of the European
        Union. The rules that apply are detailed and are outwith the scope of this
        book.

Employment

12.25   In contracts for the sale of a business, the seller receives something in
        return for his agreement to the restrictive covenant, viz. the value of the
        goodwill. This is not true in the case employees. They may only be
        persuaded to sign a contract containing a covenant to ensure that they
        obtain the job and therefore a means of livelihood. In employment cases,

---

[25] *Esso Petroleum Co. Ltd v. Harpers Garage (Stourport) Ltd* [1968] A.C. 269;
[1967] 1 All E.R. 699.

a restrictive covenant is "a *pactum illicitum* only if the restriction imposed is wider than is necessary to protect the legitimate interests of the master".[26] Plainly, the two crucial phrases in this passage are "wider than is necessary" and "legitimate interests." What do they mean? Let us begin by looking at the term "legitimate interests." It unpacks into two separate but overlapping categories: (a) trade secrets and confidential information, and (b) preservation of business connection.

Legitimate Interest (1)—Trade Secrets and Confidential Information

With good reason the area covered by trade secrets and confidential information has been described as "somewhat nebulous and ill-defined." This is because true trade secrets will normally be protected by intellectual property rights such as patents and copyrights. Moreover, independent of any express contractual term, there is an implied term in contracts of employment that an employee will not disclose confidential information to other parties.[27]   12.26

The relevant principles are as follows:

(1) The parties' obligations are *prima facie* determined by the contract of employment.
(2) The question of the use and disclosure of information is the subject of implied terms.
(3) The duty of good faith and fidelity during the employment which is implied by law depends upon the nature of the employment. The duty is broken if the employee copies or memorises customer lists.
(4) After the employment ceases, the duty of good faith is more restricted in scope. It only covers information of a type amounting to a trade secret.

Whether or not information is so confidential as to amount to a trade secret depends upon the whole circumstances of the case. Relevant factors are (a) the nature of the employment; (b) the nature of the information; (c) whether the employer impressed the confidentiality of the information upon the employee; and (d) whether the information can be easily isolated from other information which the employee possesses. Prices and customer lists can constitute trade secrets. Restrictive covenants cannot, however, extend the employer's rights to protect information which would otherwise be the subject of implied terms.   12.27

A difficult issue concerns the employers' general business methods and organisation. Does this constitute a trade secret or confidential information? In *S.O.S. Bureau v. Payne*, which involved an employee

---

[26] *Scottish Farmers' Dairy Co. (Glasgow) Ltd v. McGhee*, 1933 S.L.T. 142, 145 *per* L.P. Clyde.
[27] *Faccenda Chicken Ltd v. Fowler* [1987] Ch. 117; *Harben Pumps (Scotland) Ltd v. Lafferty*, 1989 S.L.T. 752.

who sought to leave an employment agency where she had worked, the sheriff upheld a covenant in order to prevent disclosure of the employers' "system of work, presentation of the service to the customer and in particular fee charging policy."[28] This statement would effectively cover most employees. If an employee does not know about the employer's system of work, he is more likely to be looking down the wrong end of an unfair dismissal barrel than worrying about the validity of a restrictive covenant. The more persuasive line of authority can be traced back to Lord Atkinson. He accepted that information about business organisation and methods was naturally acquired by the employee and stated that

> "he violates no obligation express or implied arising from the relation in which he stood to the [employers] by using in service of some persons other than them the general knowledge he has acquired of their scheme of organisation and methods of business."[29]

His words were echoed in a later case by Lord Pearson, who stated that the employer's scheme of organisation and methods of business are not to be counted as trade secrets.[30] Lord Ross has accepted Lord Pearson's view as a correct statement of the law.[31]

12.28   An illustration of the continuing importance of restrictive covenants where issues of trade secrets and confidential information are concerned is provided by *Bluebell Apparel v. Dickinson*[32]:

> In January 1977, D was taken on as a management trainee by Bluebell Apparel, manufacturers of "Wrangler" jeans. By June 1977, D was in sole charge of their Kilwinning factory but in August he intimated that he was leaving to take up a position with Levi Strauss and Co. Bluebell Apparel sought an interdict to prevent this on the basis of an agreement which D had signed when he joined them. It provided that except with the written permission of the employers, D would not, for a period of two years after the end of his employment with them, perform any services, either as owner, partner, employee, or consultant for any person or business entity in competition with Bluebell Apparel.

The First Division upheld the covenant on the basis that D possessed confidential information about B.A. Accordingly, D was prevented from working for a competitor anywhere in the world in any capacity for a period of two years. It may be that, even without resorting to industrial espionage, there is little that D knew about the actual products which competitors could not have found out by buying, ripping asunder and examining a few pairs of Wranglers. Nevertheless, such knowledge as he

---

[28] 1982 S.L.T. (Sh.Ct) 33.
[29] *Herbert Morris Ltd v. Saxelby* [1916] 1 A.C. 688.
[30] *Commercial Plastics Ltd v. Vincent* [1964] 3 All E.R. 546 at p.551.
[31] *Bluebell Apparel v. Dickinson*, 1980 S.L.T. 157 at 158.
[32] *Ibid.*

had after only eight months regarding pricing policy and customers was thought sufficient to justify a two-year long, worldwide restraint.

Legitimate Interest (2)—Preservation of Business Connection

Employers are not entitled to protection against competition alone. 12.29
Competition is the very essence of the market. Where there are no trade secrets or confidential information to protect, the presumption is that the employee is entitled to freely practise her trade or profession. However, there are certain qualifications to that general approach. An employer does have a legitimate interest in preserving his business connection, which can be enforced in certain circumstances.

Let us first deal with non-solicitation of clients. Prohibitions against active attempts to poach clients for a limited period are frequently upheld. It is thought reasonable by both sides that the employee will not seek to undermine the employer's business in this manner. After all, what reasonable employer intends to train "fifth columnists" to steal business out from under his nose? But when it is simply a case of competition, either by joining a competitor, or by setting up in business on one's own, the general principle is that the employee cannot be shackled.

Secondly, a reasonable restraint will be enforced when there is some 12.30
intimate relationship between the employee and the customers of the business such that he acquires a degree of influence over them. In *Scottish Farmers Dairy Co. (Glasgow) Ltd*, a milk-roundsman was the only contact between the business and the customers. His contract contained a covenant which prevented him from setting up in competition with the company for a period of two years within a one-mile radius of his employers' place of business.[33] It was held that he should not be allowed to take advantage of the position his job gave him vis-a-vis the customers. This would be unfair competition with the employer. Accordingly, the covenant was upheld:

"the preservation of his business connection is a legitimate interest of every trader; and if, to protect that interest, a prohibition against competition by the servant is made necessary by the particular nature and circumstances of the master's business, the law of Scotland recognises the prohibition as an enforceable term of the contract of employment."[34]

If the employee did not have an opportunity to exercise influence over clients or customers, it is difficult to see why he should be prevented from competing under this head.[35]

---

[33] 1933 S.C. 148; 1933 S.L.T. 133.
[34] *Scottish Farmers Dairy Co. (Glasgow) Ltd v. McGhee*, 1933 S.C. 148, 153 *per* L.P. Clyde.
[35] *Hinton and Higgs v. Murphy*, 1989 S.L.T. 450; *Office Angels Ltd v. Rainer Thomas* [1991] I.R.L.R. 214.

Wider Than is Necessary

12.31 In considering how wide the restriction is there are three matters to consider; the time for which it operates, the area over which it operates and the content of the restriction imposed.

On the following page are some examples of spatial and temporal restrictions which have been held to be valid. It will be seen that a great range of different restrictions have been enforced, from a quarter of a mile to the world in extent, from six months to life in duration. Where trade secrets are concerned, then the ambit of the restriction can be very wide as in the "Wrangler" case. In employment contracts, however, area covenants are in general looked upon with disfavour. This is because they appear to be simply an attempt to stifle competition. There is now Court of Appeal authority in England to the effect that they will not be enforced where a lesser, more precise restriction would have adequately protected the employer's interests.[36]

12.32 The restriction contained in the covenant should be directed at the legitimate interest which the employer is entitled to protect. If the clause is drafted too widely, it will be unenforceable and the employer will lose even the protection that he was entitled to seek. Determining the scope of legitimate interest requires consideration of the job which the employee did. In *Rentokil v. Hampton* the restrictive covenant sought to prevent the employee from being involved with the "marketing, sale or supply of products or services" in competition with Rentokil.[37] As he was a timber infestation surveyor, the restraint was held to be wider than was required and declared invalid. It prevented him from competing, not only in respect of his own area of work, but in respect of new areas. Similarly there was no legitimate interest in preventing him from dealing with persons with whom he had no connection during the period of his employment. If the legitimate interest is preservation of business connection by preventing contact with customers, a clause which would prevent contact with customers in relation to business other than that of the former employer is too wide.[38] Where the legitimate interest at stake is the preservation of confidential information it is very difficult to draft an effective clause that deals with that and nothing else. The nature of confidential information makes it difficult to specify what is to be protected. It is also difficult effectively to police such any prohibition on disclosure of such information. The courts therefore accept that, in some situations, the only effective means of obtaining protection for legitimate interests will be a prohibition on employment by the employer's rivals or contact with customers.[39] Accordingly, the manager of a Wrangler jeans

---

[36] *Office Angels Ltd v. Rainer Thomas, supra.*
[37] 1982 S.L.T. 422.
[38] *Aramark v. Sommerville,* 1995 S.L.T. 749.
[39] *PR Consultants Scotland Limited v. Mann,* 1997 S.L.T. 437.

factory could not take employment even as a doorman in Nicaragua for Levis or Lee Cooper.[40]

Severability

Frequently, a restrictive covenant will consist of several separate 12.33 restrictions. If each restriction is truly independent of the others, then the invalidity of each will not affect the validity of the others. Accordingly, a reasonable restriction will be enforced even where the unreasonable restriction falls. So where a salesman agreed not to canvass his employer's customers and also not to carry on business as a traveller in a particular area, the former provision was upheld but the latter rejected as too wide and too vague.[41] The divisibility of the clause can provide the subject of express stipulation in the contract.[42] If there is no such stipulation the court can only sever an unreasonable part of the clause if it can be done by simple deletion.[43] The courts will not, however, re-write the restriction so as to make it enforceable. That is to confuse the function of the parties in making the contract with that of the courts in interpreting it.[44] The parties cannot exclude the jurisidiction of the courts by declaring that terms of covenant are reasonable.[45]

Remedies for Breach of Covenant

Court procedure is of critical importance in covenant cases. Frequently, 12.34 the matter comes before the court at an interim stage. Accordingly, the decision is made on the pleadings as they then stand, together with such statements as are made by the parties' representatives at the bar of the court. There is a two-stage approach. First, the petitioner must make out a, *prima facie,* case. Secondly, he must demonstrate that on the balance of convenience, the interim interdict should be granted.[46] A *prima facie* case is one which has a seeming cogency. It is sometimes said that the pleadings disclose a case to try. The balance of convenience broadly speaking relates to the relative prejudice which will be suffered by the parties if the interim interdict is granted or refused. Among the considerations which the court will take into account are the following:

- When was the action brought?
- How long does the covenant have to run?
- What is the prejudice to the employer?
- What is the prejudice to the employee?

---

[40] *Bluebell Apparel v. Dickinson,* 1980 S.L.T. 158.
[41] *Mulvein v. Murray,* 1908 S.C. 528.
[42] *Hinton & Higgs (U.K.) Ltd v. Murphy,* 1989 S.L.T. 450.
[43] *Living Design (Home Improvements) Ltd v. Davidson,* 1994 S.L.T. 753.
[44] *Hinton & Higgs (U.K.) Ltd v. Murphy,* 1989 S.L.T. 450.
[45] *Ibid.*
[46] *Toynar v. Whitbread,* 1988 S.L.T. 433, *per* Lord Ross.

- Will the employee be deprived of his livelihood?
- Is there a remedy in damages?[47]
- Is the loss quantifiable?[48]
- Is the employee being paid for covenant?[49]

There are two other remedies which may be available to employers faced with apparent loss of confidential information. First, if the information is truly a secret, such as a trade process, it may be covered by intellectual property rights under the law relating to patents and copyrights. Secondly, if it is reasonably thought that the employee has removed trade items, customer lists, schedules of prices and the like, these may be recovered by a "dawn raid" carried out by a commissioner under section 1 of the Administration of Justice (Scotland) Act 1972. This can be an effective—but very expensive—manner of proceeding.

---

[47] *Group 4 Total Security v. Ferrier*, 1985 S.L.T. 287; 1985 S.C. 70.

[48] *Rentokil v. Kramer*, 1986 S.L.T. 116.

[49] *Agma Chemical Co. v. Hart*, 1984 S.L.T. 246.

Examples of Spatial Restrictions

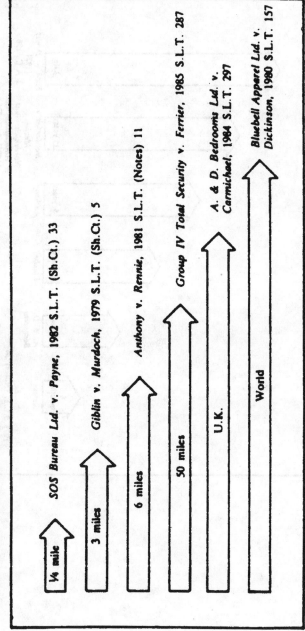

¼ mile — *SOS Bureau Ltd. v. Payne*, 1982 S.L.T. (Sh.Ct.) 33

3 miles — *Giblin v. Murdoch*, 1979 S.L.T. (Sh.Ct.) 5

6 miles — *Anthony v. Rennie*, 1981 S.L.T. (Notes) 11

50 miles — *Group IV Total Security v. Ferrier*, 1985 S.L.T. 287

U.K. — *A. & D. Bedrooms Ltd. v. Carmichael*, 1984 S.L.T. 297

World — *Bluebell Apparel Ltd. v. Dickinson*, 1980 S.L.T. 157

Examples of Temporal Restrictions

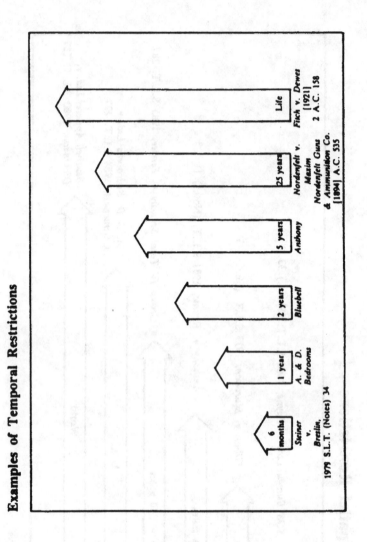

CHAPTER 13

THE EXTINCTION OF OBLIGATIONS

When does a contract come to an end? In most instances, contractual   13.1
obligations are extinguished when both parties have fully performed their
respective sides of the bargain. A contract for the sale of goods, for
example, is normally terminated when the item is delivered in return for
the correct price. The parties owe no further duties to one another under
the contract. Similarly, in unilateral obligations, once the person who has
made the promise fulfils his undertaking, the obligation is at an end. So if
a businessman promises to pay a law student £100 if she comes first in
an essay competition, the obligation will be discharged on his paying her
the money if she wins the competition. Apart from performance,
however, there are several other methods by which contractual
obligations can come to an end.

Discharge by Consent

The parties may agree to release each other from their respective   13.2
contractual obligations without performance. Put simply, the contract is
cancelled by mutual agreement. Where a creditor agrees to release the
debtor, this is known as "acceptilation". If, for example, A owes B £50 in
respect of a quantity of towels which B has delivered to him, B may
agree to waive the debt because A has done him a favour. If such a
release is not granted in the course of a business, it might qualify as a
gratuitous unilateral obligation with the result that in order to be effective
it would require to be in writing.[1]

Novation and Delegation

An obligation is extinguished when it is agreed that a fresh obligation by   13.3
the debtor be substituted for it (novation) or when a new obligation by
another debtor is substituted for it (delegation).

> *Example*: Ben owes Sid £50. Ben suggests that if Sid lends him a
> further £50 he will give him a new receipt for £100 (novation).
> Alternatively, Ben may suggest that as Alf owes him (Ben) £50, a

---

[1] Requirements of Writing Act 1995, s.1(2)(a)(ii).

new obligation should be entered into under which Alf owes Sid £50 (delegation). If Sid accepts either proposal, the original obligation by Ben will be extinguished.

There is a presumption that a new obligation is additional to an existing obligation. Accordingly, a debtor should always ensure that he obtains an express discharge of the original debt.

Compensation

13.4 Where each party owes the other a sum of money, the one debt can be compensated or set off against the other.

> *Example*: Ralph and Zeke are grain merchants who have constant dealings with each other. Ralph owes £50,000 in respect of a wheat consignment he bought from Zeke yesterday. Zeke in turn owes Ralph £120,000 for oats which he bought from him a week ago.

The two debts can be set off against each other resulting in an obligation by Zeke to pay Ralph the difference, that is £70,000. The effect of compensation is accordingly to cancel Ralph's obligation. There are some conditions which must be satisfied before the right of set-off can be used. First, both claims must be liquid, which means they must be readily ascertainable in money terms. If one of the claims is illiquid, then no right of set-off exists. A claim for damages is illiquid because until a precise figure is put upon the claim by a court, the sum is not ascertained. Secondly, the debts must be presently due. There is no right of set-off in respect of future debts. Finally, both parties must be creditor and debtor to each other in the same legal capacity. Suppose a solicitor is owed £2,000 by a client in respect of professional fees. The client cannot claim set-off on the basis that the solicitor is the trustee of an estate which is due to pay him a sum of money. But the client could claim a right of set-off if he was a joiner who had done work for the solicitor which had not been paid for.

13.5   Set-off must be distinguished from retention. The aim of set-off is to extinguish part or all of the obligation. Retention, on the other hand, is about securing performance by the other party by withholding one's own obligations under the contract.

Confusion

13.6 A person cannot be under an obligation to himself. If company A owes company B money and subsequently B were to assign all debts owed to it to A, then the obligation has been "confused" and the debt is extinguished.

Two further methods by which contractual obligations are extinguished require more detailed discussion. The first is prescription, the second frustration.

PRESCRIPTION

The principle of prescription governs the length of time for which 13.7
obligations subsist. The need for such a rule is clear. Rights cannot exist
forever. A creditor must exercise his right to enforce the debt within a
reasonable time. It would be unfair if someone were to remain silent
about a debt for ten years and then seek to take action against the other
party. Further, as time elapses, it becomes increasingly likely that
evidence will be lost. Witnesses' memories will be dimmed. They may
go abroad or die. Accordingly, the law presumes that after a period of
time has elapsed without a claim having been pursued, the creditor must
be deemed to have abandoned that right. The right is then said to have
"prescribed".

Before 1973 the law regarding prescription was in a confused and
chaotic state. On the basis, however, of work done by the Scottish Law
Commission, the Prescription and Limitation (Scotland) Act 1973 was
enacted, which signally improved and simplified this branch of the law.
It deals with three different categories: positive prescription, negative
prescription and limitation. Our main interest lies with the second of
these categories.

Negative Prescription

There are two periods of negative prescription, (a) a short negative 13.8
prescription of five years, and (b) a long negative prescription of twenty
years. Most contractual obligations are extinguished at the end of five
years.[2] So if a car is sold and the price not paid within five years, the debt
is thereafter extinguished. The main exceptions concern those obligations
which relate to land. In such cases, the 20-year period applies.[3]

Computation of Prescriptive Period

The prescriptive period commences running on the date on which the 13.9
obligation becomes enforceable.[4] In respect of a claim for breach of
contract, the action must be brought within five years of the date of the
loss, injury or damage which occurred as a result of the breach.[5] In
Greater Glasgow Health Board v. Baxter Clark & Paul the following
circumstances occurred[6]:

> Between 1969 and 1972, a firm of architects supervised works
> which were undertaken at Yorkhill hospital in Glasgow. Some
> physical damage in the form of cracks manifested in 1972. In 1978 a

---

[2] 1973 Act, s.6.
[3] 1973 Act, s.7.
[4] 1973 Act, s.6(3).
[5] 1973 Act, s.11(1).
[6] 1992 S.L.T. 35.

document was signed between the parties where the architects accepted that there were faults but not that they were liable. No action was raised until 1982. It was held that the action had prescribed. The prescriptive clock had commenced ticking in 1972. Accordingly, by the time the action was raised the obligation had prescribed.

Where there is a series of transactions between the parties, the prescriptive period commences on the date on which payment for the goods last supplied or the services last rendered became due.[7] In the case of a loan or deposit of a sum of money, the period commences on the date stipulated for repayment in the contract or, if no such stipulation is made, the date on which a written demand for repayment is made.[8] So far as obligations to pay money or execute work by instalments are concerned, the date of commencement is that on which the last of the instalments is to be paid or executed respectively.[9]

13.10   Prescription stops running when a relevant claim is made by the creditor or a relevant acknowledgement is given by the debtor. What does this mean? A relevant claim is made if the creditor has taken steps to pursue his right, either by raising a court action or referring the matter to arbitration.[10] Both courses of action clearly indicate that he has not abandoned his claim. The same principle applies if he contests any claim inconsistent with his own alleged right. For example, if he stated his right as a defence to an action brought against him by the debtor.[11] Conversely, a debtor's actions may amount to acknowledgement if they clearly indicate that he regards the claim as still subsisting. This might occur, for example, if he made part-payment of a debt allegedly owed by him.

Mora, Taciturnity and Acquiescence

13.11   There is an older, common law principle by which a claim may be time-barred. This is known as mora, taciturnity and acquiescence. Translated into modern language, this means delay, silence and consent. Even if a right has not prescribed, a person may nevertheless be personally barred because he has taken an unreasonable length of time to vindicate the right.

> *Example*: Ted and Alice sign an agreement regarding the sale of widgets. Nothing follows on from the agreement but 4 years and 8 months after it is concluded, Ted seeks to enforce it. Although the

---

[7] 1973 Act, Sched. 2, para. 1(4).
[8] 1973 Act, Sched. 2, para. 2(2).
[9] 1973 Act, Sched. 2, para. 4(2).
[10] 1973 Act, s.9.
[11] 1973 Act, s.10.

prescriptive period has not yet elapsed, Alice may argue *mora*, taciturnity and acquiescence. If the plea is successful, Ted's claim will fail.

By and large, this principle is redundant in the law of contract.

FRUSTRATION

Few people claim to be able to predict future events. Fewer can actually 13.12 do so. After a contract has been concluded, events may occur which are not the fault of either party, which are unforeseen and which have a dramatic effect on the rights and obligations of the parties. In response to this problem the doctrine of frustration has been developed. Where it operates both parties will be released from their contractual obligations. The circumstances necessary to bring about frustration of a contract were summarised in *Paal Wilson & Co. v. Blumenthal* as follows:

> "The first essential factor is that there must be some outside event or extraneous change of situation, not foreseen or provided for by the parties at the time of contracting, which either makes it impossible for the contract to be performed at all, or at least renders its performance something radically different from what the parties contemplated when they entered into it. The second essential factor is that the outside event or extraneous change of situation concerned, and the consequences of either in relation to the performance of the contract, must have occurred without either the fault or default of either party to the contract."[12]

In some cases, the courts have discharged the parties from their obligations on the basis of an implied term.[13] This approach is artificial. How can the courts imply a term on the basis of giving effect to the parties' intentions when the event is one to which, by definition, they have not directed their minds? A graphic refutation of the implied term theory was provided as long ago as 1922 by Lord Sands:

> "A tiger has escaped from a travelling menagerie. The milkgirl fails to deliver the milk. Possibly the milkman may be exonerated from any breach of contract; but, even so, it would seem hardly reasonable to base that exoneration on the ground that 'tiger days excepted' must be held as if written into milk contract."[14]

---

[12] [1983] 1 A.C. 854 *per* Lord Brandon.
[13] For example, *Taylor v. Caldwell* (1863) 3 B. & S. 826.
[14] *Scott v. Del Sel*, 1922 S.C. 592; aff'd. 1923 S.C. (H.L.) 37.

Types of Frustrating Event

13.13   Impossibility is the primary ground on which the doctrine of frustration proceeds. If one party dies and a degree of *delectus personae* is present, then frustration operates. For example, a portrait painter dies in the middle of a commission. Likewise if there is destruction of the subject-matter. Changed circumstances can make performance of the obligations impossible or at least extremely impracticable. A modern example is provided by the closure of the Shatt el Arab waterway on the outbreak of the Iran-Iraq war. Ships which had contracted to go up the waterway could no longer do so without extreme risk to life and property and the charterparties were frustrated (those, that is, which did not provide for such a contingency in the contract terms). Impossibility may affect the rights that are enjoyed under the contract as well as the obligations.

13.14   Apart from actual impossibility, there is also legal impossibility:

> *Example*: A makes a contract with B to deliver rare Scottish heather to Liberia. After the contract is made, the government passes a law forbidding the export of Scottish heather.

Clearly, A can no longer perform the contract. Otherwise he would be guilty of an offence. Accordingly, the parties are discharged from their respective obligations. The leading case on this branch of the law is *Fraser v. Denny Mott and Dickson*[15]:

> In 1929 a timber yard was let and it was agreed that the lessor should purchase all his timber from the lessee and that the lessor should have an option to purchase. On the outbreak of war, certain legislation was passed which meant that further trading between the parties could not continue. The lessor sought to exercise the option to purchase the yard.

It was held by the House of Lords that the whole agreement, including the option clause, was terminated when the relevant legislation was passed. The legislation had effectively frustrated the agreement. Another similar example of legal impossibility occurs when war breaks out between two countries. A contract between persons in two opposing states, that contract automatically falls on the outbreak of war. Thus in a contract for the supply of marine engines between an Austrian and Scottish company, the outbreak of the First World War terminated the contract.[16] Thereafter, the Austrian company was an enemy alien with whom it was illegal to do business.

13.15   There remains for consideration a third type of supervening event which we might loosely call "commercial impossibility". In such cases, performance of the contract is not physically or legally impossible, but

---

[15] 1944 S.C. (H.L.) 35; [1944] A.C. 265.
[16] *Cantiere San Rocco S.A. v. Clyde Shipbuilding & Engineering Co.*, 1923 S.C. (H.L.) 105; [1923] A.C. 226.

circumstances have changed to such a marked extent that the venture is no longer that which the parties originally envisaged. It is firmly established that frustration does not occur simply because performance has become more onerous or expensive for one of the parties. In *Tsakiroglou & Co. Ltd v. Noblee Thorl GmbH*[17]:

> A charterparty was entered into to carry freight to Britain. It was assumed by the parties that the ship would proceed through the Suez Canal although nothing was expressly stated in the contract. The Suez crisis of 1956 intervened and the canal was closed and the ship would have had to undertake its voyage round the Cape of Good Hope.

It was held that the charterparty was not frustrated. Although the voyage was longer and more expensive to perform than envisaged at the time the contract was made, that was not a ground for discharging the parties from their obligations. The court indicated, however, that if the freight had been perishable and if it were to be damaged or to perish as a result of the longer voyage, then the contract probably would be frustrated. Another example is provided by *Davis Contractors Ltd v. Fareham Urban District Council*, where inflation had caused the cost of a particular building contract to increase dramatically.[18] This would have meant the contractor would have made no profit on the contract price as originally agreed. Nevertheless he was held bound to his contract. The extra cost was no reason to invoke the doctrine of frustration. Today, building contracts are usually drawn up on special standard forms which contain provisions designed to deal with escalating costs which may arise in respect of a number of specified contingencies.

The most radical example of "commercial frustration" is provided by the English case of *Krell v. Henry*[19]:   13.16

> Rooms overlooking Pall Mall were hired at a high price to view the processions which were to take place in connection with Edward VII's coronation. Because the King had appendicitis, the coronation had to be postponed.

It was held that the contract for the hire of the rooms was terminated by frustration. The basis for the claim was that the whole rationale or purpose of the contract, the bedrock on which it was founded, had disappeared. The hirers did not want to see the Mall in its usual livery with its usual array of pedestrians and carriages. They had paid a high price to see the procession.

It has been suggested that *Krell* would not be followed in Scotland.   13.17 Lord Cooper, founding on Professor Gloag, doubted whether it is good

---

[17] [1962] A.C. 93.
[18] [1956] A.C. 696; [1956] 2 All E.R. 145.
[19] [1903] 2 K.B. 740.

authority north of the border.[20] Even south of the border its authority is in some doubt. It was decided only a few weeks apart from another "Coronation case," *Herne Bay Steamboat Co. v. Hutton*[21]:

> A pleasure boat was hired to view the naval review which was to take place off Spithead in connection with the coronation celebrations. When the review was cancelled, it was argued that the contract for the hire of the boat was frustrated.

The same court which decided *Krell* held in this case that the contract was not frustrated. What are the distinctions between the two cases? Clearly, there is very little to choose between them. The operative distinctions appear to be first, that the owners of the pleasure steamer were in the business of hiring out their craft. It was not their purpose to inquire into the reasons for the hire. Just as a taxi driver might know his vehicle was being hired to go to Musselburgh, but did not know that it was to see the races, so the boat owner could not be expected to inquire into the motives for every contract of hire into which they entered. By contrast the owner of the flat in Pall Mall was hiring it out on a special "one-off" basis.

Secondly, there was actually something to see in Herne. The distinguished jurist, Sir Frederick Pollock, went to view the British fleet assembled at Spithead and declared it to be a very impressive spectacle.[22] There was unlikely to be any special attraction in watching the usual pedestrian and vehicular traffic in Pall Mall.

13.18 It remains true, however, that distinguishing between the two cases is decidedly tricky. In Scotland, it is more likely that the presumption would be in favour of the contract being upheld if all that had occurred was the non-occurrence of an expected event as opposed to the occurrence of an unexpected event. In *Hong Kong and Whampoa Dock Co. Ltd v. Netherton Shipping Ltd*[23]:

> Shipowners sought to cancel a contract which they had made with a Hong Kong company to repair one of their ships. The shipowners claimed that it was "commercially impossible" for them to deliver the ship at Hong Kong within a reasonable time. This was because the ship lay at Singapore and the authorities there had stipulated that extensive preliminary repairs had to be carried out. Accordingly, the ship would not be ready to set out before the typhoon season, when it was dangerous for her to be at sea. Nevertheless the contract was upheld. All three judges in the Inner House expressed their unease over extending the width of the concept of commercial impossibility.

[20] Cooper, (1946) 28. J.Comp.L. 1.
[21] [1903] 2 K.B. 683.
[22] Pollock, 20 L.Q.R. 4.
[23] 1909 S.C. 34.

The Event must be Unforeseen

If the parties have foreseen a particular event and have provided for 13.19
the event in their contract, then the doctrine of frustration is not
brought into play. So if there is a danger that war will break out and
the parties make provision for such a contingency in their contract,
the term of the contract will govern the legal relations of the parties
if war does indeed break out.

Neither Party at Fault

As frustration is an equitable doctrine, it has no role to play if the 13.20
circumstances disclose that one of the parties was at fault. Where, for
example, it was known that there was a war zone and one of the parties
caused a ship to enter that zone, he could not thereafter plead
frustration.[24] It was his act which caused the detention of the ship. So it
was not possible to claim that a supervening event had occurred without
fault of either of the parties. Accordingly, the obligation was not
discharged. Self-induced frustration is, in fact, no more than breach.

> *Example*: An opera singer is engaged to appear with Scottish Opera
> for five weeks. If she loses her voice accidentally through illness, the
> contract is frustrated. But if she chooses to enter the Eastern
> European Women's Open Yodelling Championship and thereby
> loses her voice so that she cannot perform, that is breach of
> contract.[25]

Effect of Frustration

Where frustration applies, both parties to the contract are released from 13.21
their obligations. Injustice could clearly arise from this if one party had
performed all or part of their obligation and found themselves unable to
exact any performance in return. This result is avoided by rules on unjust
enrichment under which the disadvantaged party may claim against the
other.

Risk—The Alternative to Frustration

Where the subject matter of the contract has been destroyed the 13.22
alternative to discharging the contract through frustration is to determine
who must bear this loss. In early Scottish cases concerning this situation
the question asked was: on whom should the risk fall? So if a horse was
hired and then stolen whilst in the possession of the hirer the question

---

[24] *The Eugenia* [1964] 2 Q.B. 226; [1964] 1 All E.R. 161.
[25] *Cf. Poussard v. Spiers* (1876) 1 Q.B.D. 410.

was: who should bear the loss of the horse, the owner or the hirer.[26] Similarly, if goods were damaged in transit, should the owner or the carrier be liable? Out of these cases, certain rules were established regarding the passing of risk in the most common contract—sale. In a contract for the sale of goods, risk is presumed to pass when property in the goods passes, unless the parties have agreed otherwise.[27] In a sale of heritage it has been established that risk passes when the missives are completed. In *Sloans' Dairies v. Glasgow Corporation*, premises were sold under missives.[28] Before the disposition had been delivered, the subjects were badly damaged by fire and had to be demolished. It was held that the risk was the purchasers' and they therefore had to bear the loss which had occurred.[29] In either case the parties may specify when the risk of destruction passes from one to the other. Such a provision would mean that the rules on frustration would not apply.

The operation of these rules regarding the passing of risk in sale reduces considerably the problem of supervening events. In such cases, it is up to the person who bears the risk to take whatever steps he can to minimise or insure against the risk. So as soon as missives are completed for the sale of a house, the purchaser's solicitor should immediately arrange insurance cover for the property.

The Position of Leases

13.23   From earliest times, Scots law has taken the view that a lease, like any other contract, can be frustrated. In English law this is not the case, partly because a lease constitutes a separate estate in land, partly because of the belief that a person who enters a contract for a period of years must assume the risk of whatever contingencies occur in those years. Not everything can be foreseen, but it is at least likely that a variety of incidents will occur in the course of a long time. It has been stated that while it is untrue to say that a lease can never be frustrated in English law it is true to say that such a situation will hardly ever occur.[30]

Scots law is so far different in this respect that not only do we allow frustration of a lease in the event of actual destruction of the subject (*rei interitus*), but we also hold a lease frustrated in the event of constructive destruction. So where the tenants in a 19-year lease of salmon fishings were unable to take advantage of the lease when the area came to be used by the Royal Air Force as an aerial gunnery and bombing range, the lease

---

[26] See *Trotter v. Buchanan* (1688) Mor. 10080.
[27] Sale of Goods Act 1979, s.20.
[28] 1977 S.C. 223.
[29] In *Report on the Passing of Risk in Contracts for the Sale of Heritable Property* (Scot. Law Com. No. 127), a change in the law is recommended.
[30] *National Carriers Ltd.* v. *Panalpina (Northern) Ltd.* [1981] A.C. 675; [1981] 1 All E.R. 161 (emphasis added).

was held to have terminated.[31] A similar decision was reached in *Mackeson* v. *Boyd*, where a mansion which had been let was requisitioned by the authorities during the war, 14 years into a 19-year lease.[32] Despite the relatively short proportion of the lease still to run and the uncertainty, in 1940, of how long the requisition would last, the lease was nevertheless held terminated by constructive total destruction of the subject-matter. Lord President Normand said in the course of his opinion:

> "In the chapter of leases of heritage, and I think also in the chapter of *rei interitus*, our law is by no means the same as the law of England, and, to quote Lord Justice-Clerk Hope, if we were to attempt to apply that law in these cases, we should run the greatest risk of spoiling our own by mistaking theirs."[33]

---

[31] *Tay Salmon Fisheries Co.* v. *Speedie*, 1929 S.C. 593.
[32] *Mackeson* v. *Boyd*, 1942 S.C. 56.
[33] *Ibid.* at p. 63.

would have been completed. A lodging operation was decided on by Keller, W. Brown and the Commander ... who had been in close requirement by the aeroplane carrying the war 14 years and 15 years ... ... it. I respect the case that the portion of the head will be used immediately. The reply of how to the commission would have the last chance, criticisms fully confirmed by construction and ... of the ... experimental ... was given operations, and the manner of the opening ...

The principle of the aerial freight and I think also in the future ... offering our ideas as I should the same as a railway, ... the inference and reduced range. There being, I venture to ... there is enough that have in this zone ... we shall with the greatest ... of intelligence ... in selecting both ...

INDEX